365 Delicious Low-Fat Recipes

Phyllis Kohn

A JOHN BOSWELL ASSOCIATES BOOK

HarperCollins*Publishers*

FIRST EDITION

Series Editor: Susan Wyler
Design: Nigel Rollings
Index: Maro Riofrancos

Library of Congress Cataloging-in-Publication Data
Kohn, Phyllis.
    365 delicious low-fat recipes / Phyllis Kohn.
        p.   cm.
    "A John Boswell Associates book."
    Includes index.
    ISBN 0-06-017137-5
    1. Low-fat diet—Recipes.   I. Title.
RM237.7.K64   1995
641.5'638—dc20   95-23312

95   96   97   98   99   DT/HC   10   9   8   7   6   5   4   3   2   1

Contents

Stuffed Clams, and Lemon-Herbed Scallops, just for starters.

Introduction

Hardly a day goes by that I don't read a magazine or newspaper article, see a new book, or hear a report on radio or television about eating lighter and healthier. Bulletins and press releases stressing the importance of reducing dietary fat constantly cross my desk. The message is clear: We should all be attempting to eat less fat in order to look fitter and to help reduce the possible risk of heart disease, cancers, obesity, and diabetes. But if you're like me, you know it's a lot easier said than done.

Messages are confusing. The United States Department of Agriculture's Food Pyramid places great emphasis on complex carbohydrates (6 to 11 servings of whole-grain breads, cereal, rice, and pasta a day); encourages more vegetables (3 to 5 servings) and fruits (2 to 4 servings); allows just a little high-protein dairy, meats, poultry, fish, dried beans, eggs, and nuts (2 to 3 servings); and at the top tip of the pyramid, suggests sparing use of fats, oils, and sugar.

The Mediterranean Diet, one of the latest nutritional plans (at the moment), follows a similar course at the bottom of the pyramid, but puts more emphasis on fruits and vegetables, allows more fish and poultry, but reduces animal fat as much as possible, recommending red meat only occasionally (once a week at best), and is more lenient on total fat consumed if that fat is olive oil. This diet is based on some health reports, which suggest that olive oil, the most common source of fat in Mediterranean countries, lowers the incidence of coronary heart disease in men. This diet also recommends a glass of red wine with meals. Sounds good to me. But which plan is best?

What everyone seems to agree upon at the moment, including the American Heart Association, is that the most sensible course to follow is the USDA's recommendation that no more than 30 percent of all the calories you consume come from fat. That's where *365 Delicious Low-Fat Recipes* can really help, because all the recipes in this book were developed to contain a maximum of 30 percent calories from fat. Wherever possible, they are significantly lower.

With these recipes at your side, you can reduce your fat intake considerably without getting hung up on counting calories or milligrams of nutrients. It's simple if you start by making small changes that you can live with easily in your diet. Given the variety and good taste in this collection, your choices are made easy. And remember, it's the variety and combination of foods you eat over days and weeks—along with portion control—that leads to a healthful low-fat diet. One caution: If you are on a restricted diet for health reasons, it's best to check with your doctor or health care professional before changing diets.

When I began developing the recipes for *365 Delicious Low-Fat Recipes,* I surveyed supermarkets, smaller groceries, and health food stores to see what kinds of ingredients were available. Although I had already been using several reduced-fat, lower-sodium products in my daily diet. I was impressed by the extensive array of nutritionally sensible foods that are widely distributed—and more seem to be appearing every day. In these recipes, I've made an attempt to use as many of these helpful products as possible, to widen the range of dishes that can be enjoyed while keeping fat grams low.

In the dairy case are no-fat, reduced-fat, and low-fat versions of several cheeses: Swiss, lace cheese, and Cheddar, to name a few. Skim-milk mozzarella and ricotta, no-fat cream cheese and Neufchâtel, low-fat cottage cheese, buttermilk, and nonfat yogurt become excellent substitutes for their higher-fat cousins.

In place of whole eggs, I used more whites, which contain no cholesterol and little fat. Egg white works well as a crisp coating around seafood and vegetables, and it can take the place of a whole egg as a binder in meat loaf and meatballs. In baking, two egg whites can often substitute for one whole egg, and a higher proportion of egg white to yolk can allow you to enjoy reduced-fat versions of omelets and soufflés. One further note: All eggs called for in this book should be "large."

To further reduce fat, in many instances I have used liquid egg substitute, which is based on egg whites and often comes frozen. Each brand uses a different formula to replace the yolks, but all have low or no cholesterol. Read the nutrient label, and try several brands to compare cooking performance and taste before selecting the one you want to use regularly.

Lean ingredients can be found in many places. Meat counters regularly feature lean skinless, boneless chicken breasts, trimmed pork loin, and a variety of low-fat sausages made out of chicken or turkey. Fish departments, even in supermarkets, offer freshness and quality that were unheard of not so long ago. Many markets pride themselves on the quality and variety of their produce departments, which offer a range of fruits and vegetables that make good nutrition a pleasure. And on supermarket shelves are an almost endless array of low- and reduced-fat products. Take a look at "The Low-Fat Pantry" on page 4 for a list of many of my favorites.

Because many flavor components are fat-soluble, the biggest challenge that arises when you're trying to reduce the fat in cooking is to keep taste levels up. I find that infusing recipes with bright herbs, intensely flavored vinegars, soy sauce, hearty mustards, fresh ginger, hot peppers, fresh citrus juice and zest, and sometimes a splash of wine can add real punch. Mediterranean ingredients like sun-dried tomatoes, capers, and even olives (in small amounts) also add considerable brightness.

Where appropriate, just a couple of teaspoons of a fruity extra-virgin olive oil or butter can give an illusion of more richness than is really there. A few shavings of the very best quality Parmesan cheese (*Parmigiano-Reggiano*) or a couple of tablespoons of crumbled feta cheese can make all the difference in a dish.

Texture can also become thin and dry without fat, resulting in a perceptible loss of richness. Many low-fat products can help to alleviate this. Nonfat yogurt mixed with skim milk, for example can mimic the effect of heavy cream, and pureed vegetables can thicken sauces and add body without adding fat.

Technique also counts a lot when you are trying to minimize fat. How do you sauté without oil? Brown foods without frying? Bake without butter? Nonstick pots and pans are, of course, essential to low-fat cooking. The technique I like to use for sautéing involves first coating the skillet with vegetable cooking spray and then adding a very small amount of fat, preferably olive or canola oil, but sometimes reduced-fat margarine or butter for flavor. This insures that food will slide easily around even in well used, not-so-new pans and helps aid in browning.

Where larger amounts of vegetables are to be softened, I often brown them quickly first in very little oil and then cook them covered with a small amount of water, or "sweat" them, which releases their moisture and tenderizes them.

Low-fat baking is an art in itself. With too little fat, baked desserts can be dry and tough. Egg whites help, as mentioned above. So does prune puree, which can replace up to half of the butter or oil called for in a recipe. The smooth fruit retains moisture and helps keep cakes and cookies tender. And the sweet flavors you love can be enjoyed as much as ever. Ripe red strawberries, tart and zesty lemon, and all your favorite liqueurs are virtually fat free. Cocoa powder contributes that tantalizingly rich chocolate taste some of us can't live without, minus any fatty cocoa butter.

So put away your calculator and scale and pull out your skillet. Low-fat cooking has never been this easy, and low-fat dining has never tasted this delicious.

Top Twelve Equipment List

The heart of a low-fat kitchen is nonstick cookware. These pans have a special nontoxic coating that allows you to cook virtually fat free. Each manufacturer uses a different formula and trade name, but I strongly suggest you look for durable, good-quality pans. Select heavy-duty aluminum or stainless steel cookware that has an aluminum bottom or core to conduct heat evenly. Some pans have heatproof handles, which make them convenient for traveling from stovetop to oven or broiler. If it's worth the investment, it should last: Look for extended warranties for the lifetime of the cookware.

Before using nonstick cookware, most manufacturers recommend treating the inside with a film of oil, much as you might season a new wok. To prevent scratches and to extend durability, use wooden or heatproof plastic spoons and spatulas rather than metal. While some manufacturers state that their cookware is dishwasher safe, many equipment experts recommend washing by hand to extend the life of the nonstick coating.

Following is my list of the most useful nonstick pots and pans and other kitchen utensils indispensable for low-fat cooking:

1. Nonstick 10- or 12-inch (large) skillet with a lid
2. Nonstick 7- to 8-inch (medium) skillet
3. Nonstick 4- to 5-quart dutch oven, often called a flame-proof casserole, with a cover
4. An assortment of nonstick saucepans with covers: 1-quart, 2-quart, and 3-quart sizes
5. Nonstick metal cookie sheets
6. Nonstick metal baking sheets (with shallow sides)
7. Nonstick 12-cup muffin pan
8. Two 8- or 9-inch round baking pans
9. One 9-inch square baking pan
10. A full-size food processor with a metal blade for chopping and pureeing, a slicing disk for slicing and shredding vegetables, and a plastic blade to whip up low-fat salad dressings and the like
11. A medium-size kitchen scale to weigh food accurately
12. A steamer or stainless steel steamer basket for steaming vegetables

Other Important Equipment

• A set of sharp knives to make food preparation easier and safer; an 8- or 10-inch chef's knife and a small paring knife are indispensable
• An instant-reading thermometer to test internal temperature of meats and water for yeast doughs
• Colander and mesh sieve for draining and straining
• Full-size electric mixer or hand mixer for whipping up low-fat cakes and cookies
• A salad spinner for drying salad greens and herbs

The Low-Fat Pantry

The array of products is endless, but in addition to stocking a wide variety of healthful dried beans and grains in your larder and fruits and vegetables and reduced-fat or nonfat cheeses in your fridge, here are some of the low-fat products I find particularly helpful to keep on hand. You'll find most of them in your local supermarket and a few in health food stores.

Low-Fat Helpers

No-yolk noodles; no-fat refried beans; water-packed tuna and salmon; nonfat mayonnaise; frozen egg substitute; evaporated skim milk; dry skim milk powder; fat-free salad dressings; nonfat and reduced-fat Swiss, mozzarella, and cheddar cheeses; light and nonfat sour cream and cream cheese; reduced-fat and nonfat mayonnaise dressing; unsweetened cocoa powder; baked tortilla chips; 95% lean turkey bacon.

Flavor Boosters

Sun-dried tomatoes (the kind that need reconstituting, not oil-packed); capers; garlic; dried mushrooms; canned and pickled hot peppers; salsa; balsamic and sherry wine vinegar; Dijon mustard; jalapeño peppers; and fresh herbs.

Chapter 1

Sinless Appetizers and Snacks

Almost every cuisine boasts a word for appetizers, those tiny little morsels of food to tease the appetite. In Italian, they are called *antipasto*, in Greek, *meze*, in Spanish, *tapas*, in French, *hors d'oeuvres*. These little bites can be as simple as a snack, as filling as a meal, upscale for a black-tie event, or casual for a laid-back get-together. Because these before and in-between-meal nibbles are where many of us forget to watch our diets, I've given special care to creating a variety of appetizers and snacks that are as healthful as they are tasty. The recipes in this chapter incorporate low-fat ingredients and cooking techniques to keep the fat, cholesterol, sodium, and calorie count down.

Chips and dips can still be part of a low-fat diet. Substitute yogurt cheese for mayonnaise in recipes like Dilled Garlic Spread and use a silken low-fat tofu in place of oil for aïoli. Instead of greasy potato chips, surround the dips with an array of crisp vegetables, Savory Wonton Crisps, crunchy baked tortilla chips, or low-fat, low-sodium crackers. Oven-baking eggplant imparts a smoky flavor to the garlicky Baba Ghanouj waiting to be scooped up with a pita triangle.

A packaged cornmeal mix made with egg whites instead of eggs and skim milk rather than whole milk reduces fat and cholesterol for the madeleines in Cornmeal Madeleines with Smoked Salmon Spread. The spread is made with yogurt cheese, herbs, and just a small amount of smoked salmon to reduce the fat without skimping on flavor. Nonfat cream cheese stands in for its higher-fat counterpart in Smoked Trout on Pumpernickel Triangles. If your tastes run to favorites from around the world, Chinese Shrimp Toast and Sweet Potato Samosas are baked rather than fried. Pop-in-the-Mouth Meatballs are made with ground turkey rather than the higher-fat red meat or lamb. Take your pick.

1 LOW-FAT AÏOLI DIP WITH CRUDITÉS AND CROUTONS

Prep: 5 minutes   Cook: 10 to 12 minutes   Chill: 1 hour   Serves: 12

This unusual and spicy dip is for garlic lovers.

2 large unpeeled garlic cloves
1 tablespoon extra-virgin olive oil
1 (10½-ounce) package firm 1% fat silken tofu*
2 tablespoons minced onion
1 to 2 tablespoons fresh lemon juice

1 tablespoon Dijon mustard
3 cups vegetable dippers: carrot and celery sticks, cauliflower or broccoli florets, fresh green beans, sweet bell pepper strips
3 cups chunks of crusty nonfat bread (8 ounces)

1. Preheat toaster oven or oven to 425°F. Toss garlic with ¼ teaspoon of olive oil. Place on a small piece of aluminum foil. Roast 10 to 12 minutes, or until tender. Let garlic cool slightly, then slip off outer skin.

2. In a food processor, combine roasted garlic with remaining 2¾ teaspoons oil, tofu, onion, lemon juice, and mustard. Puree until smooth, about 30 seconds. Place in a bowl. Cover and refrigerate at least 1 hour for flavors to mellow.

Per Serving: Calories: 70 Total fat: 2 g Saturated fat: 0 g
Cholesterol: 0 mg Percentage calories from fat: 25%

* *Available at health food stores.*

2 DILLED GARLIC SPREAD

Prep: 5 minutes   Cook: none   Chill: 2 hours   Makes: 1 cup

This tasty spread can be spread on any crisp cracker or bagel chip. For a fancy version, tuck into the corner of endive spears and garnish with dill sprigs.

1 cup Yogurt Cheese (page 19)
2 tablespoons minced fresh dill

1 garlic clove, crushed through a press
⅛ teaspoon salt
Pinch of white pepper

In a medium bowl, combine yogurt cheese, dill, garlic, salt, and white pepper. Cover and refrigerate at least 2 hours for flavors to mellow.

Per Tablespoon: Calories: 11 Total fat: 0 g Saturated fat: 0 g
Cholesterol: 0 mg Percentage calories from fat: 0%

3 MEXICAN BLACK-EYED PEA "CAVIAR"

Prep: 15 minutes   Cook: none   Chill: overnight   Makes: 5 cups

This zippy dish gets better the longer it stands. Serve with restaurant-style fat-free tortilla chips as scoopers.

2 (16-ounce) cans black-eyed peas, rinsed and drained
¾ cup diced red bell pepper
½ cup diced red onion
½ cup minced seeded fresh jalapeño peppers
2 tablespoons minced cilantro
2 teaspoons minced garlic

1½ tablespoons canola or vegetable oil
2 tablespoons fresh lime juice
1½ teaspoons chopped fresh oregano or ½ teaspoon dried
Restaurant-style baked tortilla chips

1. In a large bowl, combine black-eyed peas, bell pepper, red onion, jalapeño peppers, cilantro, garlic, oil, lime juice, and oregano; mix lightly to combine.

2. Cover and refrigerate overnight for flavors to mellow, stirring occasionally. Drain off any liquid before serving. Serve with tortilla chips for dipping.

*Per Tablespoon: Calories: 12   Total fat: 0 g   Saturated fat: 0 g
Cholesterol: 0 mg   Percentage calories from fat: 23%*

4 HONEY MUSTARD DIP WITH VEGETABLE DIPPERS

Prep: 3 minutes   Cook: none   Chill: 1 hour   Serves: 8

This sweet-and-sour curry-flavored dip is also delicious with cooked meat, poultry, or seafood. Look for Madras-style curry powder for a more mellow flavor.

1 tablespoon curry powder
1 tablespoon Dijon mustard
1 tablespoon honey
½ cup nonfat mayonnaise dressing
½ cup nonfat plain yogurt
1 tablespoon fresh lime juice

⅛ teaspoon cayenne
4 cups dippers: raw mushrooms, sweet bell pepper strips, cherry tomatoes, raw green beans, cucumber sticks, and carrot sticks

Bagel Chips

1. In a small dry skillet, toast curry powder over low heat until fragrant, about 1 minute. Transfer to a small bowl.

2. Add mustard and honey to curry powder and mix until smooth. Stir in mayonnaise, yogurt, lime juice, and cayenne until blended. Cover and refrigerate at least 1 hour for flavors to mellow.

*Per Serving: Calories: 30   Total fat: 0 g   Saturated fat: 0 g
Cholesterol: 0 mg   Percentage calories from fat: 4%*

5   BABA GHANOUJ

Prep: 5 minutes   Cook: 15 to 20 minutes   Chill: 1 hour
Makes: 2 cups

Broiling the eggplants imparts a smoky flavor to this creamy smooth eggplant dip.

Olive oil cooking spray
2 large eggplants (1½ pounds each)
2 tablespoons tahini (Middle Eastern sesame paste)
2 tablespoons fresh lemon juice

2 garlic cloves, smashed
½ teaspoon ground cumin
2 tablespoons chopped parsley
Pita wedges

1. Preheat broiler. Line a 10 x 15-inch jelly roll pan with aluminum foil. Coat with cooking spray.

2. Cut eggplants lengthwise in half. Place, cut sides down, on prepared pan. With a fork, pierce eggplant skin in several places. Broil eggplant 5 to 6 inches from heat 15 to 20 minutes, or until eggplant is soft and skin is charred; let cool.

3. Using a tablespoon, scrape eggplant into a food processor or blender. Discard blackened skins. Add tahini, lemon juice, garlic, and cumin. Puree until smooth, about 30 seconds. Transfer to a small bowl. Cover and refrigerate at least 1 hour for flavors to mellow. Sprinkle with parsley just before serving. Serve with pita wedges for dipping.

Per Tablespoon: Calories: 16   Total fat: 1 g   Saturated fat: 0 g
Cholesterol: 0 mg   Percentage calories from fat: 30%

6   SHRIMP COCKTAIL DIP

Prep: 6 minutes   Cook: none   Chill: 1 hour   Makes: 2 cups

1 cup nonfat plain yogurt
½ cup nonfat sour cream
3 tablespoons bottled seafood cocktail sauce
2 tablespoons minced onion
Few drops of hot pepper sauce

1 (7½-ounce) can small shrimp, drained
Dippers: mini rice crackers, raw mushrooms, cherry tomatoes, zucchini rounds, celery strips, endive

In a medium bowl, blend together yogurt, sour cream, seafood cocktail sauce, onion, hot sauce, and shrimp. Cover and refrigerate at least 1 hour for flavors to mellow. Serve well chilled, with assorted dippers on the side.

Per Tablespoon: Calories: 17   Total fat: 0 g   Saturated fat: 0 g
Cholesterol: 12 mg   Percentage calories from fat: 8%

7 HUMMUS

Prep: 15 minutes   Cook: none   Chill: 1 hour   Makes: 2½ cups

This popular Middle Eastern dip takes well to pita wedges or crisp vegetables.

1 (20-ounce) can chickpeas
   (garbanzo beans)
½ cup loosely packed parsley
   leaves
1 tablespoon fresh lemon
   juice

3 tablespoons tahini (Middle
   Eastern sesame paste)
1 garlic clove, smashed
¼ teaspoon cayenne

1. Drain chickpeas, reserving ½ cup liquid. In a food processor, place chickpeas with ½ cup reserved liquid, parsley, lemon juice, tahini, garlic, and cayenne. Puree until smooth, about 30 seconds.

2. Transfer hummus to a serving bowl. Cover and refrigerate at least 1 hour for flavors to mellow.

Per Tablespoon: Calories: 24   Total fat: 1 g   Saturated fat: 0 g
Cholesterol: 0 mg   Percentage calories from fat: 28%

---

8 TUNA CAPER DIP

Prep: 10 minutes   Cook: none   Chill: 1 hour   Makes: 1⅓ cups

Silken tofu is a particular type of bean curd that has a finer texture and smoother feel than the traditional tofu. Look for it in health food stores.

½ cup nonfat mayonnaise
   dressing
½ cup firm 1% fat silken tofu
   (4 ounces)
1 (3½-ounce) can chunk light
   or white tuna in water,
   drained

¼ cup parsley leaves
1 tablespoon minced onion
1 tablespoon drained capers
1 to 1½ tablespoons fresh
   lemon juice
1 teaspoon anchovy paste

1. In a food processor, combine mayonnaise, tofu, tuna, parsley, onion, capers, lemon juice, and anchovy paste. Puree until smooth, about 30 seconds.

2. Spoon dip into a small crock or serving bowl. Cover and refrigerate at least 1 hour for flavors to mellow.

Per Tablespoon: Calories: 13   Total fat: 0 g   Saturated fat: 0 g
Cholesterol: 2 mg   Percentage calories from fat: 8%

9   MARINATED ARTICHOKE, BROCCOLI, AND CAULIFLOWER SALAD

Prep: 15 minutes   Cook: 14 minutes   Chill: 2 hours
Serves: 10 to 12

For speed, I make this easy vegetable appetizer salad using convenience foods. If you wish, you can substitute 1½ cups each fresh broccoli and cauliflower florets and steam them about 7 minutes until crisp-tender.

1 (16-ounce) package frozen
    broccoli and cauliflower
    mix
1 (9-ounce) jar artichoke
    hearts in water, drained,
    or 1 (9-ounce) package
    frozen artichoke hearts,
    cut in half if large
½ cup white wine vinegar
3 tablespoons canola oil
⅓ cup homemade or reduced-
    sodium canned chicken
    broth

2 tablespoons sliced scallions
1 tablespoon chopped cilantro
    or parsley
1½ tablespoons sugar
1 tablespoon fresh lemon
    juice
2 garlic cloves, minced
¼ teaspoon salt
⅛ teaspoon cayenne
1 cup canned chickpeas,
    rinsed and drained

1. Cook broccoli and cauliflower mix and frozen artichokes following package directions. Drain and let cool.

2. In a large bowl, combine vinegar, oil, chicken broth, scallions, cilantro, sugar, lemon juice, garlic, salt, and cayenne. Stir lightly to combine. Add vegetables and chickpeas and toss to mix.

3. Cover and refrigerate at least 2 hours for flavors to mellow, stirring occasionally. Drain before serving.

Per Serving: Calories: 66   Total fat: 2 g   Saturated fat: 0 g
Cholesterol: 0 mg   Percentage calories from fat: 28%

10   PEPPERED CHICKPEAS

Prep: 2 minutes   Cook: 3 minutes   Serves: 9

My Grandma Lena used to make this snack, which she called *nahit*, with dried chickpeas that she tossed with salt and pepper in a large kitchen towel after cooking. I've saved time by using canned chickpeas and eliminated the salt. You can add it if you want.

2 (16-ounce) cans chickpeas,
    including liquid

½ teaspoon coarsely ground
    black pepper

1. In a large skillet, place chickpeas with their liquid. Bring to a boil, reduce heat to medium-low, and simmer, stirring occasionally, until chickpeas are hot, about 3 minutes; drain.

2. On a large clean kitchen towel, rub chickpeas until dry. (Many of the outer skins will come off.) Place in a large bowl. Add pepper and toss to coat. Serve hot.

*Per Serving: Calories: 95 Total fat: 1 g Saturated fat: 0 g
                     Cholesterol: 0 mg Percentage calories from fat: 13%*

---

11   SWEET POTATO SAMOSAS
Prep: 30 minutes   Cook: 15 minutes   Makes: 24

This tasty Indian treat is usually wrapped in pastry and fried. I've rolled the filling in filo and then baked the samosas. It's important that you work quickly and that your filo be kept moist; otherwise it will be difficult to handle.

Vegetable cooking spray
1 (16-ounce) can sweet
    potatoes, drained
1 tablespoon minced seeded
    fresh jalapeño pepper
4 teaspoons curry powder
6 frozen filo pastry sheets,
    thawed

2 teaspoons butter, melted
1 (8½-ounce) jar mango
    chutney
3 tablespoons distilled white
    vinegar

1. Preheat oven to 400°F. Coat a large baking sheet with cooking spray.

2. In a food processor, combine sweet potatoes, jalapeño pepper, and curry powder. Process, using pulses, until mixture is smooth. Measure out 2 level teaspoons of sweet potato mixture into 24 mounds on a sheet of wax paper (this will save you time when filling filo strips).

3. Unfold 1 filo pastry sheet. (Keep remaining filo covered under wax paper and a slightly dampened kitchen towel to prevent drying out.) Spray filo with cooking spray. Cut lengthwise into 4 equal strips, each about 3 inches wide. Place 1 mound of potato filling in corner of one strip. Fold one corner of strip diagonally over filling so that short edge meets long edge of strip, forming a right angle. Continue folding over at right angles until you reach end of strip to form a triangular package. Place on baking sheet and cover with wax paper to prevent drying out. Repeat with remaining filo and filling, spraying each strip before cutting. Spray tops of samosas with cooking spray, then dab with a little bit of melted butter.

4. Bake 15 minutes, or until samosas are golden brown. While samosas are baking, coarsely chop chutney. Place in small bowl, add vinegar, and mix well. Use as dipping sauce for warm samosas.

*Per Samosa: Calories: 65 Total fat: 1 g Saturated fat: 0 g
                     Cholesterol: 1 mg Percentage calories from fat: 17%*

12   NEW POTATOES WITH GOLDEN GARLIC AND PARSLEY

Prep: 20 minutes   Cook: 22 minutes   Makes: 12

Small new potatoes are steamed, then topped with browned garlic and parsley. You can serve them warm or at room temperature. Try them also as a side dish to meat, fish, or poultry dishes.

12 small new red potatoes (1¼ pounds)	2 teaspoons finely chopped parsley
2 teaspoons olive oil	Coarse (kosher) salt
2 teaspoons minced garlic	Freshly cracked black
2 tablespoons chicken broth	pepper

1. Scrub potatoes well. Cut a small X in top of each potato. Place in a steamer basket and steam, covered, over boiling water until potatoes are tender, about 20 minutes. Remove from heat and let cool slightly.

2. When potatoes are cool enough to handle, gently peel back potato skin where you made the X, using a small knife. With thumb and forefinger of both hands (use potholders), press potatoes gently to pop up potato meat; fluff up slightly with a fork; set aside.

3. In a small skillet, heat olive oil over medium heat. Add garlic and cook 1 to 2 minutes, until light golden. Add chicken broth and heat slightly. Spoon ½ teaspoon of garlic and broth mixture over top of each potato. Sprinkle tops with parsley. Serve with small bowls of coarse salt and cracked pepper for guests to sprinkle over tops of potatoes. Serve warm or at room temperature.

Per Potato: Calories: 46   Total fat: 1 g   Saturated fat: 0 g
Cholesterol: 0 mg   Percentage calories from fat: 16%

13   LEMON-HERB STUFFED MUSHROOMS

Prep: 25 minutes   Cook: 8 to 10 minutes   Makes: 20

I like to use cremini mushrooms for this appetizer, as they have an earthier flavor and hold their shape when baked.

20 (1½- to 2-inch) cremini or white button mushrooms (12 ounces)	1 tablespoon reduced-fat margarine, melted
2 tablespoons finely chopped parsley	2 teaspoons fresh lemon juice
	¼ teaspoon salt
2 tablespoons finely chopped scallions	⅛ teaspoon pepper
	¼ cup bread crumbs

1. Preheat oven to 375°F. Wipe mushrooms with a damp cloth; remove stems. Chop stems finely. Place in a small bowl with parsley, scallions, margarine, lemon juice, salt, and pepper.

2. Stuff each mushroom cap with filling, mounding slightly. Sprinkle bread crumbs on top. Set stuffed mushrooms on a baking sheet.

3. Bake 8 to 10 minutes, or until filling is heated through and mushrooms are tender but still firm. Serve warm.

Per Mushroom: Calories: 12   Total fat: < 1 g   Saturated fat: 0 g
Cholesterol: 0 mg   Percentage calories from fat: 28%

---

14   PLUM TOMATOES WITH HERBED MAYONNAISE

Prep: 25 minutes   Cook: none   Chill: 1 hour   Makes: 12

½ cup nonfat mayonnaise
   dressing
¼ cup packed fresh basil
   leaves
¼ cup packed watercress
   leaves
2 tablespoons chopped fresh
   mint
2 tablespoons chopped
   parsley

2 tablespoons chopped
   scallions
2 tablespoons fresh lime juice
¼ teaspoon salt
   Pinch of pepper
6 large plum tomatoes
   (1½ pounds)
   Basil, parsley, or mint
   leaves

1. In a food processor, place mayonnaise, basil, watercress, mint, parsley, scallions, lime juice, salt, and pepper. Puree until smooth, about 15 seconds. Place in a bowl. Cover and refrigerate at least 1 hour to allow flavors to mellow.

2. When ready to serve, cut tomatoes lengthwise in half. Dollop 1 tablespoon of herbed mayonnaise onto each tomato half. Garnish with a leaf of basil, parsley, or mint.

Per Tomato: Calories: 21   Total fat: < 1 g   Saturated fat: 0 g
Cholesterol: 0 mg   Percentage calories from fat: 8%

15   FRESH TOMATO CROSTINI
Prep: 20 minutes   Cook: 1 to 2 minutes   Makes: 24

This fresh tomato crostini is best during the summer months when tomatoes are at their peak of perfection.

1 large garlic clove, halved
1 baguette (about 24 inches long), cut into ½-inch diagonal slices
1 pound firm, ripe tomatoes

1 tablespoon chopped fresh oregano or 1 teaspoon dried
¼ teaspoon salt
Freshly ground black pepper

1. Preheat broiler. Rub cut sides of garlic over top of each baguette slice. Place bread slices on a baking sheet. Toast under broiler about 1 to 2 minutes, until lightly browned, turning once. Watch carefully that bread slices don't burn.

2. Core and halve tomatoes; squeeze out seeds. Coarsely chop tomatoes. Place in a medium bowl with oregano and salt. Top each toasted baguette slice with tomato mixture. Top with a few grindings of pepper.

Per Slice: Calories: 43   Total fat: 0 g   Saturated fat: 0 g
Cholesterol: 0 mg   Percentage calories from fat: 10%

16   CORNMEAL MADELEINES WITH SMOKED SALMON SPREAD
Prep: 20 minutes   Cook: 12 to 15 minutes   Makes: 18

Make an elegant appetizer easier by using a corn muffin mix for the madeleines. For variety, you can substitute the Dilled Garlic Spread (page 8) for the Smoked Salmon Spread, or just dollop the madeleines with nonfat sour cream and caviar.

Vegetable cooking spray
1 (8½-ounce) package corn muffin mix
2 egg whites
⅓ cup skim milk

1 tablespoon chopped fresh dill or 1 teaspoon dried
Smoked Salmon Spread (page 19)
Dill sprigs

1. Preheat oven to 400°F. Coat madeleine pans with cooking spray.

2. In a large bowl, combine corn muffin mix, egg whites, milk, and dill. Mix just until moistened. Spoon 1 heaping tablespoon of batter into each madeleine hollow, spreading batter to fill evenly.

3. Bake 12 to 15 minutes, or until madeleines are golden. Let cool in pan on a wire rack 5 minutes. Unmold and let cool completely. Madeleines can be stored in an airtight container at this point, or frozen up to 1 month.

4. Dollop a scant tablespoon of Smoked Salmon Spread onto curved side of cornmeal madeleines or pipe mixture through a pastry bag fitted with a wide star-tipped tube. Garnish each with a dill sprig.

*Per Madeleine: Calories: 77   Total fat: 2 g   Saturated fat: 0 g
Cholesterol: 1 mg   Percentage calories from fat: 21%*

---

17   CHINESE SHRIMP TOAST

Prep: 15 minutes   Cook: 2 to 3 minutes   Makes: 16

This irresistible appetizer is usually fried. Substituting frozen cooked shrimp for raw shrimp and broiling the toasts gives you almost the same flavor of the original without the fat. Make sure you cover the bread slices completely with the shrimp mixture to prevent the bread from browning too much on the edges as it broils. If this happens, just trim off dark edges with a sharp knife.

1 (5½-ounce) package frozen cooked salad shrimp
2 tablespoons minced scallion
2 tablespoons finely chopped water chestnuts
1 teaspoon minced fresh ginger

½ teaspoon reduced-sodium soy sauce
¼ teaspoon sugar
⅛ to ¼ teaspoon cayenne
1 egg white
4 slices of firm white bread, toasted

1. Preheat broiler. Thaw shrimp under cold running water; squeeze dry between paper towels. Mince shrimp and place in a small bowl. Add scallions, water chestnuts, ginger, soy sauce, sugar, and cayenne. Blend in egg white until well mixed.

2. Divide shrimp mixture evenly among bread slices, spreading completely to edges. Cut each slice diagonally into 4 triangles. Place on a large baking sheet.

3. Broil 6 inches from heat about 3 minutes, or until hot and beginning to brown. Serve warm.

*Per Toast: Calories: 29   Total fat: 0 g   Saturated fat: 0 g
Cholesterol: 19 mg   Percentage calories from fat: 9%*

18   POP-IN-THE-MOUTH MEATBALLS
Prep: 16 minutes   Chill: 1 hour   Cook: 13 to 15 minutes   Makes: 30

Appetizers are called *meze* in Greek, and these savory little morsels are flavored with currants, pine nuts, mint, and cinnamon. I like to serve them with a bowl of nonfat plain yogurt for dipping, sometimes adding some of the herbs used in the meatballs.

Olive oil cooking spray	1 egg white
¾ pound ground turkey	½ teaspoon salt
½ cup minced scallions	¼ teaspoon cinnamon
⅓ cup fresh bread crumbs	⅛ teaspoon cayenne
¼ cup currants or raisins	Herbed Yogurt Sauce
2 tablespoons minced parsley	(recipe follows)
2 tablespoons minced fresh mint	

1. Coat a 10 x 15-inch jelly roll pan with cooking spray. In a large bowl, combine ground turkey, scallions, bread crumbs, currants, parsley, mint, egg white, salt, cinnamon, and cayenne. Mix lightly to combine. Shape into 1-inch balls (1 level measuring tablespoon) and place on prepared pan. Refrigerate 1 hour.

2. Preheat oven to 350°F. Bake meatballs 10 minutes. Transfer pan to broiler and broil 3 to 4 inches from heat 3 to 5 minutes, until lightly browned. Serve warm with wooden picks to pick up and dip in Herbed Yogurt Sauce.

Per Meatball: Calories: 28 Total fat: 1 g Saturated fat: 0 g
Cholesterol: 8 mg Percentage calories from fat: 29%

19   HERBED YOGURT SAUCE
Prep: 5 minutes   Stand: 30 minutes   Cook: none
Makes: about 1 cup

1 cup plain nonfat yogurt	1 tablespoon minced fresh
1 tablespoon minced scallions	mint

1. Place yogurt in a fine sieve set over a small bowl. Let drain at room temperature 30 minutes.

2. Transfer thickened yogurt to a small serving bowl. Add scallions and mint. Stir to mix. Cover and refrigerate until ready to use.

Per Tablespoon: Calories: 41 Total fat: 0 g Saturated fat: 0 g
Cholesterol: 0 mg Percentage calories from fat: 2%

20 SMOKED SALMON SPREAD

Prep: 5 minutes   Cook: none   Chill: 2 hours   Makes: 1 cup

Yogurt cheese is substituted for cream cheese in this always popular spread. Reducing the amount of smoked salmon also reduces the fat content.

1 cup Yogurt Cheese (recipe follows)
2 tablespoons minced fresh chives
1 teaspoon fresh lemon juice

2½ ounces smoked salmon, minced (3 tablespoons)
⅛ teaspoon salt (optional)
⅛ teaspoon white pepper

In a medium bowl, combine yogurt cheese, chives, lemon juice, smoked salmon, salt, if using, and white pepper. Cover and refrigerate at least 2 hours for flavors to mellow.

*Per Tablespoon: Calories: 15   Total fat: 0 g   Saturated fat: 0 g
Cholesterol: 1 mg   Percentage calories from fat: 12%*

21 YOGURT CHEESE

Prep: 20 minutes   Cook: none   Chill: overnight   Makes: 3 cups

The versatility of yogurt cheese is almost limitless. Use it as the base for many dishes that call for sour cream, cream cheese, or heavy cream.

6 cups nonfat plain yogurt

1. Line a large sieve with a double thickness of cheesecloth. Place over a large bowl; spoon yogurt in sieve and cover with plastic wrap. Refrigerate overnight to allow yogurt to drain.

2. Next day, discard whey (liquid in bowl) and scrape yogurt cheese (which will be very thick) in a bowl. Cover and refrigerate until ready to use. Yogurt cheese will keep for up to 2 weeks in the refrigerator.

*Per Cup: Calories: 160   Total fat: 0 g   Saturated fat: 0 g
Cholesterol: 0 mg   Percentage calories from fat: 0%*

22   YOGURT FRUIT DIP
Prep: 3 minutes   Cook: none   Chill: 1 hour   Makes: 1 cup

You can serve this luscious dip either as an appetizer or as a light, refreshing dessert. To prevent discoloring, brush banana, apples, and pears with a little lemon juice.

½ **cup vanilla-flavored yogurt**
½ **cup nonfat sour cream**
1 **tablespoon honey**
½ **teaspoon ground ginger**
½ **teaspoon fresh lemon juice**

Dippers: strawberries, pineapple chunks, grape clusters, melon wedges, banana chunks, apple wedges, red pear slices

In a small bowl, blend together yogurt, sour cream, honey, ginger, and lemon juice. Cover and refrigerate at least 1 hour for flavors to mellow. Serve with fruit of your choice for dipping.

Per Tablespoon: Calories: 15   Total fat: 0 g   Saturated fat: 0 g
Cholesterol: 0 mg   Percentage calories from fat: 5%

23   GARDEN-STYLE DEVILED EGG PITA BITES
Prep: 30 minutes   Cook: 15 minutes   Makes: 24

You get the tangy flavor of a deviled egg, with a fraction of the fat in these tasty mini sandwiches, great for snacking or as a cold hors d'oeuvre. The deviled egg salad can be prepared up to a day in advance and refrigerated, but to prevent the sandwiches from becoming soggy, be sure to fill the pita breads shortly before serving.

½ **of a 10-ounce package frozen chopped spinach**
6 **hard-boiled eggs**
¼ **cup nonfat mayonnaise dressing**
2 **tablespoons minced scallions or chives**

2 **tablespoons Dijon mustard**
24 **mini pita breads (3 inches in diameter)**
½ **cup alfalfa sprouts**

1. Cook spinach according to package directions; drain well and squeeze out most of liquid. Finely chop spinach and set aside.

2. Peel eggs and slice in half. Remove half of yolks; discard or save for another use. In a small bowl, chop remaining 3 egg yolks with all 6 egg whites. Mix in cooked spinach, mayonnaise, scallions, and mustard, blending well.

3. Trim a slim slice off each pita bread. Gently open to form pocket. Spoon 2 tablespoons egg salad into each. Garnish with alfalfa sprouts.

Per Pita: Calories: 103   Total fat: 2 g   Saturated fat: 0 g
Cholesterol: 27 mg   Percentage calories from fat: 14%

24 SMOKED TROUT ON PUMPERNICKEL TRIANGLES

Prep: 30 minutes   Cook: none   Chill: 3 hours   Makes: 24

Smoked fish adds an interesting flavor in this quick-to-prepare appetizer. You can also spoon the filling into scooped-out cherry tomatoes.

¼ **pound smoked trout or whitefish, skinned and boned**
½ **cup nonfat cream cheese (4 ounces)**
4 **teaspoons grated fresh onion**
1 **teaspoon fresh lemon juice**

¼ **teaspoon white pepper**
6 **square slices of Westphalian-style pumpernickel bread**
12 **small cherry tomatoes, halved**
Parsley or dill sprigs

1. In a food processor, place smoked fish, cream cheese, onion, lemon juice, and white pepper. Puree until smooth, about 30 seconds. Place in a bowl. Cover and refrigerate until mixture is firm, about 3 hours.

2. Cut bread slices into diagonal quarters. Put smoked fish spread into a pastry bag fitted with a star-tipped tube. Pipe onto bread triangles (or dollop on with a small spoon). Top each with a tomato half and a parsley or dill sprig.

Per Canapé: Calories: 31 Total fat: 0 g Saturated fat: 0 g
Cholesterol: 2 mg Percentage calories from fat: 8%

25 SAVORY WONTON CRISPS

Prep: 6 minutes   Cook: 6 to 7 minutes   Makes: 24

Vegetable cooking spray
2 **tablespoons grated fresh Parmesan cheese**
¼ **teaspoon dried basil**

¼ **teaspoon dried oregano**
¼ **teaspoon garlic powder**
1 **teaspoon olive oil**
12 **wonton skins**

1. Preheat oven to 375°F. Coat a large baking sheet with cooking spray. In a small bowl, combine Parmesan cheese, basil, oregano, and garlic powder. Stir to blend well. In small cup, mix 2 teaspoons water with olive oil.

2. Cut wonton skins in half diagonally. Place on prepared baking sheet. Brush wonton pieces lightly with water-oil mixture. Sprinkle lightly with seasoned Parmesan cheese.

3. Bake 6 to 7 minutes, or until wontons are crisp and lightly browned. Let cool on a wire rack. Store in an airtight container.

Per Crisp: Calories: 16 Total fat: 0 g Saturated fat: 0 g
Cholesterol: 1 mg Percentage calories from fat: 26%

Chapter 2

Slim Soups and Chowders

The women in my family made great soups, so it's no wonder that soup evokes fond memories for me. For many years we would go to my Grandma Lena's for Friday night dinner, and sitting on the stove would be a gargantuan pot of chicken soup with lukshen (thin noodles). It was pure ambrosia. My Aunt Helen made a hearty stick-to-the-ribs mushroom and barley soup with potato dumplings, which I have yet to duplicate. And Mom made a split pea soup so thick the spoon would stand up by itself. Nowadays, my own soups are more ethnically diverse and significantly lighter. They vary from hearty low-fat hot main-dish soups to cool, refreshing fruit soups.

Soups can start a meal, be the meal, or end the meal. Since they rely largely on broth, vegetables, and seasonings, they are naturally low in fat. The basis of a good soup is a homemade broth, and I have included recipes for beef, chicken, and vegetable broth. Chilling the broth overnight and then skimming the solidified grease on top is an easy way to remove all the fat. There are also many good-quality reduced-sodium broths available; just make sure you skim off any fat from the surface before using.

To thicken soups, I often puree part of the soup and stir it back into the pot. This technique also adds a creamy richness without any butter or cream.

Hearty soups, such as Mexican Chicken Soup and Italian Meatball and Escarole Soup, use a small amount of chicken or meat; each is a meal in itself. Soups loaded with barley, pasta, and beans are also substantial enough to be meals-in-a-bowl: Soupe au Pistou, Quick Meatless Mushroom-Barley Soup, and Hopping John Soup are a few choices. A tossed salad and crusty bread are all the accompaniments you'll need.

And on sultry summer days, try teaming cold soups, such as Moroccan Spiced Carrot Soup or Spicy Corn and Zucchini Gazpacho, with a tasty sandwich for a light supper. Or start the meal with a sandwich and serve Double Berry Cherry Soup or Cold Spiced Plum Soup as an unusual and delightful dessert.

26 MOROCCAN SPICED CARROT SOUP

Prep: 15 minutes   Cook: 23 minutes   Chill: 2 hours   Serves: 4

A delicious soup flavored with a heady blend of spices, this goes well before roast turkey or pork. You can serve the soup warm, but I like the way the spices mellow when it chills.

2 teaspoons reduced-fat margarine
½ cup chopped scallions
2 teaspoons curry powder
¼ teaspoon ground coriander
¼ teaspoon ground cardamom
4 cups chunked (1-inch) peeled carrots

3½ cups homemade or canned reduced-sodium chicken broth
½ cup nonfat plain yogurt or nonfat sour cream
Fresh mint sprigs

1. In a large saucepan, melt margarine. Add scallions and cook over medium heat until soft, about 2 minutes. Add curry powder, coriander, and cardamom; cook, stirring, 1 minute. Add carrots and chicken broth. Bring to a boil over high heat. Reduce heat, cover, and simmer until carrots are tender, about 20 minutes.

2. In a food processor or blender, puree mixture, in batches if necessary, until smooth. Pour into a bowl. Cover and refrigerate about 2 hours, or until well chilled. Dollop each serving with 1 tablespoon yogurt or sour cream. Garnish each with a mint sprig. Serve cold.

Per Serving: Calories: 102   Total fat: 3 g   Saturated fat: 1 g
Cholesterol: 0 mg   Percentage calories from fat: 24%

27 SPICY CORN AND ZUCCHINI GAZPACHO

Prep: 15 minutes   Cook: none   Chill: 3 hours   Serves: 4

This zippy Mexican-style gazpacho uses a spicy-hot vegetable juice to give it pep. Be sure to serve it ice cold.

1½ cups frozen whole-kernel corn or 1 cup canned whole-kernel corn, drained
1 cup halved cherry tomatoes
1 cup sliced zucchini
½ cup 1-inch chunks green bell pepper

⅓ cup sliced scallions
1 garlic clove, minced
2 tablespoons fresh lime juice
1 tablespoon chopped cilantro
2 cups spicy-hot vegetable juice

1. Cook frozen corn following package directions; drain and let cool. If using canned corn, eliminate this step.

2. In a food processor, place tomatoes, zucchini, bell pepper, and scallions. Process, using pulses, until vegetables are coarsely chopped. Transfer to a large bowl. Stir in corn, garlic, lime juice, cilantro, and spicy-hot vegetable juice. Cover and refrigerate 3 hours, or until very cold. Serve chilled.

Per Serving: Calories: 101   Total fat: 1 g   Saturated fat: 0 g
Cholesterol: 0 mg   Percentage calories from fat: 5%

---

28   MEXICAN CHICKEN SOUP
Prep: 15 minutes   Cook: 28 minutes   Serves: 4

Topped with Cheddar cheese, sour cream, and picante sauce, this hearty chicken soup has festive flair.

1 **pound skinless, boneless chicken breasts**
3 **cups homemade or canned reduced-sodium chicken broth**
1 **teaspoon canola or corn oil**
1 **cup chopped onion**
2 **teaspoons finely chopped garlic**
1 **(16-ounce) can red kidney beans, rinsed and drained**

1 **to 2 tablespoons minced seeded fresh jalapeño pepper**
¾ **teaspoon ground cumin**
¼ **cup coarsely shredded reduced-fat Cheddar cheese (1 ounce)**
¼ **cup nonfat sour cream**
¼ **cup prepared thick-and-chunky picante sauce**

1. Place chicken breasts and chicken broth in a large deep skillet or flame-proof casserole. Bring slowly to a simmer. Cover and simmer over low heat until chicken is tender, about 15 minutes. Remove chicken to a plate. Strain broth into a 4-cup glass measure; strain off any fat. When chicken is cool enough to handle, cut into 1-inch cubes.

2. In same skillet, heat oil. Add onion and garlic. Cook over medium heat until soft but not brown, about 3 minutes. Add kidney beans, jalapeño pepper, cumin, and chicken broth. Bring to a boil; lower heat. Cover and simmer 10 minutes.

3. Add cubed chicken and heat to serving temperature. Top each serving with 1 tablespoon each of Cheddar cheese, sour cream, and picante sauce.

Per Serving: Calories: 298   Total fat: 7 g   Saturated fat: 2 g
Cholesterol: 73 mg   Percentage calories from fat: 22%

29 HERBED CUCUMBER, RADISH, AND SCALLION SOUP

Prep: 10 minutes   Cook: none   Chill: 2 hours   Serves: 6 to 8

Yogurt forms a tart base for this refreshing, crunchy soup. If you use unwaxed cucumbers, there is no need to peel them. Serve with fresh pumpernickel rolls.

4 cups nonfat plain yogurt
1½ cups peeled, seeded, and coarsely chopped cucumber
½ cup coarsely chopped red radishes
½ cup sliced scallions
1 tablespoon minced fresh dill or ½ teaspoon dried

1 tablespoon minced fresh mint or 1 teaspoon dried
1 garlic clove, minced
¼ teaspoon salt
⅛ teaspoon freshly ground pepper
Fresh mint leaves or dill sprigs

In a large bowl, combine yogurt with 1 cup water. Mix well to blend. Stir in cucumber, radishes, scallions, dill, mint, garlic, salt, and pepper. Cover and refrigerate 2 hours, or until well chilled. Garnish with mint leaves or dill sprigs. Serve cold.

Per Serving: Calories: 81   Total fat: 0 g   Saturated fat: 0 g
Cholesterol: 3 mg   Percentage calories from fat: 3%

30 HOPPING JOHN SOUP

Prep: 8 minutes   Cook: 26 minutes   Serves: 4

Hopping John is a Southern rice and bean dish, traditionally served on New Year's Day. I've taken the same flavors and made it into a soup. This recipe can be doubled easily.

1 slice of bacon, cut into ¼-inch dice
½ cup chopped onion
½ cup thinly sliced celery
1 garlic clove, minced
1 (16-ounce) can black-eyed peas, undrained

1½ cups homemade or canned reduced-sodium chicken broth
¼ teaspoon cayenne
¼ teaspoon hot pepper sauce
¼ cup long-grain white rice
1 tablespoon chopped parsley

1. In a large saucepan, cook bacon over medium heat until crisp, about 3 minutes. Remove with a slotted spoon to paper towels to drain. Pour off all but 1 teaspoon drippings from pan.

2. Add onion, celery, and garlic to bacon drippings. Cook over medium heat until soft, about 3 minutes. Add undrained black-eyed peas, chicken broth, cayenne, and hot pepper sauce. Bring to a boil over high heat; reduce to low heat. Stir in rice. Cover and simmer until rice is tender, about 20 minutes.

3. Stir in cooked bacon pieces. Soup thickens upon standing; add water or chicken broth to thin, if necessary. Serve garnished with parsley.

*Per Serving: Calories: 168   Total fat: 3 g   Saturated fat: 1 g
              Cholesterol: 2 mg   Percentage calories from fat: 16%*

---

31   SOUPE AU PISTOU
Prep: 30 minutes   Cook: 1¼ hours   Serves: 6 to 8

As in the traditional recipe, this robust French vegetable soup is finished off with garlic, Parmesan cheese, fresh basil, and fruity olive oil.

2 cups diagonally sliced carrots

2 cups peeled and diced (½-inch) potatoes

2 cups sliced leeks (white part only)

2 teaspoons salt

¼ teaspoon pepper

1 pound zucchini, trimmed and sliced or cut into thick matchsticks

½ pound fresh green beans, trimmed and cut into 1-inch pieces

1 cup small bow ties, rotelle, elbows, or pasta of your choice

1 (16-ounce) can red kidney beans, rinsed and drained

2 tablespoons tomato paste

2 garlic cloves, minced

¼ cup grated Parmesan cheese

¼ cup chopped fresh basil

2 tablespoons extra-virgin olive oil

1. In a large soup pot or dutch oven, combine carrots, potatoes, leeks, salt, pepper, and 12 cups (3 quarts) water. Bring to a boil, reduce heat to low, and simmer, with cover slightly ajar, 1 hour, stirring several times.

2. Add zucchini, green beans, and pasta. Cover and simmer until vegetables and pasta are tender, about 15 minutes. Add kidney beans.

3. Just before serving, put tomato paste and garlic in a medium bowl. Stir in Parmesan cheese and basil. Drizzle in olive oil in a slow steady stream, mixing until combined. Add ½ cup of soup liquid to tomato paste mixture to thin; then gradually stir into soup. Serve hot.

*Per Serving: Calories: 241   Total fat: 6 g   Saturated fat: 1 g
              Cholesterol: 3 mg   Percentage calories from fat: 21%*

32   ITALIAN MEATBALL AND ESCAROLE SOUP

Prep: 20 minutes   Cook: 20 minutes   Serves: 4

Orzo, the rice-shaped pasta, escarole, which is a tart salad green, and lemon juice flavor this hearty soup. Ground turkey makes the meatballs light and nutritionally lower in fat and cholesterol than pork or beef.

½ pound ground turkey
1 egg white
1 garlic clove, minced
2 tablespoons chopped
   parsley
1 tablespoon grated Parmesan
   cheese
½ teaspoon salt

⅛ teaspoon pepper
4½ cups homemade or canned
   reduced-sodium chicken
   broth
½ cup orzo (rice-shaped pasta)
4 cups shredded escarole
2 tablespoons fresh lemon
   juice

1. In a medium bowl, combine ground turkey, egg white, garlic, parsley, Parmesan cheese, salt, and pepper. Mix lightly to blend. Shape into 16 meatballs about ¾ inch in diameter.

2. In a large soup pot, bring chicken broth to a boil. Add meatballs and orzo, reduce heat to medium-low, cover, and simmer 15 minutes, or until meatballs are cooked through. Add escarole and lemon juice. Cover and simmer 5 minutes longer, or until escarole is wilted and tender. Serve sprinkled with additional Parmesan cheese, if desired.

Per Serving: Calories: 225   Total fat: 8 g   Saturated fat: 2 g
Cholesterol: 42 mg   Percentage calories from fat: 28%

33   CARAMELIZED ONION SOUP

Prep: 15 minutes   Cook: 45 to 50 minutes   Serves: 4

Caramelizing the onions gives this soup its sweetness and robust flavor. To make thin slivers, first cut onions in half crosswise from root end, then cut into thin strips. For a sweeter-tasting soup, use large Spanish onions.

4 cups slivered onions (about
   5 medium)
1 tablespoon olive oil
2 tablespoons flour
4 cups homemade or canned
   reduced-sodium beef
   broth
1 bay leaf

½ teaspoon dried thyme leaves
¼ teaspoon hot pepper sauce,
   or to taste
¼ cup chopped parsley
4 (1-inch-thick) slices of
   French bread, toasted
4 teaspoons grated Parmesan
   cheese

1. Place onions in a large saucepan. Drizzle olive oil over onions and toss to coat. Cook over medium-low heat, stirring frequently, until onions are a deep golden brown, about 25 to 30 minutes.

2. Sprinkle flour over onions and toss to coat. Cook, stirring, 1 minute. Stir in beef broth. Add bay leaf, thyme, and hot pepper sauce. Bring to a boil. Reduce heat to low, cover, and simmer 20 minutes. Remove and discard bay leaf.

3. Ladle soup into bowls; sprinkle with parsley. Top each portion with a slice of toasted bread; sprinkle with 1 teaspoon Parmesan cheese.

Per Serving: Calories: 228   Total fat: 5 g   Saturated fat: 1 g
Cholesterol: 2 mg   Percentage calories from fat: 21%

---

34 QUICK MEATLESS MUSHROOM-BARLEY SOUP

Prep: 10 minutes   Cook: 35 minutes   Serves: 6

Using a quick-cooking barley substantially reduces the cooking time for this favorite soup. Cremini mushrooms are sometimes called "Italian brown" mushrooms. They have an intense earthy taste, which is very pleasing.

2 teaspoons canola or olive oil	1 garlic clove, minced
8 ounces cremini or white button mushrooms, trimmed and sliced	¾ cup quick-cooking barley
	½ teaspoon crumbled leaf sage
	½ teaspoon salt
½ cup sliced leeks (white part only) or ½ cup chopped onion	5 cups homemade or canned reduced-sodium beef broth
½ cup sliced celery	1 cup frozen lima beans
½ cup diced carrots	

1. In a large soup pot or dutch oven, heat oil over medium heat. Add mushrooms, leeks, celery, carrots, garlic, and 2 tablespoons water. Toss to coat with oil and water. Cover and cook over medium-low heat until vegetables are softened, about 5 minutes.

2. Add barley, sage, and salt. Stir in beef broth. Bring to a boil over high heat, reduce heat to low, cover, and simmer 15 minutes.

3. Stir in lima beans; cover and cook until barley is tender and lima beans are soft, about 15 minutes longer. Soup will thicken upon standing. Add water or additional beef broth to thin if necessary. Serve piping hot.

Per Serving: Calories: 140   Total fat: 2 g   Saturated fat: 0 g
Cholesterol: 0 mg   Percentage calories from fat: 12%

35   PUMPKIN BISQUE
Prep: 5 minutes   Cook: 10 minutes   Serves: 6

1 (16-ounce) can solid-pack pumpkin
1 (11-ounce) package frozen butternut squash, cooked according to package directions
2 cups homemade or canned reduced-sodium chicken broth

¼ teaspoon salt
¼ teaspoon ground ginger
¼ teaspoon ground cinnamon
¼ teaspoon ground nutmeg
Pinch of white pepper
1 (12-ounce) can evaporated skim milk

1. In a medium saucepan, combine pumpkin, cooked squash, chicken broth, salt, ginger, cinnamon, nutmeg, white pepper, and ¼ cup water. Mix well until smooth. Stir in evaporated skimmed milk.

2. Heat slowly to serving temperature, stirring frequently. Garnish top of each serving with a small dash of nutmeg, if you wish.

*Per Serving: Calories: 115   Total fat: 1 g   Saturated fat: 0 g
Cholesterol: 0 mg   Percentage calories from fat: 8%*

36   CHILLED RED CABBAGE AND BEET SOUP
Prep: 3 minutes   Cook: none   Chill: 2 hours   Serves: 6

This is a very refreshing soup, and very easy to prepare. Sometimes I like to top the cold soup with a sprinkling of cubed hot boiled potato. If you prefer, the soup can also be served warm.

1 (16-ounce) jar sweet-and-sour red cabbage, juices reserved
1 (16-ounce) can julienne beets, juices reserved
1 (13¾-ounce) reduced-sodium beef or chicken broth

2 tablespoons red wine vinegar
⅛ teaspoon cayenne
6 tablespoons nonfat sour cream
2 tablespoons chopped fresh dill

1. In a large bowl, combine red cabbage and beets with their juices, broth, vinegar, and cayenne. Cover and refrigerate at least 2 hours, or until very cold.

2. Top each serving with 1 tablespoon sour cream and 1 teaspoon chopped dill.

*Per Serving: Calories: 77   Total fat: 0 g   Saturated fat: 0 g
Cholesterol: 0 mg   Percentage calories from fat: 1%*

37   SOUTHWESTERN TOMATO SOUP

Prep: 20 minutes   Cook: 25 minutes   Serves: 4

This soup, while delicious hot, can also be served cold. Serve with additional baked tortilla chips on the side.

1½ **pounds ripe plum tomatoes**
½ **cup diced onion**
½ **cup diced red bell pepper**
1 **tablespoon finely chopped, seeded fresh jalapeño pepper**
2 **large garlic cloves, minced**
2½ **cups homemade or canned reduced-sodium chicken broth**

¼ **teaspoon salt**
⅛ **teaspoon cayenne**
½ **cup coarsely crumbled baked tortilla chips**
1½ **tablespoons minced fresh basil, plus 4 basil leaves**
¼ **cup nonfat sour cream**

1. Plunge plum tomatoes into a large pot of boiling water. Remove from heat and let stand 1 minute. Immediately plunge tomatoes into a bowl filled with ice and water. Peel tomatoes (the skins will come off easily), seed, and coarsely chop.

2. In a large saucepan, place onion, bell pepper, jalapeño pepper, and garlic. Add ½ cup of chicken broth and bring to a boil over high heat. Reduce heat to low, cover, and cook vegetables until soft, about 5 minutes.

3. Add chopped tomatoes, remaining 2 cups chicken broth, salt, and cayenne. Bring to a boil. Reduce heat to medium-low and simmer, uncovered, 15 minutes. Add crushed tortilla chips and minced basil; simmer 5 minutes longer. Remove from heat.

4. In a food processor or blender, puree soup, in batches if necessary, until smooth. Pour soup back into saucepan and heat to serving temperature. Top each bowl with 1 tablespoon sour cream and garnish with a basil leaf.

Per Serving: Calories: 101   Total fat: 2 g   Saturated fat: 0 g
Cholesterol: 0 mg   Percentage calories from fat: 8%

38　CREOLE SOUP
Prep: 10 minutes　Cook: 34 to 36 minutes　Serves: 4

I've used frozen cooked shrimp for this recipe, but you can substitute an equal amount of shelled and deveined fresh shrimp, if you wish. Just cook them until they turn pink.

2　teaspoons olive oil	1　to 1½ teaspoons Cajun spice
½　cup sliced scallions	blend
1　garlic clove, minced	1　cup frozen okra, slightly
3　cups low-sodium vegetable	thawed
juice	1　(5-ounce) package frozen
⅓　cup converted long-grain	cooked salad shrimp,
rice	rinsed and drained well
¾　teaspoon dried thyme leaves	⅛　teaspoon hot pepper sauce,
1　bay leaf	or more to taste

1. In a large saucepan, heat olive oil. Add scallions and garlic and cook over medium heat until soft, about 2 minutes. Add vegetable juice, rice, thyme, bay leaf, Cajun seasoning, and 1 cup water. Bring to a boil. Reduce heat to low, cover, and simmer 25 minutes.

2. Add okra and cook, covered, 6 to 8 minutes, or until okra is cooked. Stir in shrimp and hot sauce; heat through. If using fresh shrimp, cook just until shrimp turn pink. Remove and discard bay leaf before serving.

Per Serving:　Calories: 216　Total fat: 4 g　Saturated fat: 1 g
*　　　　　　　Cholesterol: 69 mg　Percentage calories from fat: 16%*

39　CURRIED YELLOW SPLIT PEA SOUP WITH SPINACH
Prep: 10 minutes　Cook: 50 to 53 minutes　Serves: 6 to 8

Indian spices add zest to this thick, hearty soup. Be sure to add the spinach just shortly before serving to keep it colorful and bright green.

2　teaspoons canola oil	¼　teaspoon turmeric
1　cup chopped onion	¼　teaspoon ground coriander
1　large garlic clove, minced	¼　teaspoon cayenne
1½　teaspoons finely chopped	2　cups dry yellow split peas
fresh ginger	1½　cups trimmed shredded
½　teaspoon ground cumin	fresh spinach
½　teaspoon curry powder	½　teaspoon salt

1. In a large soup pot or dutch oven, heat oil over medium heat. Add onion and garlic and cook until soft, 3 to 5 minutes. Add ginger, cumin, curry powder, turmeric, coriander, and cayenne. Cook, stirring, 1 minute, to toast the spices.

2. Add yellow split peas and 8 cups water. Bring to a boil over high heat. Reduce heat to medium-low, cover, and simmer until split peas are soft, about 45 minutes.

3. Add spinach and salt. Cook until spinach wilts, about 1 to 2 minutes. Soup will thicken upon standing. Add additional water to thin.

*Per Serving: Calories: 217   Total fat: 2 g   Saturated fat: 0 g
                Cholesterol: 0 mg   Percentage calories from fat: 8%*

---

40   COLD POTATO AND LEEK SOUP

Prep: 15 minutes   Cook: 12 to 15 minutes   Chill: 3 hours   Serves: 4

Evaporated skim milk replaces the heavy cream traditionally used in this classic vichyssoise. You get all the richness of flavor without the fat and calories.

1 teaspoon olive oil	1 cup evaporated skim milk
½ cup sliced leeks (white part only)	¼ teaspoon salt
	¼ teaspoon white pepper
2 cups peeled and diced (½-inch) yellow potatoes, such as Yukon Gold	⅛ teaspoon ground nutmeg
	¼ cup nonfat sour cream
	Fresh chives
2 cups homemade or canned reduced-sodium chicken broth	

1. In a medium saucepan, heat olive oil over medium heat. Add leeks and cook until soft but not brown, 2 to 3 minutes. Add potatoes and chicken broth. Bring to a boil over high heat. Reduce heat to medium-low, cover, and simmer until potatoes are fork-tender, 10 to 12 minutes. Remove from heat; let cool slightly.

2. In a food processor or blender, puree soup until smooth. Pour into a large bowl. Whisk in evaporated skimmed milk, salt, white pepper, nutmeg, and sour cream. Cover and refrigerate 3 hours, or until well chilled. Garnish with chives. Serve cold.

*Per Serving: Calories: 152   Total fat: 2 g   Saturated fat: 0 g
                Cholesterol: 3 mg   Percentage calories from fat: 14%*

41 BEEF BROTH

Prep: 10 minutes   Cook: 2½ to 3 hours   Chill: 8 hours
Makes: 2 quarts

Browning the beef and vegetables gives the broth a rich, deep flavor. Chilling the broth overnight makes it easier to remove the fat that accumulates on top.

3 pounds meaty beef chuck neck bones or beef soup bones

1 large unpeeled onion, quartered

2 large unpeeled carrots, washed and cut into chunks

1 large leafy celery rib, cut into chunks

8 sprigs of fresh parsley

3 sprigs of fresh thyme or ½ teaspoon dried

1 bay leaf

¼ teaspoon black peppercorns

1. Preheat oven to 400°F. Roast bones in a shallow roasting pan lined with foil, turning occasionally with a slotted spoon, until they begin to brown, about 30 minutes. Drain off fat. Add onion, carrots, and celery to pan. Continue to roast until bones and vegetables are browned, about 30 minutes longer.

2. With a slotted spoon, transfer bones and vegetables to a large heavy soup pot or dutch oven. Add 12 cups (3 quarts) water, parsley, thyme, bay leaf, and peppercorns. Bring to a boil; skim foam from surface.

3. Cook broth, uncovered, over medium-low heat until reduced by one-third, about 2½ to 3 hours. Reduce heat to low if liquid begins to boil.

4. Strain broth through a large fine-mesh strainer or colander set over a large bowl. (Note: If you wish, shred meat from bones, discarding fat; reserve for soup.) Refrigerate overnight. Skim solid fat from surface and discard. If not using within 2 days, ladle broth into 2-cup containers and freeze.

Per Serving: Calories: 15   Total fat: 0 g   Saturated fat: 0 g
Cholesterol: 0 mg   Percentage calories from fat: 1%

42 SPINACH TORTELLINI EN BRODO

Prep: 15 minutes   Cook: 12 to 17 minutes   Serves: 4

This soup couldn't be simpler to prepare, and it is a veritable meal in a bowl.

8 ounces frozen spinach and cheese tortellini or frozen mini cheese ravioli

2 cups homemade or canned reduced-sodium chicken broth

* fresh Ginger

1 cup shredded fresh spinach leaves (2 ounces)

2 tablespoons sliced scallions

¼ cup grated Parmesan cheese Freshly ground black pepper

1. In a medium saucepan, cook tortellini or mini ravioli in boiling water until tender, 10 to 15 minutes; drain.

2. In same saucepan, heat chicken broth with ⅔ cup water. Add tortellini, spinach, and scallions. Cook over medium heat until tortellini are hot and spinach is wilted, about 2 minutes. Serve sprinkled with Parmesan cheese and a few grindings of black pepper.

Per Serving: Calories: 376 Total fat: 10 g Saturated fat: 5 g
Cholesterol: 76 mg Percentage calories from fat: 24%

---

43 COLD SPICED PLUM SOUP

Prep: 6 minutes   Cook: 10 minutes   Chill: 3 hours   Serves: 4

Here is a delicately spiced soup, thickened with yogurt, which can be served at the beginning of a meal or as a dessert.

¾ cup frozen apple juice concentrate, thawed

2 (2-inch) cinnamon sticks

1 (2-inch) strip of lemon zest

1 pound red ripe plums

1½ cups nonfat plain yogurt Fresh plum slices and mint sprigs for garnish (optional)

1. In a large saucepan, place thawed apple juice, cinnamon sticks, and lemon zest. Halve, pit, and thinly slice plums directly into saucepan. Bring to a boil. Reduce heat to medium-low, cover, and simmer until plums are tender, about 10 minutes. Remove from heat; let cool slightly. Remove and discard cinnamon sticks. Leave lemon zest in soup.

2. In a food processor or blender, puree plum mixture until smooth. Pour into a large bowl. Stir in yogurt. Cover and refrigerate at least 3 hours, or until very cold. Serve well chilled, garnished with plum slices and mint sprigs.

Per Serving: Calories: 195 Total fat: 1 g Saturated fat: 0 g
Cholesterol: 2 mg Percentage calories from fat: 4%

44   WINTER VEGETABLE SOUP
Prep: 30 minutes   Cook: 30 minutes   Serves: 8

Once you have all the ingredients assembled and cut up, this savory root vegetable soup cooks up in 30 minutes. It is just perfect on a cold winter's night with crusty semolina bread, a crisp salad, and a glass of wine.

1 tablespoon olive oil
1 teaspoon finely chopped fresh garlic
8 cups (2 quarts) homemade or canned reduced-sodium chicken broth
1 pound potatoes, peeled and cut into thin strips
1 pound purple-topped turnips or rutabaga, peeled and cut into thin strips

1 pound carrots, peeled and cut into thin strips
1 tablespoon minced fresh dill
1 tablespoon chopped fresh parsley
1 teaspoon dried marjoram
½ teaspoon salt
½ teaspoon pepper
1 cup slivered escarole leaves

1. In a large soup pot or dutch oven, heat olive oil over medium heat. Add garlic and cook until soft and fragrant, about 1 minute. Stir in chicken broth, potatoes, turnips or rutabaga, and carrots. Bring to a boil over high heat. Reduce heat to medium-low and simmer, with cover slightly ajar, until vegetables are tender, about 20 minutes.

2. Stir in dill, parsley, marjoram, salt, pepper, and escarole. Simmer 5 minutes longer. Serve hot.

*Per Serving: Calories: 112   Total fat: 4 g   Saturated fat: 1 g
Cholesterol: 0 mg   Percentage calories from fat: 18%*

45   CHICKEN BROTH
*Prep: 10 minutes   Cook: 2½ to 3 hours   Chill: 8 hours
Makes: 2 quarts*

To get a rich-flavored broth, simmer the soup slowly. Chilling the broth overnight makes it easier to remove the fat that accumulates on top.

3 pounds chicken backs and wings
1 large onion, peeled and quartered
2 large unpeeled carrots, washed and cut into chunks

1 large leafy celery rib, cut into chunks
8 sprigs of fresh parsley
2 sprigs of fresh thyme or ¼ teaspoon dried
1 bay leaf
¼ teaspoon black peppercorns

1. Rinse chicken thoroughly. Place in a large heavy soup pot or dutch oven with 12 cups (3 quarts) water. Bring to a boil; skim off foam from surface. Add onion, carrots, celery, parsley, thyme, bay leaf, and peppercorns. Bring to a boil; skim foam from surface.

2. Cook broth, uncovered, over medium-low heat until reduced by one-third, about 2½ to 3 hours. Reduce heat to low if liquid begins to boil.

3. Strain broth through a large fine-mesh strainer or colander set over a large bowl. Refrigerate broth overnight. Skim solid fat from surface and discard. If not using within 2 days, ladle broth into 2-cup containers and freeze.

Per Serving: Calories: 20   Total fat: 1 g   Saturated fat: 0 g
Cholesterol: 0 mg   Percentage calories from fat: 1%

---

46   DOUBLE BERRY CHERRY SOUP
Prep: 10 minutes   Cook: 8 minutes   Chill: 3 hours   Serves: 4

Strawberries and raspberries heighten the flavor of this tart cherry soup. You can serve it at the beginning of a meal or as a dessert.

1 (16-ounce) can tart red pitted
  cherries in water
2 cups hulled and sliced fresh
  strawberries
1 cup fresh raspberries
⅓ cup sugar
¼ teaspoon cinnamon
½ cup dry red wine
1 tablespoon cornstarch
  mixed with 2 tablespoons
  water

1 tablespoon fresh lemon
  juice
¼ cup low-fat vanilla-flavored
  yogurt
Fresh strawberries,
  raspberries, and mint
  sprigs (optional)

1. Drain cherries, reserving juice and 8 perfect cherries for garnish. Place remaining cherries and reserved juice in food processor or blender. Add strawberries, raspberries, sugar, and cinnamon. Puree until smooth. Pour pureed fruit into a large nonreactive saucepan. Stir in wine. Bring to a boil over medium-low heat, stirring constantly. Reduce heat to low and simmer, uncovered, 5 minutes.

2. To remove seeds, pour mixture into a sieve set over a large bowl; press on pulp using back of a wooden spoon. Return mixture to saucepan. Stir cornstarch mixture again and stir into pureed fruit in saucepan. Cook over medium-high heat, stirring, until soup comes to a boil and thickens slightly, about 1 minute.

3. Pour soup into a bowl. Stir in lemon juice. Cover and refrigerate 3 hours, or until well chilled. Refrigerate reserved cherries. When ready to serve, top each serving with 1 tablespoon of yogurt. Garnish with reserved cherries and additional fresh strawberries, raspberries, and a mint sprig, if desired. Serve cold.

Per Serving: Calories: 185   Total fat: 1 g   Saturated fat: 0 g
Cholesterol: 1 mg   Percentage calories from fat: 4%

47   SUMMER SQUASH SOUP WITH FRESH BASIL

Prep: 15 minutes   Cook: 20 minutes   Chill: 3 hours   Serves: 4

½ cup chopped scallions
½ cup chopped celery
1 garlic clove, minced
2 teaspoons olive oil
2 cups coarsely shredded zucchini
2 cups coarsely shredded yellow summer squash

2 cups homemade or canned reduced-sodium chicken broth
¼ teaspoon salt
¼ teaspoon freshly ground pepper
¼ cup shredded fresh basil
½ cup buttermilk
4 fresh basil leaves

1. In a large nonstick saucepan, combine scallions, celery, garlic, olive oil, and 2 tablespoons water. Cover and cook over medium-low heat until vegetables are soft, 3 to 5 minutes. Add zucchini, yellow squash, chicken broth, salt, and pepper. Bring to a boil. Reduce heat to medium-low, cover, and simmer, with cover slightly ajar, until squash is tender, about 15 minutes. Remove from heat; let cool slightly.

2. In a food processor or blender, puree soup with shredded basil until smooth. Pour into a large bowl. Stir in buttermilk. Cover and refrigerate 3 hours, or until well chilled. Serve cold, garnishing each portion with a basil leaf.

*Per Serving: Calories: 65 Total fat: 2 g Saturated fat: 1 g
Cholesterol: 1 mg Percentage calories from fat: 29%*

48   VEGETABLE BROTH

Prep: 20 minutes   Cook: 2¼ hours   Chill: 8 hours   Makes: 2 quarts

Browning the vegetables heightens the flavor of this vegetable broth. It is not necessary to peel the carrots and parsnip, just wash them thoroughly.

2 cups chopped onions
1½ cups sliced leeks (white part only)
1 cup scrubbed and sliced carrots
1 cup sliced celery with leafy tops
1 cup scrubbed and sliced parsnips
2 unpeeled garlic cloves

1 teaspoon extra-virgin olive oil
1 cup sliced mushrooms
12 ounces fresh spinach, washed but not trimmed
12 sprigs of fresh parsley
6 sprigs of fresh thyme or ¾ teaspoon dried
1 bay leaf

1. In a large nonstick soup pot or dutch oven, place onions, leeks, carrots, celery, parsnips, and garlic. Add olive oil and stir to blend. Cook, uncovered, over medium-low heat until vegetables wilt and begin to brown, about 15 minutes.

2. Add mushrooms, spinach, parsley, thyme, bay leaf, and 12 cups (3 quarts) water; stir to combine. Bring to a boil. Cook broth, uncovered, over medium heat until reduced by one-third, about 2 hours. Reduce heat to low if liquid begins to boil.

3. Strain broth through a large fine-mesh strainer or colander set over a large bowl. If not using within 2 days, ladle broth into 2-cup containers and freeze.

Per Serving: Calories: 24 Total fat: 1 g Saturated fat: 0 g
Cholesterol: 0 mg Percentage calories from fat: 24%

---

49 CREAMY VEGETABLE CHOWDER
Prep: 10 minutes   Cook: 23 minutes   Serves: 4

Pureed potatoes thicken this soup and give it a creamy texture and taste with no added flour or cream.

Vegetable cooking spray
½ **cup chopped onion**
2 **cups diced (½-inch) peeled baking or all-purpose potatoes**
2½ **cups homemade or canned reduced-sodium chicken broth**
1 **(10-ounce) package frozen mixed vegetables, thawed**

½ **cup chopped red bell pepper**
1 **teaspoon chopped fresh thyme leaves or** ¼ **teaspoon dried**
⅛ **teaspoon crushed hot pepper flakes, or to taste**
1 **tablespoon chopped fresh basil or 1 teaspoon dried**

1. Coat a large saucepan with vegetable spray and heat saucepan. Add onion and cook over medium heat until it begins to soften, about 3 minutes. Add potatoes and 2 cups of chicken broth. Bring to a boil. Reduce heat to medium-low and simmer, with cover partially ajar, until potatoes are tender, about 10 minutes. Remove from heat; let cool slightly.

2. In a food processor, puree potato mixture until smooth. Pour soup back into saucepan. Stir in remaining ½ cup chicken broth, mixed vegetables, bell pepper, thyme, and hot pepper flakes. Return to a boil, stirring occasionally. Reduce heat to low, cover, and simmer until vegetables are tender, about 8 minutes. Stir in basil.

Per Serving: Calories: 135 Total fat: 2 g Saturated fat: 0 g
Cholesterol: 0 mg Percentage calories from fat: 2%

50   RIBOLITA

Prep: 15 minutes   Cook: 23 minutes   Serves: 6

Ribolita is a hearty Tuscan-style bean and cabbage soup, which is thickened with bread.

4   slices of semolina, French, or Italian bread, cut ¼ inch thick
3   garlic cloves
2   teaspoons extra-virgin olive oil
1   medium onion, chopped
3   medium carrots, peeled and sliced
1   (19-ounce) can cannellini (white kidney beans), drained and rinsed

1¾   cups homemade or reduced-sodium chicken broth
1   (14½-ounce) can Italian plum tomatoes, liquid reserved
2   cups chopped cabbage
1   medium zucchini, sliced
¼   teaspoon crumbled rosemary
⅛   teaspoon dried thyme leaves

1. Preheat oven to 350°F. Place bread on a large baking sheet. Bake 15 minutes, or until golden brown, turning once. Remove bread from oven. Cut 1 garlic clove in half and rub each slice of bread on both sides with cut side of garlic. Set garlic toasts aside.

2. Mince remaining 2 garlic cloves. In a large soup pot, heat olive oil over medium heat. Add onion, carrots, and minced garlic. Cook, stirring, until onion and garlic are softened, 3 to 5 minutes.

3. Add cannellini beans, chicken broth, tomatoes with their juices, cabbage, zucchini, rosemary, and thyme. Bring to a boil over medium heat. Reduce heat to low and simmer 20 minutes, or until vegetables are tender and flavors are blended. To serve, place a slice of garlic toast in the bottom of 6 shallow soup bowls. Ladle 1 cup of the soup over each.

Per Serving: Calories: 157   Total fat: 3 g   Saturated fat: 0 g
Cholesterol: 0 g   Percentage calories from fat: 14%

Chapter 3

Light Pasta Pleasers

Pasta has come into its own as a great-tasting staple that fits into our health-conscious way of eating. It's low in sodium, calories, fat, and cholesterol, while concentrated in carbohydrates, protein, vitamins, and minerals.

In addition, new dietary guidelines recommend 6 to 11 servings of complex carbohydrates daily. Pasta also plays a major role in today's healthy and popular Mediterranean cuisine, consisting of whole grains, olive oil, fresh vegetables, seafood, and legumes. Combined with healthy low-fat toppings, sauces, and accompaniments, pasta is perfect!

Pasta should be cooked, uncovered, in rapidly boiling water, at least 4 cups to every 4 ounces of pasta. To keep the fat and sodium levels down, do not add oil or salt to the cooking water. When adding pasta to the boiling water, do so gradually so as not to stop the water from boiling, and stir the first minute or two to prevent the pasta from sticking.

Follow the package directions for cooking times. Each pasta, due to its characteristic size and thickness, cooks up differently. Most pasta packages give a range of cooking times. Since I like my pasta fairly firm (al dente) I start checking the pasta at the lower range of time. Drain pasta in a colander and do not rinse unless the recipe says to do so. Though there are no specific rules for selecting pasta shapes with specific sauces, a rule of thumb is to combine thin pasta shapes with light sauces, and thick pasta shapes with heartier sauces.

I had fun developing lean versions of many of my classic Italian favorites. Believe it or not, the sauce for fettuccine Alfredo offered here is low-fat and low-calorie. A sauce of lightly thickened skim milk takes the place of the traditional cream. Nonfat cream cheese and just a touch of excellent freshly grated Parmesan cheese pulls the dish together. I make Spaghetti Carbonara, usually laden with eggs, cream, and bacon, with an egg substitute, evaporated skim milk, and reduced-fat turkey bacon.

Another family favorite is macaroni and cheese. My recipe for Quick Macaroni and Cheese uses low-fat cottage cheese, evaporated skim milk, and seasonings, all whirled in a blender. Then the mixture is heated and a small amount of Cheddar cheese is added at the end. Low-fat ricotta and skim milk with fresh herbs is another low-fat blender sauce for Pasta with Fresh Herbs. To reduce the fat in traditional oil-based pasta sauces, reserve part of the pasta cooking water, or add reduced-sodium chicken broth to moisten the pasta without adding fat.

51 ANGEL HAIR PASTA WITH LEMON DILL SAUCE

Prep: 8 minutes   Cook: 8 to 10 minutes   Serves: 3 to 4

8 ounces angel hair pasta,
     capellini, or spaghettini
2 tablespoons flour
1½ cups skim milk
1 tablespoon butter
½ cup dry white wine
2 tablespoons nonfat cream
     cheese

2 teaspoons grated lemon zest
2 tablespoons chopped fresh
     dill or 1½ teaspoons dried
¼ teaspoon salt
⅛ teaspoon cayenne

1. In a large saucepan filled with boiling water, cook pasta, without adding salt or oil, until tender but still firm, 5 to 7 minutes; drain.

2. Meanwhile, place flour in a small bowl. Gradually whisk in milk until mixture is smooth. In a medium saucepan, melt butter over medium heat. Gradually stir milk mixture into saucepan. Cook over medium-low heat, stirring often, until sauce boils and thickens, about 3 minutes. Gradually add wine, stirring constantly; if you add the wine too fast, the mixture will curdle. Whisk in cream cheese until smooth. Stir in lemon zest, dill, salt, and cayenne.

3. Transfer pasta to a large bowl. Pour on sauce; toss to coat. Serve hot.

*Per Serving: Calories: 310   Total fat: 4 g   Saturated fat: 2 g
                Cholesterol: 10 mg   Percentage calories from fat: 12%*

52   ASIAN NOODLES WITH VEGETABLES IN PEANUT SAUCE

Prep: 25 minutes   Cook: 14 to 16 minutes   Serves: 6 to 8

Soba noodles, snow peas, straw mushrooms, and baby corn in a creamy spiced peanut sauce make a delightful party or buffet dish.

4 medium scallions, cut into 1-inch lengths	¼ pound fresh snow peas, cut into thin strips
4 garlic cloves, smashed	3 medium carrots, cut into very thin strips (1 cup)
½ to ¾ teaspoon crushed hot red pepper, to taste	1 medium red bell pepper, cut into thin strips
6 tablespoons reduced-fat creamy peanut butter	1 (15-ounce) can medium peeled straw mushrooms, rinsed and drained
¾ cup homemade or canned reduced-sodium chicken broth	1 (8-ounce) can baby corn, rinsed and drained, large spears cut in half lengthwise
5 tablespoons rice wine vinegar	
16 ounces Japanese soba noodles, Chinese egg noodles, or spaghettini	

1. In a food processor, place scallions and garlic; process until finely chopped. Add hot pepper, peanut butter, ¼ cup chicken broth, and 3 tablespoons rice wine vinegar; puree until blended. Transfer peanut sauce to a small bowl.

2. In a large saucepan filled with boiling water, cook pasta, without adding salt or oil, until tender but still firm, 10 to 12 minutes; drain.

3. Meanwhile, in a large skillet, bring remaining ½ cup chicken broth to a boil. Add snow peas, carrots, and bell pepper. Cook until crisp-tender, about 2 minutes. Add mushrooms and baby corn. Cook until vegetables are heated through and liquid has evaporated in pan, about 2 minutes longer. Sprinkle with remaining 2 tablespoons rice wine vinegar; toss to blend.

4. Transfer pasta to a large bowl. Add peanut sauce, top with vegetables, and toss to combine. Serve warm or at room temperature.

Per Serving: Calories: 350   Total fat: 6 g   Saturated fat: 1 g
Cholesterol: 0 mg   Percentage calories from fat: 15%

53 CAVATELLI WITH TOMATO, CAPER, AND OLIVE SAUCE

Prep: 10 minutes   Cook: 15 to 18 minutes   Serves: 4

Greek olives, capers, and fennel accent the flavor of this quick tomato sauce.

8 ounces cavatelli
1 tablespoon extra-virgin
  olive oil
1 pint cherry tomatoes, halved
2 tablespoons pitted and
  sliced Kalamata olives

¼ cup chopped parsley
1 tablespoon drained capers
½ teaspoon fennel seeds,
  slightly crushed
1 teaspoon grated lemon zest

1. In a large saucepan filled with boiling water, cook pasta, without adding salt or oil, until tender but still firm, about 12 to 15 minutes; drain.

2. Meanwhile, in a large nonstick skillet, heat olive oil over medium heat. Add tomatoes, olives, parsley, capers, and fennel seeds. Cook until tomatoes soften, about 3 minutes. Stir in lemon zest.

3. Transfer pasta to a large bowl. Pour on sauce; toss to combine. Serve hot or at room temperature.

*Per Serving: Calories: 266 Total fat: 6 g Saturated fat: 1 g
Cholesterol: 0 mg Percentage calories from fat: 19%*

54 LINGUINE WITH FRESH TOMATO, BASIL, AND MOZZARELLA

Prep: 15 minutes   Chill: 1 hour   Cook: 10 minutes   Serves: 3 to 4

When summer rolls around, I run to the farmers' market to pick up vine-ripened tomatoes and fresh basil to make this cold sauce wrapped around hot pasta.

1 pound ripe tomatoes or
  plum tomatoes, halved,
  seeded, and cut into thin
  strips (3 cups)
1 medium green bell pepper,
  cut into thin strips (1 cup)
¼ cup slivered fresh basil
  leaves
2 garlic cloves, minced
1½ tablespoons extra-virgin
  olive oil

½ teaspoon salt
⅛ teaspoon pepper
8 ounces dried spinach
  linguine or regular
  linguine or fusilli
4 ounces reduced-fat part-
  skim milk mozzarella,
  cut into ½-inch cubes
  (1 cup)

1. In a medium bowl, combine tomatoes, bell pepper, basil, garlic, olive oil, salt, and pepper. Cover and refrigerate 1 hour.

2. In a large saucepan filled with boiling water, cook pasta, without adding salt or oil, until tender but still firm, about 10 minutes; drain. Transfer to a large bowl. Top with chilled tomato mixture and mozzarella; toss to combine. Serve at once.

Per Serving: *Calories: 350 Total fat: 10 g Saturated fat: 3 g*
Cholesterol: 10 mg Percentage calories from fat: 24%

---

55 CHEESY FETTUCCINE FLORENTINE
Prep: 10 minutes Cook: 23 to 25 minutes Serves: 6

Fettuccine Florentine is a combination of regular and spinach pasta sometimes called straw and hay. If you cannot find the mixture in the supermarket, use 6 ounces each regular fettuccine and spinach fettuccine. I've combined a frozen vegetable mélange with Cheddar cheese and a Mexican beer for this hearty pasta dish. If you prefer not to use beer, use chicken broth.

1 (12-ounce) package
   fettuccine Florentine or 6
   ounces *each* regular
   fettuccine and spinach
   fettuccine
1 (16-ounce) package frozen
   vegetables olé (broccoli,
   carrots, Italian green
   beans, small white beans,
   garbanzo beans, red
   kidney beans, red bell
   peppers)

6 tablespoons flour
¾ teaspoon salt
¼ teaspoon cayenne
1½ cups skim milk
½ cup Mexican beer or chicken
   broth
1½ cups shredded reduced-fat
   sharp Cheddar cheese
   (6 ounces)

1. In a large saucepan filled with boiling water, cook pasta, without adding salt or oil, until tender but still firm, 10 to 12 minutes; drain.

2. While pasta is cooking, in a medium saucepan, cook frozen vegetables in ½ cup boiling water until tender, about 8 minutes; drain.

3. In a medium saucepan, place flour, salt, and cayenne. Gradually whisk in milk until mixture is smooth. Stir in beer. Bring to a boil over medium-low heat, stirring until sauce is thickened, about 5 minutes. Remove from heat. Stir in Cheddar cheese until melted.

4. Transfer pasta to a large bowl. Add cooked vegetables. Pour on cheese sauce; toss to combine. Serve hot.

Per Serving: *Calories: 417 Total fat: 8 g Saturated fat: 4 g*
Cholesterol: 75 mg Percentage calories from fat: 18%

56   MOROCCAN COUSCOUS
Prep: 15 minutes   Cook: 3 minutes   Serves: 6

Couscous is a tiny pasta, which many think of as a grain. The addition of spices and herbs makes for a flavorful side dish.

1½ cups homemade or reduced-sodium chicken broth
⅓ cup currants or raisins
1½ teaspoons curry powder
¾ teaspoon ground cumin
1 cup couscous
¼ cup sliced scallions
¼ cup finely chopped parsley

¼ cup finely chopped fresh mint
2 tablespoons slivered almonds, preferably toasted
2 tablespoons fresh lemon juice
1 teaspoon grated lemon zest
Salt and pepper

1. In a medium saucepan, combine chicken broth, currants, curry powder, and cumin. Bring to a boil over high heat; remove from heat. Stir in couscous and scallions. Cover and let stand 5 minutes, or until liquid is absorbed.

2. Add parsley, mint, almonds, lemon juice, lemon zest, and salt and pepper if you wish. Stir with a fork to combine and fluff up couscous.

*Per Serving: Calories: 45   Total fat: 1 g   Saturated fat: 0 g
Cholesterol: 0 mg   Percentage calories from fat: 27%*

57   LOW-FAT FETTUCCINE ALFREDO   9 ·15
Prep: 20 minutes   Cook: 13 to 16 minutes   Serves: 3 to 4

An Alfredo sauce is usually made with heavy cream, but I've made a béchamel sauce using skim milk and thickened with a nonfat cream cheese product. Use freshly grated Parmesan, as it gives better flavor to the sauce.

8 ounces dried fettuccine
1 tablespoon reduced-fat margarine
2 teaspoons finely chopped garlic

1 tablespoon flour
1¼ cups skim milk
¼ cup nonfat cream cheese
1 cup grated Parmesan cheese
1 tablespoon chopped parsley

1. In a large saucepan filled with boiling water, cook pasta, without adding salt or oil, until tender but still firm, 8 to 10 minutes; drain.

2. Meanwhile, in a medium saucepan, melt margarine over medium heat. Add garlic and cook 1 minute. Add flour and cook, stirring, 1 minute. Gradually whisk in milk until mixture is smooth. Bring to a boil, stirring, until sauce is smooth and slightly thickened, 1 to 2 minutes. Whisk in cream cheese until melted. Add Parmesan cheese, stirring constantly until cheese melts, about 2 minutes.

3. Transfer pasta to a large bowl. Pour on sauce and toss lightly to coat. Sprinkle parsley on top. Serve hot.

*Per Serving: Calories: 369   Total fat: 10 g   Saturated fat: 5 g
Cholesterol: 73 mg   Percentage calories from fat: 24%*

---

58   BOW TIES WITH ROASTED EGGPLANT AND RED PEPPERS

*Prep: 15 minutes   Stand: 30 minutes   Cook: 20 to 22 minutes
Serves: 4*

Salting the eggplant and letting it stand removes the bitter taste that sometimes occurs. Here the eggplant is broiled to eliminate the need for oil. Farfalle, pronounced *far-FAH-leh,* is a frilly bow tie-shaped pasta sometimes referred to as butterflies.

1 **small eggplant (¾ pound), cut into ½-inch cubes**	½ **cup homemade or canned reduced-sodium chicken broth**
½ **teaspoon salt**	
Vegetable cooking spray	1 **garlic clove, minced**
1 **medium red bell pepper, cut in ½-inch strips**	1½ **teaspoons olive oil**
	½ **teaspoon dried oregano**
8 **ounces farfalle, rigatoni, or ziti**	1 **cup shredded fresh basil**
	¼ **cup crumbled feta cheese**

1. Place eggplant on paper towels and sprinkle with salt. Cover with more paper towels. Let stand 30 minutes; pat dry.

2. Preheat broiler. Coat a 10 x 15-inch jelly roll pan with cooking spray. Arrange eggplant and bell pepper on pan in a single layer. Broil 4 to 6 inches from heat 10 minutes, turning once, until eggplant has browned and bell pepper is slightly charred. Set aside, covered to keep warm.

3. Meanwhile, in a large saucepan filled with boiling water, cook pasta, without salt or oil, until tender but still firm, 10 to 12 minutes; drain. Transfer pasta to a large bowl.

4. In a small skillet, bring chicken broth, garlic, olive oil, and oregano to a boil. Pour over pasta. Add eggplant, bell pepper, basil, and feta; toss to combine. Serve hot.

*Per Serving: Calories: 286   Total fat: 5 g   Saturated fat: 2 g
Cholesterol: 7 mg   Percentage calories from fat: 16%*

59 FUSILLI WITH RED CLAM SAUCE
Prep: 10 minutes   Cook: 22 to 24 minutes   Serves: 4

12 ounces fusilli or spaghetti
1 tablespoon extra-virgin
    olive oil
½ cup coarsely chopped onion
½ cup coarsely chopped green
    bell pepper
1 teaspoon finely chopped
    garlic
1½ cups seeded and coarsely
    chopped plum tomatoes
    or 1 (14½-ounce) can
    Italian peeled tomatoes,
    drained and coarsely
    chopped

½ cup dry white wine
1 (10-ounce) can baby clams,
    drained, with juice
    reserved
¼ cup chopped parsley
1½ teaspoons chopped fresh
    thyme or ½ teaspoon
    dried
⅛ to ¼ teaspoon cayenne, to
    taste

1. In a large saucepan filled with boiling water, cook pasta, without adding salt or oil, until tender but still firm, 10 to 12 minutes; drain.

2. Meanwhile, in a medium saucepan, heat olive oil over medium heat. Add onion, bell pepper, and garlic. Cook, stirring occasionally, until vegetables soften, about 3 minutes. Add tomatoes and cook 3 minutes longer. Add wine and reserved clam juice. Bring to a simmer, reduce heat to low, and cook 5 minutes. Stir in parsley, thyme, cayenne, and clams. Heat until hot, about 1 minute; do not boil.

3. Transfer pasta to a large bowl. Pour clam sauce over pasta and toss lightly to combine. Serve hot.

Per Serving: Calories: 449   Total fat: 6 g   Saturated fat: 1 g
Cholesterol: 25 mg   Percentage calories from fat: 12%

60 QUICK MACARONI AND CHEESE
Prep: 5 minutes   Cook: 15 to 18 minutes   Serves: 4

8 ounces elbow twists, wagon
    wheels, or rotelle
1½ cups low-fat cottage cheese
1 (5-ounce) can evaporated
    skim milk
1 tablespoon flour
¾ teaspoon dry mustard

¾ teaspoon salt
½ teaspoon paprika
¼ teaspoon cayenne
½ cup coarsely shredded
    reduced-fat sharp
    Cheddar cheese
    (2 ounces)

1. In a large saucepan filled with boiling water, cook pasta, without adding salt or oil, until tender but still firm, about 9 to 12 minutes; drain.

2. Meanwhile, in a food processor or blender, combine cottage cheese, evaporated milk, flour, dry mustard, salt, paprika, and cayenne. Puree until smooth. Pour sauce into a medium saucepan. Cook over medium-low heat, stirring constantly, until sauce boils and thickens, about 5 minutes. Add Cheddar cheese and stir until cheese is melted, about 1 minute.

3. Transfer pasta to a large bowl. Pour on sauce; toss to coat. Serve hot.

*Per Serving: Calories: 364   Total fat: 5 g   Saturated fat: 3 g
Cholesterol: 18 mg   Percentage calories from fat: 13%*

---

61 FUSILLI WITH ROASTED RED PEPPER SAUCE

*Prep: 10 minutes   Stand: 30 minutes   Cook: 10 to 12 minutes
Serves: 4*

I prefer this sauce at room temperature, but you can heat it, if you wish. Serve as a starter or side dish.

1 **(12-ounce) jar roasted red peppers, drained**	1 **teaspoon finely chopped garlic**
¼ **cup finely chopped red onion**	⅛ **teaspoon salt**
1 **tablespoon red wine vinegar**	⅛ **teaspoon cayenne**
1 **tablespoon extra-virgin olive oil**	2 **tablespoons chopped parsley**
	8 **ounces fusilli or spaghetti**

1. In a food processor, combine roasted red peppers, red onion, vinegar, olive oil, garlic, salt, and cayenne. Pour into a bowl; stir in parsley. Let stand at room temperature 30 minutes for flavors to mellow.

2. In a large saucepan filled with boiling water, cook pasta, without adding salt or oil, until tender but still firm, 10 to 12 minutes; drain. Transfer to a large bowl. Pour on sauce; toss to combine. Serve hot.

*Per Serving: Calories: 277   Total fat: 4 g   Saturated fat: 1 g
Cholesterol: 0 mg   Percentage calories from fat: 15%*

62 ORECCHIETTE WITH BROCCOLI RABE
Prep: 8 minutes   Cook: 14 to 17 minutes   Serves: 6

Broccoli rabe is a strong-flavored green and to some people an addictive taste. In the recipe, the broccoli rabe is cooked with the pasta to flavor the cooking liquid, part of which is used to replace oil.

1 bunch of broccoli rabe (1 to 1¼ pounds), tough stems removed, rinsed, and cut into 1-inch lengths
16 ounces orecchiette
1½ tablespoons extra-virgin olive oil

2 teaspoons finely chopped garlic
¼ teaspoon crushed hot red pepper
½ teaspoon salt

1. In a large saucepan filled with boiling water, cook pasta, without adding salt or oil, 5 minutes. Stir in broccoli rabe and cook together until pasta is tender but still firm and broccoli rabe is tender, 8 to 10 minutes longer. Drain pasta, reserving ½ cup cooking liquid. Transfer pasta to a large bowl.

2. Meanwhile, in a small skillet, heat olive oil over medium heat. Add garlic and hot pepper. Cook, stirring, until garlic just begins to brown, 1 to 2 minutes. Pour over pasta. Toss to coat. Add ½ cup cooking liquid and salt and toss to coat. Serve hot.

Per Serving: Calories: 331 Total fat: 5 g Saturated fat: 1 g
Cholesterol: 0 mg Percentage calories from fat: 13%

63 ORZO WITH PEAS
Prep: 5 minutes   Cook: 10 to 12 minutes   Serves: 6

8 ounces orzo (about 1¼ cups)
1 cup frozen peas, thawed
1 tablespoon butter
2 teaspoons fresh lemon juice

½ teaspoon salt
⅛ teaspoon white pepper
2 tablespoons chopped fresh dill

1. In a large saucepan filled with boiling water, cook orzo, without adding salt or oil, until tender but still firm, 9 to 11 minutes; drain. Transfer orzo to a large bowl. Add peas; toss to combine.

2. In a small skillet, combine butter with 2 tablespoons water and lemon juice. Bring to a boil. Stir in salt, pepper, and dill. Pour over orzo; toss to combine. Serve hot.

Per Serving: Calories: 177 Total fat: 3 g Saturated fat: 1 g
Cholesterol: 5 mg Percentage calories from fat: 13%

64 PASTA SHELLS WITH LIGHT MARINARA SAUCE

Prep: 10 minutes   Cook: 33 to 37 minutes   Serves: 3 to 4

Here is a quick and easy—and, of course low-fat—fresh tomato sauce to be served over pasta or ravioli.

1 tablespoon olive oil	¼ teaspoon salt
½ cup chopped onion	⅛ teaspoon crushed hot red
1 large garlic clove, minced	pepper
1½ pounds ripe tomatoes, seeded and coarsely chopped	1 tablespoon finely chopped fresh basil or 1 teaspoon dried
8 ounces pasta shells	

1. In a nonreactive medium saucepan, heat olive oil over medium heat. Add onion and garlic. Cook, stirring occasionally, until onion is soft and translucent, 3 to 5 minutes. Add tomatoes; stir to combine. Cover and simmer until tomatoes are soft and juices begin to run, about 15 minutes.

2. Meanwhile, in a large saucepan of boiling salted water, cook pasta until tender but still firm, 10 to 12 minutes. Drain into a colander and transfer to a deep serving dish.

3. In a food processor, puree tomato sauce until smooth. Return to saucepan. Season with salt and hot pepper. Simmer, uncovered, 5 minutes longer. Stir in basil. Pour sauce over pasta, toss, and serve.

Per Serving: Calories: 283   Total fat: 5 g   Saturated fat: 1 g
Cholesterol: 0 mg   Percentage calories from fat: 15%

65 PASTA WITH FRESH HERBS

Prep: 20 minutes   Cook: 10 to 12 minutes   Serves: 4

Use *only* fresh herbs for this pasta dish.

12 ounces fettuccine, linguine, or fusilli	1 garlic clove, minced
½ cup minced fresh parsley	¾ cup low-fat ricotta cheese
½ cup minced fresh basil	1 cup skim milk
1 tablespoon minced chives	½ teaspoon salt
	¼ teaspoon pepper

1. In a large saucepan filled with boiling water, cook pasta, without adding salt or oil, until tender but still firm, about 10 to 12 minutes; drain.

2. In a food processor, combine parsley, basil, chives, garlic, ricotta, milk, salt, and pepper. Puree until smooth, about 1 minute.

3. Transfer pasta to a large bowl. Pour on sauce; toss to combine. Serve hot.

Per Serving: Calories: 408   Total fat: 7 g   Saturated fat: 2 g
Cholesterol: 89 mg   Percentage calories from fat: 15%

66   PASTA PRIMAVERA WITH GOAT CHEESE
Prep: 20 minutes   Cook: 13 to 15 minutes   Serves: 3 to 4

This creamy pasta dish is perfect for a late summer brunch.

8 ounces linguine or fusilli
¾ cup homemade or canned reduced-sodium chicken broth
½ pound asparagus, trimmed and cut into 2-inch pieces
1 medium green bell pepper, seeded and cut into thin strips
¼ cup (2 ounces) coarsely chopped sun-dried tomatoes (not packed in oil)

1 medium zucchini, halved lengthwise, then cut crosswise into thin diagonal slices
3 ounces crumbled goat cheese with chives
½ cup slivered fresh basil leaves
3 plum tomatoes (6 ounces), seeded and diced

1. In a large saucepan filled with boiling water, cook pasta, without adding salt or oil, until tender but still firm, 10 to 12 minutes; drain.

2. Meanwhile, in a large skillet, bring chicken broth to a boil over medium heat. Add asparagus, bell pepper, and sun-dried tomatoes. Cover and cook 2 minutes, stirring once. Add zucchini and cook, uncovered, 1 minute.

3. Transfer pasta to a large bowl. Add cooked vegetables, goat cheese, basil, and plum tomatoes. Toss until cheese coats pasta and vegetables. Serve hot.

Per Serving: Calories: 338   Total fat: 8 g   Saturated fat: 5 g
Cholesterol: 17 mg   Percentage calories from fat: 21%

67   SPAGHETTI CARBONARA
Prep: 5 minutes   Cook: 19 to 21 minutes   Serves: 4

This pasta dish is usually laden with eggs, cream, and bacon. Using egg substitute, evaporated skim milk, and reduced-fat turkey bacon lowers the fat content considerably.

12 ounces spaghetti or rigatoni Vegetable cooking spray
3 slices of 95% fat-free smoked turkey bacon, cut crosswise into ¼-inch strips
1½ cups evaporated skim milk

⅓ cup egg substitute
¼ teaspoon crushed hot red pepper
⅓ cup grated Parmesan cheese Freshly ground black pepper

1. In a large saucepan filled with boiling water, cook pasta, without adding salt or oil, until tender but still firm, about 10 to 12 minutes; drain.

2. Meanwhile, coat a medium nonstick saucepan with cooking spray and heat pan over medium heat. Add turkey bacon and cook until it sizzles and browns lightly, about 3 minutes. Drain on paper towels.

3. In same saucepan, combine evaporated milk, egg substitute, and hot pepper. Cook over medium heat, stirring occasionally, until sauce coats a spoon, about 4 minutes. Do not boil. Stir in cooked bacon and Parmesan cheese. Cook, stirring, until cheese melts, about 2 minutes.

4. Transfer pasta to a large bowl. Pour on sauce; toss to coat. Top each serving with a few grindings of pepper. Serve hot.

Per Serving: Calories: 455   Total fat: 6 g   Saturated fat: 2 g
            Cholesterol: 16 mg   Percentage calories from fat: 11%

---

68   PASTA WITH SPINACH, MUSHROOMS, AND BACON

Prep: 15 minutes   Cook: 19 to 21 minutes   Serves: 4 to 6

One of my favorite salads is spinach with mushrooms and bacon tossed with a mustard-based vinaigrette. Here it is warm with pasta.

12   ounces fusilli, farfalle (bow ties), or a spiral pasta
 4   slices of reduced-fat, reduced-sodium bacon
 ½   cup chopped scallions
 ½   cup diced red bell pepper
 8   ounces mushrooms, trimmed and sliced (2 cups)
 ¾   cup homemade or canned reduced-sodium chicken broth

 2   tablespoons red wine vinegar
 1   tablespoon Dijon mustard
 ¼   teaspoon pepper
 4   cups firmly packed fresh washed and trimmed spinach, torn into bite-size pieces

1. In a large saucepan filled with boiling water, cook pasta, without adding salt or oil, until tender but still firm, about 10 to 12 minutes.

2. Meanwhile, cook bacon in a large skillet over medium heat until crisp, about 5 minutes. Drain on paper towels. Drain off all but 1 teaspoon bacon fat.

3. Add scallions and bell pepper to skillet. Cook over medium heat until softened, about 2 minutes. Add mushrooms and chicken broth. Bring to a boil. Reduce heat and simmer 2 minutes. Whisk in vinegar, mustard, and pepper.

4. Drain pasta. Place in a large bowl. Add spinach, pour on hot sauce, and toss until spinach has wilted. Serve at once.

Per Serving: Calories: 320   Total fat: 5 g   Saturated fat: 1 g
            Cholesterol: 6 mg   Percentage calories from fat: 13%

69 SPAGHETTI WITH TURKEY MEATBALLS

Prep: 15 minutes   Cook: 1¼ hours   Serves: 8

I would be remiss if I didn't include a spaghetti and meatball recipe in this pasta chapter. You can make up the hearty tomato sauce and serve it plain over the spaghetti or add the meatballs. It's your choice.

- 1 cup finely chopped onions
- 1 cup finely chopped carrots
- 1 cup finely chopped celery
- 2 garlic cloves, minced
- 1 (28-ounce) can Italian-style whole tomatoes, liquid reserved
- 1 (6-ounce) can tomato paste

- ½ cup dry red wine
- 1 teaspoon dried oregano
- 1 teaspoon dried basil
- ½ teaspoon sugar
  Turkey Meatballs (recipe follows)
- 16 ounces spaghetti

1. In a large nonreactive saucepan, place onions, carrots, celery, garlic, and ½ cup water. Bring to a boil, reduce heat to low, cover, and cook vegetables until soft, about 15 minutes, stirring once or twice. Add tomatoes with their liquid, tomato paste, wine, oregano, basil, and sugar. Bring slowly to a boil over medium heat. Reduce heat to a simmer and add meatballs. Cover and simmer 30 minutes. If you like the sauce thicker, uncover and simmer until sauce has thickened to desired consistency.

2. While sauce is cooking, in a large saucepan filled with boiling water, cook pasta, without adding any salt or oil, until tender but still firm, 9 to 11 minutes; drain. Transfer pasta to a large bowl. Spoon meatballs with sauce over pasta; toss to combine. Serve hot.

TURKEY MEATBALLS

You can add these meatballs to the preceding spaghetti and meatball recipe or prepare them separately and use with bottled spaghetti sauce.

- Vegetable cooking spray
- 1 pound ground turkey
- 1 egg white
- ½ cup fresh bread crumbs
- 2 tablespoons minced parsley

- ½ teaspoon dried oregano
- ½ teaspoon dried basil
- ½ teaspoon salt
- ¼ teaspoon pepper

1. Preheat oven to 375°F. Coat a 10 x 15-inch jelly-roll pan with cooking spray.

2. In a large bowl, combine turkey, egg white, 2 tablespoons water, bread crumbs, parsley, oregano, basil, salt, and pepper; mix lightly to combine. Shape into 24 walnut-size meatballs (each about 1 measuring tablespoon) with moistened hands. Place on prepared baking sheet.

3. Bake 20 minutes, or until meatballs are cooked through. If you wish to brown the meatballs, place under broiler about 5 minutes.

Per Serving: Calories: 494 Total fat: 8 g Saturated fat: 2 g
Cholesterol: 55 mg Percentage calories from fat: 15%

70 SPAGHETTINI WITH SMOTHERED ONIONS

Prep: 12 minutes   Cook: 27 to 29 minutes   Serves: 4

I wondered what would happen if I took the flavors of an onion soup and tossed it with pasta. This is the delicious result.

1½ tablespoons extra-virgin olive oil

2 large (12-ounce) sweet onions, quartered, then cut into thin wedges (about 4 cups)

2 large garlic cloves, minced

½ cup homemade or canned reduced-sodium chicken broth

½ teaspoon dried thyme leaves

⅛ teaspoon pepper

8 ounces spaghettini

1½ cups frozen peas, thawed

¼ cup shredded reduced-fat Swiss cheese (1 ounce)

¼ cup chopped parsley

Salt and pepper

1. In a large skillet, heat olive oil over medium heat. Add onions and garlic and toss to coat with oil. Reduce heat to low, cover, and cook, stirring occasionally, until onions are very tender and a deep golden color, about 20 minutes. Stir in chicken broth, thyme, and pepper.

2. Meanwhile, in a large saucepan filled with boiling water, cook pasta, without adding salt or oil, until tender but still firm, 7 to 9 minutes; drain.

3. Place pasta in a large bowl. Add peas and browned onions; toss to combine. Add cheese and parsley and toss again. Season with salt and pepper to taste. Serve hot.

Per Serving: Calories: 362   Total fat: 8 g   Saturated fat: 2 g
Cholesterol: 5 mg   Percentage calories from fat: 20%

71   SPAGHETTI WITH BASIL AND PIGNOLI
Prep: 10 minutes   Cook: 11 to 13 minutes   Serves: 4

Pignoli is another name for pine nuts. Instead of coating the spaghetti with loads of oil, I've used chicken broth as a base. If you want to make this dish completely vegetarian, substitute vegetable broth.

8 ounces spaghettini or capellini	½ cup homemade or canned reduced-sodium chicken broth or vegetable broth
2 teaspoons extra-virgin olive oil	3 tablespoons pignoli (pine nuts)
1 teaspoon finely chopped garlic	½ teaspoon grated lemon zest (optional)
½ cup shredded fresh basil leaves	2 tablespoons grated Parmesan cheese

1. In a large saucepan filled with boiling water, cook pasta, without adding salt or oil, until tender but still firm, 8 to 10 minutes; drain.

2. While pasta cooks, in a medium saucepan, heat olive oil over medium heat. Add garlic and cook 30 seconds. Add basil and chicken broth; bring to a simmer.

3. Transfer pasta to a large bowl. Pour on sauce; toss lightly to coat. Sprinkle with pignoli, lemon zest, and Parmesan cheese; toss to combine. Serve hot. Pass additional grated cheese at table, if desired.

Per Serving: Calories: 287   Total fat: 8 g   Saturated fat: 2 g
Cholesterol: 2 mg   Percentage of calories from fat: 24%

---

72   PENNE WITH SPINACH AND FETA
Prep: 10 minutes   Cook: 20 to 22 minutes   Serves: 6 to 8

The flavors of a Greek spinach pie are used in this hearty pasta dish.

1 (10-ounce) package frozen chopped spinach	½ cup homemade or canned reduced-sodium chicken broth
16 ounces penne or ziti	½ cup crumbled feta cheese
Olive oil cooking spray	3 tablespoons minced fresh dill
½ cup diced red onion	
2 tablespoons flour	3 tablespoons fresh lemon juice
1 (12-ounce) can evaporated skim milk or ¾ cup skim milk	⅛ teaspoon pepper

1. In a medium saucepan, cook spinach following package directions, about 4 to 6 minutes; drain.

2. In a large saucepan filled with boiling water, cook pasta, without adding salt or oil, until tender but still firm, about 10 minutes; drain.

3. Meanwhile, coat a medium saucepan with cooking spray. Add red onion and cook until softened, about 3 minutes. Place flour in a medium bowl. Whisk in milk and chicken broth. Gradually stir flour mixture into onions. Bring to a boil over medium heat, stirring, until mixture thickens, about 3 minutes. Stir in cooked spinach and feta cheese. Cook and stir until heated through. Stir in dill, lemon juice, and pepper.

4. Transfer pasta to a large bowl. Pour on sauce; toss to coat. Serve hot.

Per Serving: Calories: 336   Total fat: 4 g   Saturated fat: 2 g   Cholesterol: 11 mg   Percentage calories from fat: 10%

---

73   ZITI WITH MUSHROOMS AND ARTICHOKES

Prep: 12 minutes   Cook: 16 minutes   Serves: 4

Lemon, parsley, and sage are perfect flavor accents for this elegant dish.

8   ounces ziti or other tubular pasta
1   tablespoon extra-virgin olive oil
¼   cup minced shallots
10   ounces mushrooms, trimmed and sliced (3 cups)
¼   cup chopped parsley

1   (9-ounce) package frozen artichoke hearts, cooked and drained, large hearts cut in half
2   teaspoons fresh lemon juice
1   teaspoon grated lemon zest
¾   teaspoon crumbled leaf sage
½   teaspoon salt
⅛   teaspoon pepper

1. In a large saucepan filled with boiling water, cook pasta, without adding salt or oil, until tender but still firm, about 12 minutes; drain.

2. Meanwhile, in a large skillet, heat olive oil over medium-high heat. Add shallots and mushrooms. Cook, stirring often, just until mushrooms begin to give up their liquid, about 4 minutes. Stir in parsley, artichoke hearts, lemon juice, lemon zest, sage, salt, and pepper; toss to combine.

3. Drain pasta, reserving ⅓ cup cooking liquid. Place pasta in a large bowl. Pour mushroom-artichoke mixture over pasta; toss to combine. Add reserved cooking liquid; toss to moisten. Serve hot.

Per Serving: Calories: 292   Total fat: 5 g   Saturated fat: 1 g   Cholesterol: 0 mg   Percentage calories from fat: 15%

74 MEXICAN HOT PASTA
Prep: 15 minutes   Cook: 26 minutes   Serves: 4

This dish is really spicy. If you want to tame it a bit, reduce the amount of pickled jalapeño peppers. Be sure to serve an ice cold Mexican beer to quench the heat.

½ cup dry sherry or canned reduced-sodium chicken broth
2 teaspoons canola oil
½ cup finely chopped onion
2 tablespoons finely chopped garlic
1 (28-ounce) can Italian peeled tomatoes, drained and coarsely chopped

8 sun-dried tomato halves (not packed in oil), cut into small pieces
¼ cup finely chopped pickled jalapeño peppers
12 ounces fusilli or spaghetti
¼ cup finely chopped cilantro

1. In a large skillet, bring sherry and oil to a boil over medium-high heat. Add onion and garlic. Cook, stirring, 2 minutes. Add Italian tomatoes, sun-dried tomatoes, and pickled jalapeño peppers. Reduce heat and simmer, covered, until sauce is thickened, about 12 minutes, stirring occasionally.

2. While sauce is cooking, in a large saucepan filled with boiling water, cook pasta, without adding salt or oil, until tender but still firm, about 12 minutes. Drain pasta, reserving ¾ cup cooking liquid. Stir reserved cooking liquid into tomato sauce in skillet.

3. Place pasta in a large bowl. Add sauce; toss to combine. Sprinkle with cilantro; toss again. Serve hot.

Per Serving: Calories: 447   Total fat: 4 g   Saturated fat: 4 g
Cholesterol: 0 mg   Percentage calories from fat: 9%

Chapter 4

Thin Pizzas and Sandwiches

Pizza is no longer just a slice to go. This staple of the American diet has gone from the Neapolitan baked dough topped with tomato sauce, stringy mozzarella, and oily pepperoni to trendier versions, which are often individual rounds rolled thin, thin, thin. Now lighter and healthier pizzas are topped with fresh vegetables, wild mushrooms, lower-fat sausages, beans, reduced-fat cheeses, and fresh herbs, which increase flavor while cutting fat and reducing calories.

The base for all pizzas is the crust. The pizza crust recipe in this chapter is for a thin crust made with a bread machine yeast, which cuts the rising time in half. If you cannot find bread machine yeast, use a quick-rising yeast. The inclusion of whole wheat flour in the pizza dough gives the dough a slightly nutty flavor, and a cornmeal variation, used with the Mexican Hot Bean Pizza, has a crunchy texture.

In the ever-popular Sausage, Onion, and Pepper Pizza I've eliminated the cheese (I promise you won't even miss it) and substituted a low-fat turkey sausage for the higher-fat pork sausage. White pizzas are another type enjoying current popularity. Made without a tomato sauce base, these pizzas have become a pizza parlor favorite. One that I usually order is a Broccoli and Mushroom Pizza, which you will find in this chapter made with a low-fat mozzarella cheese. For unusual pizza choices, try the Tomato, Swiss Cheese, and Fennel Pizza or Wild Mushroom, Red Onion, and Sage Pizza.

Each pizza recipe in this chapter makes one 12-inch round—enough to serve 6. You can also divide the dough into 6 equal portions to make individual pizzas, as I did for the Roasted Garlic and Potato Pizzas.

Sandwiches, too, have become trendy. Now they are served on a variety of breads with unusual fillings and savory condiments. I've given a Mexican twist to the Grilled Cheese and Green Chile Sandwich and reduced the fat with a part-skim milk Monterey Jack cheese. An egg substitute takes the place of eggs. Kibbee is a Mediterranean meatball made with bulgur and a little bit of meat, flavored with fresh herbs. I've tucked the meatballs in a pita and topped it with a tomato yogurt sauce for a flavorful sandwich. Roasted vegetables form the base for the hearty knife-and-fork Grilled Eggplant, Zucchini, and Tomato Melt served on sourdough bread.

Whichever you choose, this chapter is designed to keep the fun in picking up a bite to eat while taking out as much of the fat as possible.

75   MEXICAN HOT BEAN PIZZA
Prep: 20 minutes   Cook: 12 minutes   Serves: 6

This gives you the familiar taste of a black bean burrito transformed into a pizza packed with a lot of flavor.

1 (16-ounce) can black beans, drained but not rinsed
1 teaspoon ground cumin
1 teaspoon hot Mexican chili powder
   Low-Fat Cornmeal Pizza Crust (page 61)
1 pound tomatoes, seeded and coarsely chopped
½ cup chopped scallions

1 tablespoon seeded minced fresh jalapeño pepper
½ cup coarsely shredded low-fat Monterey Jack cheese (2 ounces)
½ cup coarsely shredded reduced-fat sharp Cheddar cheese (2 ounces)
1 tablespoon chopped cilantro

1. Preheat oven to 500°F. In a large bowl, mash beans with cumin and chili powder until chunky. Spread over prepared crust. Top with tomatoes, scallions, and jalapeño pepper. Sprinkle with Monterey Jack and Cheddar cheeses.

2. Bake pizza about 12 minutes, until crust is golden and cheeses have melted. Sprinkle with cilantro. Slide pizza onto a large cutting board; let rest 5 minutes. Cut into wedges to serve.

Per Serving: Calories: 317   Total fat: 5 g   Saturated fat: 3 g
Cholesterol: 13 mg   Percentage calories from fat: 15%

76   BROCCOLI AND MUSHROOM PIZZA
Prep: 11 minutes   Cook: 16 minutes   Serves: 6

Pizzas without a tomato sauce are called white pizzas. This is one popular variation.

2½ cups coarsely chopped broccoli (about 6 ounces)
1 cup sliced mushrooms
1 garlic clove, minced
1 teaspoon extra-virgin olive oil
   Low-Fat Cornmeal Pizza Crust (page 61)

1 cup coarsely shredded low-fat, part-skim mozzarella (4 ounces)
2 tablespoons shredded fresh basil or 1 teaspoon dried

1. Preheat oven to 500°F. Steam broccoli, covered, in a vegetable steamer over boiling water until crisp-tender, about 2 minutes. Drain broccoli on paper towels; blot dry.

2. In a small bowl, toss together mushrooms, garlic, and olive oil. Cook in a large nonstick skillet over medium-high heat, stirring constantly, until mushrooms wilt, about 2 minutes. Add broccoli and toss to mix. Spoon broccoli mixture over crust. Sprinkle with half of cheese.

3. Bake pizza about 12 minutes, until crust is golden. Slide pizza onto a large cutting board. Sprinkle with remaining cheese and basil; let rest 5 minutes. Cut into wedges to serve.

Per Serving: Calories: 241   Total fat: 5 g   Saturated fat: 2 g
Cholesterol: 11 mg   Percentage calories from fat: 20%

---

77   LOW-FAT PIZZA CRUST
Prep: 14 minutes (includes resting time)   Cook: 12 to 15 minutes
Serves: 6

Using a quick-rising yeast cuts down on the rising time usually required in making a pizza dough. You can also use bread machine yeast, which is the same as quick-rising. If you want to make individual pizzas, divide the dough into 6 equal pieces and pat out each piece to a 6-inch round. Then just follow directions for individual recipes, dividing ingredients proportionately.

1½ **cups all-purpose flour**
½ **cup whole wheat flour**
2¼ **teaspoons (¼ ounce) quick-rising yeast**
1 **teaspoon salt**

1 **teaspoon sugar**
1 **teaspoon olive oil**
¾ **cup warm water (105° to 115°F.)**
Olive oil cooking spray

1. In a food processor, combine all-purpose and whole wheat flours with yeast, salt, and sugar. With machine on, add olive oil; gradually pour warm water through feed tube. Process, adding up to 1 tablespoon cold water, until dough forms a ball; then process 1 minute to knead. Dough should be slightly sticky. Turn dough out onto a lightly floured surface; cover and let rest 10 minutes.

2. Coat a 12-inch pizza pan with cooking spray. Pat dough out in prepared pan, building up edges to form a rim. Top and bake according to recipe directions. For a fully baked plain crust, bake in a preheated 500°F. oven 12 to 15 minutes.

Per Serving: Calories: 166   Total fat: 1 g   Saturated fat: 0 g
Cholesterol: 0 mg   Percentage calories from fat: 8%

Variation: **LOW-FAT CORNMEAL PIZZA CRUST**
Substitute ½ cup yellow cornmeal for whole wheat flour.

Per Serving: Calories: 175   Total fat: 1 g   Saturated fat: 0 g
Cholesterol: 0 mg   Percentage calories from fat: 8%

78   TOMATO, SWISS CHEESE, AND FENNEL PIZZA

Prep: 12 minutes   Cook: 12 minutes   Serves: 6

Fennel, a licorice-flavored spice, adds an interesting flavor to this pizza.

1 cup coarsely shredded low-fat, low-sodium Swiss cheese (about 4 ounces)
Low-Fat Pizza Crust (page 61)
1 to 2 tablespoons dried marjoram or oregano
1 teaspoon fennel seeds

3 large ripe tomatoes (1½ pounds), cut into ¼-inch slices
¼ teaspoon coarse (kosher) salt
⅛ teaspoon cracked black pepper
1 teaspoon extra-virgin olive oil

1. Preheat oven to 500°F. Sprinkle Swiss cheese over prepared crust. Sprinkle with marjoram and fennel. Arrange tomato slices, overlapping slightly, over cheese. Season with salt and pepper. Drizzle olive oil over pizza.

2. Bake pizza about 12 minutes, until crust is golden. Slide pizza onto a large cutting board; let rest 5 minutes. Cut into wedges to serve.

Per Serving: Calories: 266   Total fat: 7 g   Saturated fat: 0 g
Cholesterol: 6 mg   Percentage calories from fat: 23%

79   ROASTED GARLIC AND POTATO PIZZAS

Prep: 20 minutes   Cook: 17 to 22 minutes   Serves: 4

There's no need to peel the potatoes here, but it's important to cut them paper-thin so they will cook in the allotted time. A mandoline helps, but you can also slice the potatoes thinly with a large sharp knife.

Roasted Garlic (recipe follows)
Low-Fat Pizza Crust (page 61)
2 medium baking potatoes (¾ pound), scrubbed and cut into paper-thin slices

1 tablespoon extra-virgin olive oil
½ teaspoon salt
1½ teaspoons coarsely chopped fresh rosemary or ½ teaspoon dried, crumbled

1. Preheat oven to 500°F. Mash enough roasted garlic to equal 4 teaspoons (save remaining garlic for another use); set aside.

2. Divide pizza dough into 4 equal pieces. Pat out each piece to a 6-inch round, building up edges to form a ½-inch rim. Place on 2 large baking sheets.

3. In a large bowl, place potatoes and olive oil; toss to coat. Spread 1 teaspoon of mashed roasted garlic over each prepared pizza round. Overlap potato slices, pinwheel fashion, over prepared crusts. Season with salt and rosemary.

4. Bake pizzas 17 to 22 minutes, until crust is golden brown and potatoes are tender.

Per Serving: Calories: 367   Total fat: 6 g   Saturated fat: 1 g
Cholesterol: 0 mg   Percentage calories from fat: 14%

---

80   ROASTED GARLIC
Prep: 1 minute   Cook: 45 minutes   Makes: about 2 tablespoons

A toaster oven is really convenient for roasting something as small as a head of garlic. But if you don't have one, this recipe will work just as well in an ordinary oven.

1 medium-large garlic bulb

1. Remove some outer papery skin from garlic bulb, but do not separate cloves. With a sharp knife, cut thin slice off pointed end of garlic bulb to expose cloves. Wrap bulb in aluminum foil.

2. Toast in toaster oven set at 425°F. (no need to preheat) for 45 minutes, or until garlic cloves are soft. Remove foil; cool slightly. Squeeze out garlic and mash with a fork. Store in a small container and refrigerate. Use as directed in individual recipes.

Per Tablespoon: Calories: 54   Total fat: 1 g   Saturated fat: 0 g
Cholesterol: 0 mg   Percentage calories from fat: 3%

---

81   CREAMY DATE NUT SANDWICH
Prep: 8 minutes   Cook: none   Serves: 2

A nutted-cheese sandwich and a cup of coffee is one of my comfy lunches. I've embellished the sandwich with dates and apple slices and used a nonfat cream cheese product to reduce the fat content. Coat the apple slices with lemon juice if you plan to tote it in a lunch box.

⅓ **cup nonfat cream cheese product**
¼ **cup pitted chopped dates**
2 **tablespoons chopped pecans, almonds, or walnuts**

4 **slices of cinnamon-raisin bread, toasted, if desired**
1 **small sweet red apple, cored and cut into thin slices**

In a small bowl, stir together cream cheese, dates, and nuts. Spread equal amounts of the mixture on half of bread slices. Top with apple slices and cover with remaining bread slice. Cut into diagonal halves.

Per Serving: Calories: 311   Total fat: 7 g   Saturated fat: 1 g
Cholesterol: 4 mg   Percentage calories from fat: 20%

82 EGG SALAD POCKETS
Prep: 15 minutes   Cook: none   Serves: 4

Because half of the egg yolks are eliminated, the amount of fat is reduced in this popular sandwich. You can now purchase nonfat pita rounds in flavors—oat bran, onion, and garlic.

6 hard-boiled eggs
½ cup coarsely chopped celery
¼ cup coarsely chopped scallions
2 tablespoons nonfat sour cream
1 tablespoon reduced-fat mayonnaise dressing
2 teaspoons horseradish mustard

⅛ teaspoon salt
4 (6-inch) nonfat onion pita rounds
4 leaves of green leaf lettuce
4 tomato slices, cut ¼ inch thick
1 cup alfalfa sprouts

1. Scoop out egg yolks; discard half or save for another use. Coarsely chop or mash 3 remaining egg yolks with all of egg whites. Place in a medium bowl. Add celery, scallions, sour cream, mayonnaise, mustard, and salt. Mix thoroughly to combine.

2. Cut a thin slice off each pita round. Open up to form a pocket. Tuck in a lettuce leaf and a tomato slice. Spoon ½ cup egg salad into each. Top each with ¼ cup sprouts.

Per Serving: Calories: 273 Total fat: 7 g Saturated fat: 2 g
Cholesterol: 159 mg Percentage calories from fat: 21%

83 SAUSAGE, ONION, AND PEPPER PIZZA
Prep: 15 minutes   Cook: 22 minutes   Serves: 6

Substituting turkey sausage cuts the fat for this popular pizza.

Olive oil cooking spray
2 hot or sweet Italian-style turkey sausage, casings removed
1 large green bell pepper, cut into thin strips
1 large red bell pepper, cut into thin strips
1 medium onion, cut into thin wedges

1 garlic clove, minced
1 teaspoon dried marjoram
⅛ teaspoon crushed hot red pepper
1 cup Basic Tomato Sauce (recipe follows)
Low-Fat Pizza Crust (page 61)
1 tablespoon grated Parmesan cheese

1. Preheat oven to 500°F. Coat a nonstick skillet with cooking spray. Add sausage and flatten with a spoon. Cook over medium-high heat, breaking up sausage with a wooden spoon into small pieces, until browned, about 5 minutes. Drain sausage on paper towels. Wipe out skillet, if necessary.

2. Coat skillet with cooking spray; heat over medium-high heat. Add green and red bell peppers, onion, and garlic. Coat vegetables lightly with cooking spray. Cook, stirring often, until crisp-tender, about 5 minutes. Stir in marjoram and hot pepper.

3. Spread tomato sauce over crust. Top with vegetable mixture. Dot with sausages and sprinkle cheese over all.

4. Bake pizza about 12 minutes, until crust is golden. Slide pizza onto a large cutting board; let rest 5 minutes. Cut into wedges to serve.

*Per Serving: Calories: 239   Total fat: 4 g   Saturated fat: 0 g
Cholesterol: 15 mg   Percentage calories from fat: 15%*

---

84   BASIC TOMATO SAUCE
Prep: 3 minutes   Cook: 32 minutes   Makes: 2½ cups

Sauces for pizza should be fairly thick, otherwise you will get a soggy crust. The addition of tomato paste aids as a thickening agent. Now you can buy tomato paste in a tube, which is a great convenience when you just need a few tablespoons. This sauce freezes well.

1½ teaspoons extra-virgin olive oil
1 tablespoon finely chopped garlic
1 (28-ounce) can Italian-style plum tomatoes with tomato puree

2 tablespoons tomato paste
½ teaspoon dried marjoram or oregano
¼ teaspoon dried thyme leaves

In a large nonreactive saucepan, heat olive oil over medium heat. Add garlic and cook, stirring often, until lightly browned, about 2 minutes. Add tomatoes with puree, tomato paste, marjoram, and thyme; break up tomatoes with back of a wooden spoon. Simmer, uncovered, stirring occasionally, until sauce is thick, about 30 minutes.

*Per Serving: Calories: 52   Total fat: 1 g   Saturated fat: 0 g
Cholesterol: 0 mg   Percentage calories from fat: 19%*

85 WILD MUSHROOM, RED ONION, AND SAGE PIZZA

Prep: 15 minutes   Cook: 15 to 17 minutes   Serves: 6

A combination of wild and domestic mushrooms gives an earthy flavor to this pizza.

- 2 cups sliced cultivated mushrooms, such as white button or Italian brown (about 6 ounces)
- 2 cups wild mushrooms, such as chanterelles, cèpes, shiitake, or oyster (about 6 ounces)
- 1 cup red onion slivers
- 1 teaspoon extra-virgin olive oil
- ¼ teaspoon salt
- ¼ teaspoon cracked black pepper
- Low-Fat Pizza Crust (page 61) or Low-Fat Cornmeal Pizza Crust (page 61)
- 1 tablespoon shredded fresh sage leaves or 1 teaspoon dried
- 1 cup coarsely shredded part-skim mozzarella cheese (4 ounces)
- 1 tablespoon chopped parsley

1. Preheat oven to 500°F. In a large bowl, place mushrooms with onions. Add olive oil and toss to coat.

2. In a large nonstick skillet, cook mushrooms and onions over medium-high heat, stirring frequently, until mushrooms soften, 3 to 5 minutes. Season with salt and pepper. Place mushroom mixture on paper towels; blot dry. Spoon mushroom-onion mixture over crust. Sprinkle with sage. Top with half of cheese.

3. Bake pizza about 12 minutes, until crust is golden. Remove from oven. Slide pizza onto a large cutting board. Top with remaining cheese and sprinkle with parsley; let rest 5 minutes. Cut into wedges to serve.

Per Serving: Calories: 244   Total fat: 5 g   Saturated fat: 2 g
Cholesterol: 11 mg   Percentage calories from fat: 20%

86 FALAFEL WITH TAHINI SAUCE
Prep: 30 minutes (includes standing time)
Cook: 4 minutes   Serves: 4

This favorite Middle Eastern sandwich is made easier by using a prepared falafel mix. Instead of deep-frying the patties, I've baked them on a griddle.

1 cup prepared falafel mix
2 tablespoons finely chopped parsley
2 tablespoons finely chopped scallions
  Olive oil cooking spray
4 (6-inch) nonfat oat bran or onion pita rounds

1 cup shredded romaine lettuce leaves
½ cup halved cherry tomatoes
½ cup diced zucchini or cucumber
¼ cup radish or alfalfa sprouts
  Tahini Sauce (recipe follows)

1. In a medium bowl, combine falafel mix with parsley and scallions. Stir in ½ cup water. Let stand 10 minutes. Shape into 12 (2¾-inch) patties, about 1 tablespoon each.

2. Coat a nonstick griddle with cooking spray. Heat griddle until a few drops of water dance about. Add falafel patties and cook until brown on bottom, about 2 minutes. Turn and cook 2 minutes longer, or until brown on second side.

3. Cut a thin slice off each pita. Open up to form a pocket. Tuck 3 patties into each pocket; smash slightly with a fork. Tuck in equal amounts of lettuce, tomatoes, zucchini, and sprouts. Drizzle each sandwich with 2 tablespoons tahini sauce.

TAHINI SAUCE
Makes: ½ cup

Using yogurt as the base for this sauce and a little bit of the tahini (sesame seed paste) gives you the flavor of the richer version without the fat or calories.

½ cup nonfat plain yogurt
2 tablespoons tahini (Middle Eastern sesame seed paste)
1 teaspoon fresh lemon juice

1 garlic clove, minced
  Few drops of hot pepper sauce

In a small bowl, combine yogurt, tahini, lemon juice, garlic, and hot pepper sauce. Stir until well blended. Mix in 1 to 2 tablespoons water to thin to a sauce consistency.

Per Serving: Calories: 343 Total fat: 7 g Saturated fat: 1 g
Cholesterol: 1 mg Percentage calories from fat: 22%

87　GREEK SALAD IN A SANDWICH

Prep: 20 minutes　Cook: none　Serves: 6

1 (6⅛-ounce) can solid white albacore tuna in water, drained and broken into chunks
1 cup halved cherry tomatoes, quartered if large
1 cup green or red bell pepper slivers
½ cup peeled and seeded cucumber slices
½ cup diced red onion
2 tablespoons sliced black olives, preferably Kalamata
2 ounces crumbled feta cheese
1 tablespoon extra-virgin olive oil
1 tablespoon water or chicken broth
2 teaspoons red wine vinegar
2 teaspoons fresh lemon juice
½ teaspoon dried oregano
6 crusty rolls, such as kaiser or 5-inch oblong hero rolls
6 large leaves of leafy green lettuce

1. In a large bowl, combine tuna, tomatoes, bell pepper, cucumber, red onion, olives, feta, olive oil, water or broth, vinegar, lemon juice, and oregano. Toss Greek salad to mix.

2. Cut off top third of rolls. Scoop out some of soft center in bottom, leaving a ½-inch shell. Line shells with lettuce. Spoon Greek salad into shells. Cover with tops of rolls.

Per Serving:　Calories: 275　Total fat: 8 g　Saturated fat: 2 g
Cholesterol: 20 mg　Percentage calories from fat: 27%

88　GRILLED EGGPLANT, ZUCCHINI, AND TOMATO MELT

Prep: 20 minutes　Cook: 7 minutes　Serves: 4

Eat this hot and hearty open-faced sandwich with a knife and fork.

Olive oil cooking spray
2 teaspoons red wine vinegar
2 large tomatoes (about 1 pound), each cut into 4 thick slices
½ teaspoon fennel seeds, crushed
½ teaspoon Italian seasoning
1 medium zucchini (about 10 ounces), cut in half crosswise, then cut lengthwise into ½-inch slices
1 small eggplant (¾ pound), cut crosswise into ½-inch slices
3 garlic cloves—2 minced, 1 halved
4 slices of sourdough bread, cut ½ inch thick
2 (1-ounce) slices of provolone cheese, each cut into 6 strips

1. Preheat broiler. Coat a large baking sheet with cooking spray.

2. Drizzle vinegar over tomato slices. Sprinkle with fennel seeds and Italian seasoning.

3. Arrange zucchini and eggplant on prepared baking sheet. Sprinkle minced garlic over vegetables. Lightly coat vegetables with cooking spray. Broil about 3 inches from heat 3 minutes, or until eggplant is lightly browned. Turn vegetables over and broil about 3 minutes longer, or until eggplant is lightly browned and zucchini has softened.

4. Toast bread slices in toaster oven or under broiler. Rub cut garlic over 1 side of each bread slice. Top bread slices with eggplant, zucchini, and tomato slices, dividing evenly. Top vegetables with 3 strips of cheese. Broil 3 inches from heat until cheese melts, about 10 seconds.

Per Serving: Calories: 185   Total fat: 6 g   Saturated fat: 3 g
Cholesterol: 10 mg   Percentage calories from fat: 27%

---

89 GRILLED CHEESE AND GREEN CHILE SANDWICH
Prep: 16 minutes   Cook: 4 minutes   Serves: 4

If you like your food very hot, use canned jalapeño peppers and a spicy salsa.

1 cup coarsely shredded part-skim Monterey Jack cheese (4 ounces)
8 slices of firm white sandwich bread
1 (4-ounce) can chopped green chiles, drained
4 teaspoons chopped cilantro

¾ cup frozen egg substitute, thawed
½ cup skim milk
Vegetable cooking spray
¼ cup nonfat sour cream
¼ cup chunky salsa
4 teaspoons sliced scallions

1. Divide Monterey Jack cheese among 4 bread slices. Sprinkle green chiles and cilantro over cheese. Top with remaining bread slices.

2. In a shallow 9 x 13-inch baking dish, beat together the thawed egg substitute and milk. Dip sandwiches, one at a time, into egg mixture, coating both sides. Let stand until egg mixture is absorbed, turning sandwiches once with a wide spatula.

3. Coat a griddle with cooking spray. Heat griddle until a few drops of water dance about. Add sandwiches and toast, turning once, until golden brown, about 2 minutes for each side. To serve, cut sandwiches in diagonal halves. Top each sandwich with 1 tablespoon each sour cream and salsa and 1 teaspoon scallions.

Per Serving: Calories: 271   Total fat: 7 g   Saturated fat: 4 g
Cholesterol: 21 mg   Percentage calories from fat: 24%

90   KIBBEE SANDWICH WITH TOMATO YOGURT SAUCE

Prep: 15 minutes   Stand: 30 minutes
Cook: 25 to 30 minutes   Serves: 6

Bulgur forms the base of this spicy meatball and stretches the amount of meat used in this delicious sandwich.

½ cup bulgur
½ cup boiling water
½ pound extra-lean ground beef
½ cup minced scallions
½ cup minced parsley
¼ cup frozen egg substitute, thawed
1 teaspoon finely chopped garlic

1 teaspoon salt
½ teaspoon ground cumin
½ teaspoon ground coriander
   Olive oil cooking spray
6 (6-inch) oat bran or whole wheat pita rounds
1½ cups shredded iceberg or romaine lettuce
   Tomato Yogurt Sauce (recipe follows)

1. Place bulgur in a medium bowl. Pour on boiling water to cover. Let stand until water is absorbed, about 30 minutes.

2. Add beef, scallions, parsley, egg substitute, garlic, salt, cumin, and coriander. Blend with a fork until mixture comes together. Shape into 18 (1½-inch) meatballs, about 2 tablespoons each.

3. Preheat oven to 350°F. Coat a 10 x 15-inch jelly roll pan with cooking spray. Place meatballs 1 inch apart on pan. Bake 25 to 30 minutes, or until meatballs are browned.

4. Cut thin slice off pita rounds. Open up to form a pocket. Tuck ¼ cup lettuce and 3 meatballs into each. Top with ¼ cup tomato yogurt sauce.

Per Serving: Calories: 315 Total fat: 6 g Saturated fat: 2 g
Cholesterol: 24 mg Percentage calories from fat: 16%

91   TOMATO YOGURT SAUCE

Prep: 5 minutes   Cook: none   Makes: 1½ cups

1 cup nonfat plain yogurt
⅔ cup seeded, diced, firm-ripe plum tomatoes

2 tablespoons minced fresh dill

In a small bowl, combine yogurt, tomatoes, and dill. Stir to mix well. Cover and refrigerate until ready to use.

Per ¼-Cup Serving: Calories: 26 Total fat: < 1 g Saturated fat: 0 g
Cholesterol: 1 mg Percentage calories from fat: 4%

Chapter 5

Lean Meats

When you're cutting back to 30 percent fat or less, the hardest food to calculate into your diet is red meat. In a quest for healthier eating, some people have given up meat entirely. Many of us, however, still love the taste of meat and occasionally crave a savory stew or roast, juicy barbecue, or nice crusty chop. It's good to keep in mind, too, that meat is high in iron and niacin, and a little meat can help our bodies to absorb many of the vitamins and minerals that are contained in vegetables, beans, and grains.

The trick to keeping some meat in your menu while still reducing fat and cholesterol is to choose the leanest cuts, trim them of all visible fat, cook them with little or no added fat, and, especially, combine the meat with plenty of healthy carbohydrates—vegetables, beans, grains, fruits, and starches. In this way, the meat adds flavor and satisfying texture, but does not act as a heavy filler. The demand for less fat has helped bring about a revolution in meat marketing; you can buy 98 percent lean ground beef in many supermarkets, and the pork we purchase today is substantially leaner than the same meat of only a decade ago.

This chapter offers over two dozen tempting ways to enjoy beef, veal, pork, and lamb and still keep your fat count low. Some, such as Sauerbraten with Potato Dumplings, Lamb Stew with Fall Vegetables, and Pork Chops with Sauerkraut, are hearty traditional dishes. Others, such as Cajun Veal with Julienned Vegetables, Chinese Pepper Steak, and Pork Medallions with Apricots and Prunes, offer a more contemporary and international approach. And for anyone who has trouble giving up what they've always enjoyed eating, I've even included a couple of meaty low-fat burgers.

92   BEEF GOULASH WITH LEMON POPPY SEED NOODLES

Prep: 10 minutes   Cook: 1½ hours   Serves: 4 to 6

You can also serve this easy, saucy goulash with mashed potatoes.

Vegetable cooking spray
1 teaspoon canola oil
1 pound trimmed beef round steak, cut into 1-inch cubes
3 cups thinly sliced onions
1 tablespoon finely chopped garlic
2 tablespoons hot Hungarian paprika

¼ teaspoon caraway seeds (optional)
2 cups homemade or canned reduced-sodium beef broth
½ cup nonfat sour cream, at room temperature
1 tablespoon chopped parsley
Lemon Poppy Seed Noodles (recipe follows)

1. Coat a large nonstick skillet with cooking spray. Add oil and heat over medium-high heat. Add beef and cook, turning, until brown all over, about 5 minutes. Remove with a slotted spoon to a bowl.

2. Add onions, garlic, and ¼ cup water to skillet. Toss to coat. Reduce heat to low, cover, and cook 10 minutes, stirring occasionally, until onions are soft.

3. Return browned beef to skillet. Add paprika, caraway seeds, and beef broth; stir to mix. Bring to a boil, reduce heat to low, cover, and simmer 1 hour and 15 minutes, or until meat is tender.

4. Remove from heat. Gradually blend sour cream into goulash. Return to low heat. Cook, stirring, just until mixture is hot, about 1 minute. Do not boil. Spoon goulash into a bowl, sprinkle with parsley, and serve with lemon poppy seed noodles.

Per Serving: Calories: 256   Total fat: 8 g   Saturated fat: 2 g
Cholesterol: 66 mg   Percentage calories from fat: 27%

93   LEMON POPPY SEED NOODLES

Prep: 5 minutes   Cook: 6 minutes   Serves: 4 to 6

A hint of lemon zest accents the flavor of this noodle side dish.

8 ounces egg-free noodles
2 teaspoons reduced-fat margarine
2 teaspoons grated lemon zest

1 teaspoon poppy seeds
1 teaspoon sugar
Pinch of salt

1. In a large saucepan filled with boiling water, cook noodles, without adding salt or oil, until tender but still firm, about 6 minutes. Drain, reserving 2 tablespoons cooking liquid.

2. Place noodles in a large bowl. Add margarine, lemon zest, poppy seeds, sugar, salt, and the reserved 2 tablespoons cooking liquid; toss to combine. Serve hot.

Per Serving: Calories: 108   Total fat: 1 g   Saturated fat: 0 g
Cholesterol: 0 mg   Percentage calories from fat: 10%

---

94   STIR-FRIED BEEF WITH BROCCOLI
Prep: 30 minutes (includes standing time)
Cook: 7 minutes   Serves: 4

Sun-dried tomatoes are added to this favorite Chinese dish. Serve with brown rice.

8 dried Chinese mushrooms
1½ ounces sun-dried tomatoes (without oil) (about 24)
1 pound lean, boneless top round steak
1 large bunch of broccoli Vegetable cooking spray
1 teaspoon vegetable oil
½ cup (1-inch pieces) scallions
1 teaspoon finely chopped garlic
1 teaspoon finely chopped fresh ginger
4 teaspoons cornstarch
¾ cup dry white wine or canned reduced-sodium chicken broth
½ cup reduced-sodium soy sauce

1. In a small bowl, place mushrooms and sun-dried tomatoes; pour on ¾ cup boiling water; let stand 10 minutes to soften. Drain and discard liquid. Cut tomatoes in thin strips. Remove and discard stems from mushrooms; cut caps into ½-inch strips.

2. Trim fat from steak; cut meat diagonally across grain to thin strips. Trim broccoli, removing stems. Cut broccoli into florets to equal 3 cups; slice tender stalks to equal 1 cup.

3. Coat a wok or large nonstick skillet with cooking spray; heat wok or skillet over high heat. Add steak and stir-fry 2 minutes; remove to a bowl and keep warm. Add oil to wok or skillet; heat over medium-high heat until hot. Add broccoli and stir-fry 3 minutes. Add mushrooms, sun-dried tomatoes, scallions, garlic, and ginger; stir-fry 1 minute.

4. Stir together cornstarch, wine or broth, and soy sauce. Add to wok or skillet with the cooked beef and juices in the bowl. Stir-fry until sauce has thickened, is bubbly, and coats the meat and vegetables, about 1 minute.

Per Serving: Calories: 344   Total fat: 7 g   Saturated fat: 2 g
Cholesterol: 65 mg   Percentage calories from fat: 17%

95 CHINESE PEPPER STEAK

Prep: 20 minutes   Stand: 20 minutes
Cook: 5 to 8 minutes   Serves: 4 to 6

Chinese black mushrooms are also known as tree-ear or wood-ear mushrooms. They can be purchased in some supermarkets and in Asian food stores. To make the steak easier to slice neatly into thin slices, place in the freezer for about 30 minutes, until partially frozen.

12 ounces lean sirloin steak, trimmed of all visible fat	2 teaspoons finely chopped garlic
3 tablespoons reduced-sodium soy sauce	¼ cup minced scallions
3 tablespoons rice wine vinegar	1 large green bell pepper, seeded and cut into 1-inch pieces
1 tablespoon cornstarch	1 large red bell pepper, seeded and cut into 1-inch pieces
1 teaspoon sugar	
¾ teaspoon hot pepper sauce	
8 dried Chinese black mushrooms	2 ounces snow peas, trimmed and cut in half
1½ teaspoons canola oil	1 (8-ounce) can sliced water chestnuts, drained
2 teaspoons finely chopped ginger	Toasted sesame seeds (optional)

1. Cut steak in half lengthwise, then cut crosswise on a diagonal into ¼-inch-thick slices. In a medium bowl, combine soy sauce, rice wine vinegar, cornstarch, sugar, and hot sauce. Add steak to marinade; toss to coat. Let stand at room temperature 20 minutes, mixing occasionally.

2. Meanwhile, in a small bowl, pour 1 cup boiling water over mushrooms. Let soak 15 minutes to soften; drain. Remove and discard stems; cut mushroom caps into thin strips.

3. Drain beef, reserving marinade. In a large nonstick skillet, heat 1 teaspoon of oil over high heat. Add ginger, garlic, and scallions; stir-fry 30 seconds. Add beef; stir-fry until brown outside but still pink inside, 1 to 3 minutes. Place meat in a large bowl.

4. Add remaining ½ teaspoon oil to skillet. Add mushrooms, green and red bell peppers, snow peas, water chestnuts, and 2 tablespoons water. Stir to combine. Cover and steam over medium heat until vegetables are slightly softened, about 3 minutes. Add beef with bowl juices and the reserved marinade to the skillet. Cook, stirring, until sauce is slightly thickened and mixture is heated through, about 1 minute. Sprinkle sesame seeds on top and serve.

Per Serving: Calories: 167   Total fat: 4 g   Saturated fat: 1 g
Cholesterol: 41 mg   Percentage calories from fat: 24%

96 SAUERBRATEN WITH POTATO DUMPLINGS

Prep: 15 minutes   Cook: 2½ hours   Serves: 12

Usually sauerbraten has to marinate 2 to 3 days. In this recipe you can make it early in the day and serve it in the evening or the next day. The trick is to cook the meat partially, remove it from the broth, slice it, and return the meat to the pan to cook with the remaining incredients. I like to serve this tasty meat with potato dumplings and sweet-and-sour red cabbage.

Vegetable cooking spray
4 pounds bottom round roast, well trimmed
¾ cup balsamic or red wine vinegar
2 tablespoons light brown sugar
2 teaspoons salt
1½ teaspoons cracked or coarsely ground pepper

1 teaspoon ground ginger
⅛ teaspoon ground cloves
⅛ teaspoon ground allspice
1 bay leaf
1 cup sliced onions
1 cup sliced carrots
3 tablespoons flour
Potato Dumplings (recipe follows)

1. Coat a heavy saucepan or dutch oven with cooking spray. Brown meat on all sides. Pour off any fat from pan and wipe out saucepan. Place a small rack in pan. Add meat and ¾ cup water. Bring to a boil; reduce heat. Cover and steam 1 hour (meat will not be done).

2. Place meat on a cutting board set over a 10 x 15-inch jelly roll pan. Cut into ½-inch-thick slices. Return meat to heavy saucepan with juices in jelly roll pan. Add ¾ cup water, vinegar, brown sugar, salt, pepper, ginger, cloves, allspice, bay leaf, onions, and carrots. Bring to a boil; lower heat. Cover and simmer until tender, about 1½ hours. Remove meat to a serving platter with a slotted spoon; cover and keep warm.

3. Pour juices in pan in a large sieve set over a bowl; discard vegetables. Allow fat to rise to the top and skim off. Measure liquid. You should have 3 cups (add water, if necessary, to make 3 cups). Pour liquid back into saucepan and heat to a simmer.

4. In a small cup, blend together the flour with 3 tablespoons water. Slowly stir into hot liquid in pan. Cook and stir until gravy has thickened slightly, about 5 minutes. Spoon some of the gravy over meat. Pour remainder into gravy boat to pass at the table. Serve with potato dumplings.

Per Serving: Calories: 325   Total fat: 10 g   Saturated fat: 4 g
Cholesterol: 92 mg   Percentage calories from fat: 28%

97   RANCHERO STEAK WITH TOASTED CORN SALSA

Prep: 7 minutes   Stand: 1 to 4 hours
Cook: 15 to 17 minutes   Serves: 6

The steak is marinated in a barbecue-type sauce, quickly broiled, and thinly sliced. Serve with cole slaw and beer.

⅓ cup apple cider or unsweetened apple juice
2 tablespoons apple cider vinegar
1 tablespoon honey
1 tablespoon tomato paste or ketchup
¼ cup minced scallions
2 garlic cloves, minced

2 teaspoons hot Mexican chili powder
½ teaspoon ground cumin
¼ teaspoon dried oregano
¼ teaspoon salt
1 flank steak (1½ pounds), trimmed of all visible fat
   Toasted Corn Salsa (recipe follows)

1. In a small bowl, combine apple cider or apple juice, apple cider vinegar, honey, tomato paste or ketchup, scallions, garlic, chili powder, cumin, oregano, and salt; stir to combine. Place meat in a large zip-top heavy-duty plastic bag and pour on marinade; squeeze marinade around steak and close bag securely. Place in a bowl. Marinate at room temperature 1 hour or refrigerate up to 4 hours.

98   TOASTED CORN SALSA

Prep: 20 minutes   Cook: 9 to 13 minutes   Serves: 6

4 ears of corn
   Vegetable cooking spray
1 large red bell pepper
1½ teaspoons cumin seeds
1½ tablespoons lime juice

1 tablespoon minced pickled jalapeño peppers
3 tablespoons minced scallions
¼ teaspoon salt

1. Preheat broiler. Shuck corn and coat kernels with cooking spray. Set corn and bell pepper on a shallow baking sheet and broil about 4 inches from heat, turning, until corn is lightly browned and pepper is charred, 5 to 7 minutes for corn, 7 to 10 minutes for pepper.

2. Place pepper in a brown paper bag and set aside for about 10 minutes. As soon as corn is cool enough to handle, cut kernels off cob. Place corn in a medium bowl. Peel and seed pepper and cut into ⅜-inch dice. Add to corn.

3. In a small dry skillet, toast cumin seeds until fragrant and lightly browned, 2 to 3 minutes. Immediately pour over corn and pepper. Add lime juice, jalapeño peppers, scallions, and salt. Toss to mix. Serve at room temperature.

*Per Serving: Calories: 75   Total fat: 2 g   Saturated fat: 0 g
            Cholesterol: 0 mg   Percentage calories from fat: 17%*

2. Preheat broiler. Lift steak from marinade; save marinade. Place steak on broiler rack and broil 4 inches from heat 5 minutes per side for medium-rare, 6 minutes for well-done, turning once.

3. While meat is cooking, place marinade in a small skillet. Bring to a boil over high heat; lower heat. Simmer marinade for 5 minutes, stirring frequently.

4. Remove meat to a cutting board; let stand 5 minutes. Cut meat diagonally across grain into thin slices. Place slices, slightly overlapping, on a large serving platter. Using a pastry brush, brush cooked marinade over meat slices. Spoon toasted corn salsa over steak and serve.

Per Serving: Calories: 299 Total fat: 10 g Saturated fat: 4 g
Cholesterol: 57 mg Percentage calories from fat: 30%

---

99 LEMON BURGERS
Prep: 10 minutes   Cook: 4 to 6 minutes   Serves: 4

Using extra-lean ground beef cuts back on the fat count of an American favorite—burgers. You can also substitute 8 ounces of ground turkey for 8 ounces of the beef. The lemon gives this burger a refreshing taste, and I sometimes substitute chives for the parsley. Serve on buns with all the trimmings.

1 **pound ground beef**
   (98% lean)
	⅛ **teaspoon pepper**
	   Vegetable cooking spray

2 **tablespoons fresh lemon**
   juice
	4 **sourdough rolls (3 ounces**
	   each)

1 **teaspoon grated lemon zest**	4 **lettuce leaves**
1 **tablespoon finely chopped** **parsley**	4 **large slices of sweet onion**
¾ **teaspoon salt**	4 **large slices of tomato**

1. In a large bowl, combine beef, lemon juice, lemon zest, parsley, salt, and pepper. Mix lightly to combine. Shape into 4 patties.

2. Coat a large nonstick skillet with cooking spray. Heat skillet over medium-high heat. Add burgers and cook, turning, until brown on both sides, about 4 to 6 minutes, or to desired doneness.

3. Split rolls. Place lettuce leaf on bottom half. Top with burger, onion, tomato, and top of roll.

Per Serving: Calories: 449 Total fat: 14 g Saturated fat: 5 g
Cholesterol: 70 mg Percentage calories from fat: 29%

100 POTATO DUMPLINGS

Prep: 19 minutes   Cook: 24 minutes   Makes: 12

Tiny cubes of sautéed bread are tucked into the center of these dumplings. You can make the dumplings in advance up to 4 hours before cooking. Serve them with sauerbraten, or drop into a hearty vegetable soup.

3 to 4 medium all-purpose potatoes (1½ pounds), peeled and cut into 1-inch cubes	6 tablespoons frozen egg substitute, thawed
1 slice of firm-textured white bread	⅓ cup flour
1 tablespoon butter	⅓ cup uncooked farina
	1½ teaspoons salt
	¼ teaspoon pepper
	¼ teaspoon grated nutmeg

1. Place potatoes in a large saucepan with enough cold water to cover. Bring to a boil over high heat. Reduce heat to medium and cook, covered, at a low boil, 15 minutes, or until potatoes are tender.

2. While potatoes are cooking, cut bread into 36 (¼-inch) cubes. In a small nonstick skillet, melt butter over medium heat. Add bread cubes and cook, tossing, until golden, about 3 minutes.

3. Drain potatoes. Return to saucepan and toss over low heat to dry, about 1 minute. Put potatoes through a ricer or mash until smooth in a large bowl. Add egg substitute, flour, farina, salt, pepper, and nutmeg; stir until well blended.

4. In a large saucepan, bring 4 quarts water to a boil. Divide potato mixture into 12 equal parts, each slightly larger than a golf ball. Shape each mound in a round ball around 3 bread cubes, dusting hands with flour to keep dumplings from sticking.

5. Drop dumplings into boiling water. Cook, uncovered, until dumplings float to surface of water, about 5 minutes. Remove with slotted spoon to serving platter. Dust with additional nutmeg, if desired.

Per Serving: Calories: 83 Total fat: 1 g Saturated fat: 1 g
Cholesterol: 3 mg Percentage calories from fat: 12%

101 MEATBALLS AND RICE WITH AVGOLEMONO SAUCE

Prep: 30 minutes   Cook: 50 minutes   Serves: 6 to 8

In these meatballs flavored with dill and mint and topped with the classic Greek lemon and egg sauce, the eggs are replaced with an egg substitute to reduce the fat.

1 pound lean ground veal	1 (8-ounce) container frozen
¾ cup finely chopped onion	egg substitute, thawed
2 teaspoons finely chopped garlic	(1 cup)
2 cups long-grain white rice	1 teaspoon salt
2 tablespoons finely chopped fresh dill	⅛ teaspoon pepper
2 tablespoons finely chopped fresh mint	About 3 cups homemade or canned reduced-sodium chicken broth
	1 tablespoon cornstarch
	¼ cup fresh lemon juice

1. In a large bowl, combine ground veal, onion, garlic, ½ cup of rice, dill, mint, ¼ cup of egg substitute, ½ teaspoon salt, and pepper. Mix with hands or a wooden spoon until thoroughly combined. Shape into 24 meatballs (about 1½ tablespoons each).

2. In a large skillet, bring 2 cups of chicken broth to a boil. Place meatballs in a single layer in skillet. Cover, reduce heat, and simmer 30 minutes.

3. Meanwhile, in a large saucepan, bring 3 cups water with remaining ½ teaspoon salt to a boil. Add remaining 1½ cups rice, cover, and reduce heat to low. Cook 18 minutes, or until rice is tender and liquid is absorbed.

4. Lift meatballs out with a slotted spoon and place on a plate; cover and keep warm. Measure broth in saucepan into a 2-cup measure. Add enough of remaining broth to make 1½ cups liquid. Pour back into skillet and bring to a simmer.

5. In small bowl of an electric mixer, place remaining ¾ cup egg substitute and beat on high speed until mixture is thick, light, and lemon-colored, about 3 minutes. Beat in cornstarch and lemon juice. Gradually beat in hot broth. Return mixture to saucepan and bring to a simmer over low heat, stirring constantly, until sauce thickens, about 2 minutes. Do not boil. Pour sauce over meatballs and serve at once with cooked rice.

*Per Serving: Calories: 308 Total fat: 3 g Saturated fat: 1 g
Cholesterol: 56 mg Percentage calories from fat: 10%*

102 CAJUN VEAL WITH JULIENNED VEGETABLES

Prep: 30 minutes   Cook: 22 to 28 minutes   Serves: 6

6 veal scallops, cut from
   leg (1¼ pounds)
¼ cup flour
½ teaspoon Hungarian hot
   paprika
¼ teaspoon dried basil
⅛ teaspoon pepper
1 large red bell pepper (8
   ounces), seeded and cut
   into thin strips

1 medium zucchini, cut into
   2 x ¼-inch strips
2 medium carrots, peeled and
   cut into 2 x ¼-inch strips
4 teaspoons olive oil
¾ cup homemade or canned
   reduced-sodium chicken
   broth
1 garlic clove, minced
¼ teaspoon dried thyme leaves

1. Pound veal between sheets of plastic wrap to a thickness of ⅛ inch. On a sheet of wax paper, combine flour, paprika, basil, and pepper; stir to mix. Dredge veal in seasoned flour to coat both sides; shake excess back onto paper. In a medium bowl, combine bell pepper, zucchini, and carrots; set aside.

2. In a large nonstick skillet, heat 2 teaspoons olive oil over medium-high heat. Add 3 veal slices. Cook, turning, until lightly browned, 2 to 3 minutes on each side. Place veal on a plate; cover to keep warm. Repeat with remaining 2 teaspoons oil and veal slices.

3. Pour chicken broth into skillet and add garlic. Bring to a boil; reduce heat. Place veal slices in broth. Top with the vegetables; sprinkle with thyme. Cover and simmer 10 minutes, or until veal is tender and vegetables are crisp-tender. With a wide spatula, place veal with vegetables on a large serving platter. Spoon on pan juices.

Per Serving: Calories: 174   Total fat: 5 g   Saturated fat: 1 g
Cholesterol: 74 mg   Percentage calories from fat: 27%

103 VEAL WITH APPLES
Prep: 12 minutes   Cook: 8 to 13 minutes   Serves: 4

4 veal scallops, cut from
   leg (4 ounces each)
½ teaspoon salt
¼ teaspoon pepper
¼ cup flour
1 tablespoon butter
¼ cup apple brandy, dry white
   wine, or vermouth

2 medium Granny Smith
   apples, cored and thinly
   sliced
¼ cup homemade or canned
   reduced-sodium chicken
   broth
½ cup nonfat sour cream

1. Pound veal between sheets of plastic wrap to a thickness of ⅛ inch. Season on both sides with salt and pepper. Place flour on a sheet of wax paper. Dredge veal in flour to coat.

2. In a large nonstick skillet, melt 1½ teaspoons butter over medium-high heat. Add 2 veal slices and cook, turning until lightly browned on both sides, 2 to 3 minutes. Place veal on a large platter; cover to keep warm. Repeat with remaining butter and veal slices, placing on platter after cooking.

3. Add apple brandy to skillet. Bring to a boil, scraping up browned bits on bottom of pan. Add apple slices; cover. Cook over low heat until apples soften, 3 to 5 minutes. Stir in chicken stock and sour cream until sauce is smooth. Simmer 1 to 2 minutes. Spoon apples and sauce over veal and serve at once.

*Per Serving: Calories: 248   Total fat: 5 g   Saturated fat: 2 g
                Cholesterol: 96 mg   Percentage calories from fat: 21%*

---

104   VEAL WITH ARTICHOKES, POTATOES, AND SUN-DRIED TOMATOES

Prep: 20 minutes   Cook: 21 minutes   Serves: 4

Veal with artichokes and lemon is a classic combination. The addition of sun-dried tomatoes adds an assertive flavor to the dish.

1 ounce sun-dried tomatoes (without oil), about ⅓ cup	Olive oil cooking spray
2 large red potatoes, peeled and cut into ½-inch dice	1 tablespoon olive oil
¼ cup flour	2 teaspoons fresh lemon juice
¼ teaspoon salt	2 tablespoons dry white wine, vermouth, or reduced-sodium chicken broth
⅛ teaspoon cayenne	
4 veal scallops, cut from leg (4 ounces each)	1 (9-ounce) package frozen artichoke hearts, thawed

1. In a small bowl, pour ½ cup boiling water over sun-dried tomatoes. Let soak 10 minutes to soften; drain. Cut tomatoes into thin strips.

2. In medium saucepan of boiling salted water, cook potatoes until tender, about 10 minutes. Drain and set aside.

3. On a sheet of wax paper, combine flour, salt, and cayenne. Pound veal between sheets of plastic wrap to a thickness of ⅛ inch. Dredge veal in seasoned flour. Coat a large nonstick skillet with cooking spray. Add 1½ teaspoons olive oil and heat skillet over medium-high heat. Add 2 veal slices and cook, turning, until lightly browned on both sides, about 2 minutes per side. Transfer to a large platter; cover to keep warm. Repeat with remaining 1½ teaspoons oil and veal slices.

4. Add lemon juice and wine to skillet, scraping up any browned bits in bottom of pan. Stir in artichokes, potatoes, and sun-dried tomatoes, cover, and cook 3 minutes, or until vegetables are heated through. Spoon vegetables and sauce over veal and serve at once.

*Per Serving: Calories: 297   Total fat: 6 g   Saturated fat: 1 g
                Cholesterol: 88 mg   Percentage calories from fat: 19%*

105 VEAL SCALLOPS WITH RED ONIONS AND FENNEL

Prep: 10 minutes   Cook: 11 to 16 minutes   Serves: 4

4 veal scallops, cut from
   leg (4 ounces each)
½ teaspoon salt
¼ cup flour
   Olive oil cooking spray
2 teaspoons extra-virgin
   olive oil
2 large red onions (¾ pound),
   thinly sliced

2 teaspoons sugar
2 teaspoons crushed fennel
   seeds
⅛ to ¼ teaspoon crushed hot
   red pepper
1 tablespoon red wine vinegar

1. Pound veal between sheets of plastic wrap to a thickness of ⅛ inch. Season veal on both sides with salt and dust with flour.

2. Coat a large nonstick skillet with cooking spray. Add 1 teaspoon olive oil and heat skillet over medium-high heat. Add 2 veal slices and cook, turning, until lightly browned on both sides, about 2 to 3 minutes for each side. Place veal on a large serving platter; cover to keep warm. Repeat with remaining 1 teaspoon oil and veal slices.

3. Coat skillet with cooking spray. Add onions, sugar, fennel, and hot pepper; toss to mix. Cook over medium heat, stirring often, until onions are wilted and tender, 3 to 4 minutes. Stir in vinegar. Spoon onions over veal and serve.

*Per Serving: Calories: 220 Total fat: 5 g Saturated fat: 1 g
             Cholesterol: 88 mg Percentage calories from fat: 21%*

106 SAVORY VEAL WITH MUSHROOMS

Prep: 12 minutes   Cook: 8 to 10 minutes   Serves: 4

Veal and mushrooms have always been a winning combination. Here they are in a creamy sauce with a horseradish-flavored mustard.

4 veal scallops, cut from
   leg (4 ounces each)
   Olive oil cooking spray
2 teaspoons olive oil
1 cup sliced mushrooms (3
   ounces)
1 medium onion, sliced

3 garlic cloves, minced
¼ cup dry white wine
2 tablespoons Dijon mustard
   with horseradish
¼ cup nonfat sour cream
1 tablespoon chopped fresh
   dill weed or parsley

1. Pound veal slightly between sheets of plastic wrap to even out slightly. Cut into 1½ x 1-inch strips.

2. Coat a large nonstick skillet with cooking spray. Add olive oil and heat skillet over medium-high heat. Add mushrooms, onion, and garlic. Cook, stirring occasionally, until onion is soft but not brown, 2 to 3 minutes. Push vegetables to one side.

3. Add veal strips to skillet and cook over medium-high heat, tossing, until veal is tender and white throughout, 3 to 4 minutes. Add wine and mustard to skillet and stir until blended. Reduce heat to low. Stir in sour cream. Simmer, uncovered, for flavors to mellow, about 3 minutes, stirring occasionally. Serve, garnished with dill.

Per Serving: Calories: 195   Total fat: 5 g   Saturated fat: 1 g
Cholesterol: 88 mg   Percentage calories from fat: 23%

107   PORK WITH DRIED CRANBERRY SAUCE AND WILD RICE
Prep: 15 minutes   Cook: 64 to 68 minutes   Serves: 4

Dried cranberries, cranberry juice, and port flavor the sauce for this pork dish. The sauce could also be served with sautéed chicken breasts or turkey cutlets.

1 cup wild rice
1 teaspoon salt
1 pound pork tenderloin, trimmed
⅛ teaspoon pepper
2 teaspoons olive oil
½ cup cranberry juice cocktail
½ cup ruby port
3 tablespoons sugar

1½ teaspoons finely chopped fresh sage leaves or ½ teaspoon dried
¼ cup dried cranberries
1 tablespoon balsamic vinegar
1 tablespoon cornstarch
½ teaspoon lemon juice
Fresh sage leaves (optional)

1. Rinse wild rice well. In a medium saucepan, bring 6 cups water to a boil. Add wild rice and ½ teaspoon of salt. Cook over medium heat until rice is tender but pleasantly chewy, about 45 minutes. Drain well.

2. Meanwhile, cut pork tenderloin on a diagonal into 8 (¾-inch-thick) slices. Sprinkle with remaining ½ teaspoon salt and pepper. In a large nonstick skillet, place 1 teaspoon olive oil. Heat oil over medium-high heat. Add half of pork slices and cook 3 to 4 minutes on each side, until pork is brown and tender. Place pork on a serving platter; cover and keep warm. Repeat with remaining oil and pork slices.

3. Add cranberry juice, port, sugar, sage, dried cranberries, and vinegar to skillet and bring to a boil; lower heat. Cover and simmer 5 minutes. In a small bowl, combine cornstarch with 2 tablespoons water; stir into cranberry mixture. Bring to a boil, stirring constantly, until mixture thickens slightly, about 1 minute. Boil 1 minute longer. Stir in lemon juice.

4. Spoon wild rice onto platter alongside pork. Spoon part of sauce over pork. Pour remainder of sauce in a sauce boat and pass at table. Garnish platter with fresh sage leaves.

Per Serving: Calories: 430   Total fat: 7 g   Saturated fat: 2 g
Cholesterol: 74 mg   Percentage calories from fat: 15%

☆ 108 BARBECUED PORK ON A BUN
Prep: 10 minutes   Cook: 40 to 48 minutes   Serves: 4

Several years ago, my friend Babs and I pigged out at a hole-in-the-wall eatery in Hot Springs, Arkansas. One of the many superb pork dishes we had was BBQ pork on white bread. We loved every lip-smacking bite.

1 **(12-ounce) pork tenderloin, trimmed**	2 **tablespoons dark brown sugar**
¼ **teaspoon salt**	1 **teaspoon dried mustard**
⅛ **teaspoon pepper**	¼ **teaspoon crushed hot red**
1 **cup finely chopped onion**	**pepper**
1 **(8-ounce) can tomato sauce** /BBQ sauce	4 **soft hamburger buns**
¼ **cup apple cider vinegar**	

1. Preheat oven to 400°F. Sprinkle tenderloin with salt and pepper. Place meat on a rack in a shallow baking pan. Roast 30 to 35 minutes, or when internal temperature reads 160°F. on an instant-reading thermometer; let cool. Cut tenderloins into ½-inch lengths, then shred with a knife or pull apart with fingers.

2. Meanwhile, in a medium nonstick skillet, place onion and 2 tablespoons water; cook and stir until onion is soft and water has evaporated, about 5 minutes. Stir in tomato sauce, cider vinegar, brown sugar, dried mustard, and hot red pepper; stir to combine. Bring to a boil, stirring constantly; lower heat. Cover and simmer 5 to 8 minutes, or until slightly thickened but still juicy. Stir in pork. Spoon meat onto buns. Serve hot.

Per Serving: Calories: 289 Total fat: 6 g Saturated fat: 2 g
Cholesterol: 49 mg Percentage calories from fat: 17%

109 PORK CHOPS WITH PEARS AND ROSEMARY
Prep: 6 minutes   Cook: 10 to 13 minutes   Serves: 4

Pork and fruit make a perfect combination. Here pork is paired, no pun intended, with pears and rosemary.

2 **teaspoons butter**	¼ **teaspoon white pepper**
3 **small firm-ripe pears (5 ounces each), such as Bartlett or Comice, cored and thinly sliced**	1 **tablespoon cornstarch**
	1 **cup homemade or canned reduced-sodium chicken broth**
1 **teaspoon sugar**	1 **tablespoon balsamic vinegar**
4 **(½-inch-thick) boneless pork loin chops (1 pound), trimmed of all fat**	¼ **teaspoon crumbled dried rosemary**

1. In a large nonstick skillet, melt butter over medium heat. Add pears and sprinkle with sugar. Cook and gently stir until pears have softened, about 2 to 3 minutes. Place pears on a serving platter; cover and keep warm.

2. Sprinkle chops with white pepper. Heat skillet over medium heat. Add chops; brown 5 to 7 minutes on each side, or until pork is tender. Place on platter with pears.

3. Place cornstarch in skillet. Gradually stir in chicken broth until cornstarch is dissolved. Add vinegar and rosemary. Cook and stir over medium heat until sauce thickens and bubbles, about 2 minutes. Spoon some sauce over pork and pears. Place remaining sauce in gravy boat and pass at the table.

*Per Serving: Calories: 253   Total fat: 9 g   Saturated fat: 3 g
          Cholesterol: 77 mg   Percentage calories from fat: 30%*

110   PORK AND VEGETABLE SATAY
Prep: 15 minutes   Cook: 5 to 7 minutes   Serves: 6

Tiny cubes of pork are marinated in a creamy reduced-fat peanut butter flavored with hot pepper flakes and soy. You can easily turn this into an appetizer, threading the cubes of pork onto short bamboo skewers that have been soaked in water for 20 minutes.

2 tablespoons reduced-fat creamy peanut butter	1½ tablespoons brown sugar
½ cup minced scallions	1 pound boneless pork loin, cut in ½-inch cubes
2 garlic cloves, halved	18 cherry tomatoes
½ to ¾ teaspoon crushed hot red pepper	2 medium zucchini, cut into 1-inch chunks
3 tablespoons reduced-sodium soy sauce	1 large white onion, cut into 1-inch squares about ¼ inch thick
3 tablespoons fresh lime juice	

1. In a small food processor, place peanut butter, scallions, garlic, hot pepper, soy sauce, lime juice, brown sugar, and 1 tablespoon water; process until smooth. Pour into a large shallow baking dish.

2. Thread pork equally onto long metal skewers (if using bamboo skewers, soak in cold water 20 minutes). Place skewers into marinade and turn to coat. Let stand at least 20 minutes, or refrigerate, covered, until ready to cook.

3. Thread cherry tomatoes, zucchini, and onion onto 6 skewers, alternating vegetables. Turn vegetable kebabs in pork marinade to coat lightly.

4. Preheat broiler. Remove skewers of pork from marinade; reserve marinade. Place pork and vegetable kebabs on cold broiler rack and broil 4 to 6 inches from heat, turning once and basting with reserved marinade, until vegetables are just tender and pork is browned outside and white in center, 5 to 7 minutes. Serve hot.

*Per Serving: Calories: 199   Total fat: 7 g   Saturated fat: 2 g
          Cholesterol: 47 mg   Percentage calories from fat: 30%*

111 CUMIN-SCENTED PORK WITH BANANA-CUCUMBER RAITA

Prep: 5 minutes   Stand: 30 minutes   Cook: 35 to 40 minutes
Serves: 6

Here pork tenderloin is lightly coated with a yogurt-cumin marinade. When roasted, its red appearance is similar to Chinese roasted pork, with different flavors. It's served thinly sliced with a refreshingly cool raita.

1 teaspoon nonfat plain
    yogurt
1 teaspoon fresh lemon juice
1 teaspoon paprika
1 teaspoon finely chopped
    garlic
¼ teaspoon ground cumin

Pinch of cayenne
1 (1-pound) pork tenderloin,
    trimmed
Banana-Cucumber Raita
    (recipe follows)
Mint sprigs (optional)

1. In a small bowl, combine yogurt, lemon juice, paprika, garlic, cumin, and cayenne; mix well. With a pastry brush or fingertips, rub mixture all over pork. Let stand at room temperature 30 minutes.

2. Preheat oven to 400°F. Place pork on a rack in a shallow roasting pan. Roast 35 to 40 minutes, or until internal temperature reads 160° on an instant-reading thermometer. Let stand 10 minutes. Cut into thin diagonal slices. Place slices, slightly overlapping, on a serving platter. Spoon part of the banana-cucumber raita along 1 edge of the slices. Garnish with mint leaves. Place remaining raita in a sauce bowl and pass at table.

Per Serving: Calories: 113 Total fat: 3 g Saturated fat: 1 g
Cholesterol: 50 mg Percentage calories from fat: 22%

---

112 BANANA-CUCUMBER RAITA

Prep: 8 minutes   Cook: none   Makes: 1 cup

Banana adds a sweet touch to this raita. You can also serve it with curry or on broiled fish.

½ cup nonfat plain
    yogurt
⅓ cup peeled, halved, seeded,
    and coarsely chopped
    cucumber

⅓ cup peeled, diced (¼-inch)
    banana (½ of a small
    banana)
⅛ teaspoon ground cardamom
Pinch of salt

In a small bowl, combine yogurt, cucumber, banana, cardamom, and salt; mix well. Cover and refrigerate at least 30 minutes to mellow flavors.

Per Serving: Calories: 7 Total fat: > 1 g Saturated fat: 0 g
Cholesterol: 0 mg Percentage calories from fat: 2%

113 PORK MEDALLIONS WITH APRICOTS AND PRUNES

Prep: 10 minutes   Cook: 11 to 18 minutes   Serves: 4

Dried fruits always marry well with pork. Apricots and prunes are macerated in port and served warm over the sautéed pork chops.

12 pitted prunes	¼ teaspoon salt
12 dried apricot halves	⅛ teaspoon pepper
⅓ cup white or ruby port	⅛ teaspoon dried thyme or
¼ cup homemade or canned	sage
reduced-sodium chicken	Vegetable cooking spray
broth	4 teaspoons butter
4 (½-inch-thick) boneless pork	
loin chops (1 pound),	
trimmed of all fat	

1. In a small bowl, combine prunes, apricot halves, and port; let stand 10 minutes. Stir in chicken broth.

2. Season chops with salt, pepper, and thyme. Coat a large nonstick skillet with cooking spray. Add 2 teaspoons butter to skillet and melt over medium heat. Add chops; cook until browned on both sides and white in center, 5 to 8 minutes on each side. Place chops on a serving platter; cover and keep warm.

3. Add dried fruit mixture to skillet with remaining 2 teaspoons butter. Bring to a boil over high heat, stirring constantly, until sauce thickens slightly, 1 to 2 minutes. Spoon fruit sauce over chops and serve.

Per Serving: Calories: 316 Total fat: 10 g Saturated fat: 4 g
Cholesterol: 82 mg Percentage calories from fat: 30%

114   PORK CHOPS WITH SAUERKRAUT
Prep: 12 minutes   Cook: 10 to 15 minutes   Serves: 4

Pork with sauerkraut and apples is a classic combination. If you use the apple juice instead of the dry white wine, the dish is slightly sweeter.

4 (½-inch-thick) boneless pork
    loin chops (1 pound),
    trimmed of all fat
¼ teaspoon pepper
    Vegetable cooking spray
1 (16-ounce) package
    sauerkraut, rinsed and
    drained
1 cup diced red onion
2 tablespoons dark or light
    brown sugar

1 medium Granny Smith
    apple (6 ounces),
    unpeeled, cored, and
    thinly sliced
1 teaspoon caraway seeds
⅓ cup dry white wine, apple
    juice, or reduced-sodium
    chicken broth
1 tablespoon chopped parsley
    (optional)

1. Sprinkle chops with pepper. Coat a large nonstick skillet with cooking spray. Heat skillet over medium-high heat. Add chops; brown on both sides, about 2 to 3 minutes.

2. While chops are cooking, in a medium bowl, combine sauerkraut, red onion, brown sugar, apple slices, and caraway seeds. Spoon over chops, covering completely. Pour on wine, apple juice, or chicken broth. Cover and simmer over low heat 8 to 12 minutes, or until pork is tender and apple slices have softened. Place chops with sauerkraut mixture onto a serving platter; sprinkle with parsley.

Per Serving: Calories: 252   Total fat: 6 g   Saturated fat: 2 g
Cholesterol: 71 mg   Percentage calories from fat: 24%

115   LAMB STEW WITH FALL VEGETABLES
Prep: 20 minutes   Cook: 49 to 56 minutes   Serves: 6

Lots of vegetables add extra flavor to this quick and easy lamb stew. Serve with a tossed green salad and crusty bread.

Vegetable cooking spray
1½ **pounds lean, boneless leg of lamb, cut into 1-inch cubes**
3 **tablespoons flour**
1 **teaspoon dried rosemary**
½ **teaspoon pepper**
1½ **cups homemade or canned reduced-sodium beef broth**
1 **(10-ounce) container fresh brussels sprouts**

2 **medium all-purpose potatoes (12 ounces)**
2 **medium white turnips**
1½ **cups peeled baby carrots (½ a 1-pound package) or 3 to 4 large carrots, peeled and cut into ½-inch diagonal slices**
½ **teaspoon salt (optional)**

1. Preheat broiler. Coat a cold broiler rack with cooking spray. Place lamb on broiler pan and broil 4 to 5 inches from heat 3 to 4 minutes, or until rare, turning once.

2. In a large nonstick skillet, place browned lamb, 1 tablespoon flour, rosemary, and pepper; toss to coat. Add beef broth and ½ cup water. Bring to a boil. Reduce heat to low, cover, and simmer 30 minutes.

3. Meanwhile, trim brussels sprouts; cut in half. Peel potatoes; cut into ¾-inch cubes. Peel turnips; cut in quarters, then cut each quarter into ½-inch triangular slices. Add brussels sprouts, potatoes, turnips, and carrots to lamb in skillet. Continue to simmer, covered, 15 to 20 minutes, or until meat and vegetables are tender.

4. Remove lamb and vegetables with a slotted spoon to a large serving bowl; keep warm. In a small bowl, stir together the remaining 2 tablespoons flour and ¼ cup water. Gradually stir into liquid in skillet. Cook and stir over medium heat until mixture comes to a boil and thickens slightly, 1 to 2 minutes. Pour over lamb and vegetables; toss gently to coat. Add salt, if desired.

Per Serving: Calories: 256   Total fat: 7 g   Saturated fat: 2 g
         Cholesterol: 76 mg   Percentage calories from fat: 25%

116 LAMB IN ACORN SQUASH HALVES
Prep: 20 minutes   Cook: 1 hour 20 minutes   Serves: 6

The flavors of Greece—cinnamon, mint, and pine nuts—flavor the lamb and rice filling nestled into squash halves.

3   medium golden acorn squash, halved, seeded, and stringy fibers removed (about 1 pound each)
Olive oil cooking spray
1   teaspoon olive oil
½   pound lean ground lamb (from leg)
1   cup chopped onion
1   teaspoon finely chopped garlic

2   tablespoons minced parsley
2   tablespoons minced fresh mint
¼   cup currants or raisins
2   tablespoons pine nuts
1   teaspoon cinnamon
¼   teaspoon salt
⅛   teaspoon pepper
1½ cups cooked long-grain white rice
1   cup tomato sauce

1. Preheat oven to 400°F. Place squash, cut side down, in a 9 x 13-inch baking pan; add ¼ inch water and cover with foil. Bake 50 minutes, or until squash are tender.

2. While squash are baking, coat a large nonstick skillet with cooking spray. Add olive oil and tilt skillet to coat bottom with the oil; heat oil over medium-high heat. Add lamb, onion, and garlic; sauté until lamb is brown, about 5 minutes. Drain off any fat. Add parsley, mint, currants, pine nuts, cinnamon, salt, and pepper; stir to combine. Cover and simmer 10 minutes. Stir in rice and tomato sauce; remove from heat.

3. Remove squash from oven. Reduce oven temperature to 350°F. Drain off liquid from pan and blot squash dry with paper towels. Place squash, cut side up, in pan. Fill each hollow with ½ cup of the meat filling. Cover pan loosely with aluminum foil and bake 15 minutes longer, or until filling is hot.

Per Serving: Calories: 250   Total fat: 5 g   Saturated fat: 1 g
Cholesterol: 24 mg   Percentage calories from fat: 16%

117 LAMB KEBABS

Prep: 20 minutes   Marinate: 3 hours   Cook: 15 minutes
Serves: 4

Lamb cubes are marinated in a savory herb marinade, then threaded with colorful vegetables. You can either broil the kebabs or cook them outdoors on the grill. Serve with orzo or a white and wild rice blend.

¼ cup homemade or canned
  reduced-sodium beef or
  chicken broth
¼ cup fresh lemon juice
¼ cup finely chopped onion
2 tablespoons finely chopped
  parsley
1 large garlic clove, minced
1 teaspoon dried marjoram
½ teaspoon dried oregano
1 pound boneless lean lamb
  (from leg), cut in 12
  (1½-inch) cubes
1 Italian eggplant (6 ounces),
  cut in 1-inch cubes

1 medium red bell pepper
  (6 ounces), seeded and cut
  into 12 chunks
1 medium summer squash
  (6 ounces), cut into ½-inch
  rounds
1 large Vidalia or other sweet
  onion, cut into 1-inch
  chunks
12 medium cremini
  mushrooms, trimmed
  (about ½ pound)
  Olive oil cooking spray

1. In a small bowl, place chicken broth, lemon juice, onion, parsley, garlic, marjoram, and oregano. Place meat in a large zip-top heavy-duty plastic bag and pour on marinade; squeeze marinade around meat and close bag securely. Place in a bowl. Refrigerate at least 3 hours, or overnight.

2. Preheat broiler. Remove meat from marinade and save marinade. Thread lamb on 2 long metal skewers. Thread vegetables alternately on 4 long metal skewers. Coat lamb and vegetables lightly with cooking spray.

3. Broil kebabs 4 to 6 inches from heat 15 minutes, until lamb is done and vegetables have softened. Turn once and baste with the reserved marinade.

Per Serving: Calories: 227 Total fat: 6 g Saturated fat: 2 g
Cholesterol: 73 mg Percentage calories from fat: 24%

118   LAMB PILAF
Prep: 17 minutes   Cook: 30 minutes   Serves: 4

A small amount of ground lamb is stretched in this savory rice dish chock-full of dried fruits and spices.

1 envelope low-sodium beef broth granules (2 teaspoons)	¾ cup lean ground lamb (from leg)
1 teaspoon cinnamon	1 cup chopped onion
½ cup chopped pitted prunes	¾ teaspoon curry powder
¼ cup golden raisins	¼ teaspoon pepper
¾ cup converted long-grain rice	3 tablespoons fresh lemon juice
Vegetable cooking spray	3 tablespoons chopped parsley
	2 tablespoons toasted slivered almonds or pine nuts

1. In a medium saucepan, bring 2½ cups water to a boil. Add beef granules, cinnamon, prunes, raisins, and rice; stir once to combine. Bring back to a boil; lower heat. Cover and simmer 20 minutes, until liquid is absorbed and rice is tender.

2. While rice is cooking, coat a large nonstick skillet with cooking spray. Heat skillet over medium heat. Add lamb, onion, curry powder, and pepper; cook and stir just until meat turns color, about 4 to 5 minutes. Do not brown meat. Drain off any fat.

3. Add cooked rice mixture to meat in skillet along with lemon juice, 2 tablespoons parsley, and almonds or pine nuts; stir with a fork to combine. Cover and simmer over low heat 5 minutes for flavors to mellow. Spoon into a serving bowl; sprinkle with remaining 1 tablespoon parsley.

Per Serving: Calories: 299   Total fat: 4 g   Saturated fat: 1 g
Cholesterol: 20 mg   Percentage calories from fat: 13%

119   LAMB TAGINE
Prep: 10 minutes   Cook: 48 to 54 minutes   Serves: 6

Tagine, a Moroccan lamb stew, has a delicious blend of flavors and orange-flower water is added. Serve over couscous.

Vegetable cooking spray
1 pound lean, boneless leg of lamb, cut into 1-inch cubes
½ teaspoon salt
½ teaspoon ground ginger
½ teaspoon cinnamon
½ teaspoon saffron threads, crushed
1 large onion, chopped
2 tablespoons chopped parsley
½ cup prunes or dried apricots, quartered

2 medium white turnips, peeled and cut into ¾-inch chunks
3 medium carrots, peeled and cut into ½-inch diagonal slices
2 medium all-purpose potatoes, peeled and cut into ¾-inch chunks
2 tablespoons honey
½ teaspoon orange-flower water (optional)

1. Preheat broiler. Coat a cold broiler pan with cooking spray. Place lamb on broiler pan and broil 4 to 5 inches from heat 3 to 4 minutes, or until rare, turning once.

2. In a large nonstick skillet, place lamb, salt, ginger, cinnamon, and saffron; toss to coat lamb. Add onion, parsley, and 2 cups water. Bring to a boil. Reduce heat to low, cover, and simmer 30 minutes.

3. Add prunes, potatoes, turnips, carrots, honey, and orange-flower water to skillet. Stir to mix. Continue to simmer, covered, until meat and vegetables are tender and prunes are plump, 15 to 20 minutes.

*Per Serving: Calories: 240   Total fat: 5 g   Saturated fat: 2 g
Cholesterol: 50 mg   Percentage calories from fat: 18%*

120   STIR-FRIED LAMB AND PEPPERS

Prep: 15 minutes   Cook: 8 to 9 minutes   Serves: 4

It takes longer to prepare this dish than to cook it. As with any stir-fry dish, it is important that you have all the ingredients ready to go before beginning to cook.

1 pound lean boneless lamb (from leg), cut in 1-inch cubes
1 tablespoon cornstarch
½ teaspoon sugar
2 tablespoons reduced-sodium soy sauce
1 tablespoon dry sherry
Vegetable cooking spray
1½ teaspoons canola oil
1 medium green bell pepper (6 ounces), seeded and cut in thin strips

1 medium red bell pepper (6 ounces), seeded and cut in thin strips
1 large red onion, cut in thin wedges
3 thin slices peeled ginger
1 garlic clove, minced
½ teaspoon crushed hot red pepper
2 small tomatoes, cut into 8 thin wedges each

1. In a medium bowl, place lamb, cornstarch, sugar, soy sauce, and sherry; toss to combine.

2. Coat a large nonstick skillet or wok with cooking spray. Add ½ teaspoon oil and heat skillet or wok over medium-high heat. Add green and red bell pepper and red onion; stir-fry until vegetables are crisp-tender, about 3 minutes. Remove vegetables to a bowl.

3. Coat skillet or wok with cooking spray. Add remaining 1 teaspoon oil and heat skillet or wok over medium-high heat. Add lamb mixture, ginger, garlic, and hot red pepper; stir-fry until meat turns color and is done, about 3 to 4 minutes. Add cooked vegetables with the tomatoes; cook and stir until heated through, about 2 minutes. Remove ginger slices.

Per Serving: Calories: 238   Total fat: 8 g   Saturated fat: 2 g
Cholesterol: 73 mg   Percentage calories from fat: 29%

Chapter 6

Low-Fat Chicken and Turkey

We've come a long way from chicken every Sunday and turkey just at Thanksgiving. The emphasis on eating lighter and reducing cholesterol has inspired a potpourri of chicken and turkey products. Individual chicken and turkey parts, skinless chicken breasts, thin-sliced chicken cutlets, turkey breast fillets, turkey tenderloins, ground chicken, ground turkey, and turkey sausage give us an endless array of ways to prepare them. Lean chicken and turkey combine with other foods—vegetables, fruits, grains, beans, pasta, spices, and herbs—in countless flavor combinations. There's a bird—or some part of one—to suit everyone's taste.

To keep fat and cholesterol as low as possible, remove all skin and visible fat from chicken or turkey parts before using. Skinning whole birds is difficult to do, so I recommend roasting them with the skin on, then removing all the skin before serving. The skin also helps to keep the meat moist when dry-roasting—such as broiling or grilling. You need to compensate for moisture by basting with chicken stock, wine, a marinade, or apple juice. All these recipes have great taste, some have an ethnic bent, and others are old-fashioned favorites.

Just about everyone loves fried chicken, but nowadays, no one wants the fat. To eliminate every gram I could, I double-dipped and cereal coated Crusty Oven "Fried" Chicken, which bakes in the oven to a golden crispness. Chicken Breasts Paprikash and Turkey Mushroom Stroganoff each take less than 30 minutes from stovetop to tabletop. Turkey Fajitas and Spicy Turkey Fingers with Honey-Mustard Dip are contemporary culinary fixings. Ground turkey and turkey sausage are combined for Meat Loaf and Mashed Potatoes, elegant enough to set out on a buffet table. Moroccan-Style Chicken with Couscous and Turkey Curry offer some exotic seasonings for variety.

121   CHICKEN BREASTS OREGANO WITH VEGETABLE BROCHETTES

Prep: 15 minutes   Stand: 30 minutes   Cook: 14 minutes   Serves: 4

Chicken breasts with a classic Greek combination of lemon and oregano are teamed with artichoke hearts, cherry tomatoes, and yellow squash, for a colorful, light meal that needs only some rice or small pasta, such as orzo, to accompany it.

2 teaspoons olive oil	1 (9-ounce) package frozen
2 tablespoons fresh lemon	artichoke hearts
juice	Vegetable cooking spray
1 garlic clove, minced	2 small yellow squash, cut
1 teaspoon dried oregano	into 1-inch rounds
½ teaspoon salt	12 cherry tomatoes
½ teaspoon pepper	
4 skinless, boneless	
chicken breast halves	
(1¼ pounds), trimmed of	
all visible fat	

1. In a shallow nonreactive pan, combine olive oil, lemon juice, garlic, oregano, salt, and pepper with 2 teaspoons water. Add chicken breasts and turn to coat. Let stand at room temperature 30 minutes or refrigerate 1 hour, turning a few times.

2. Meanwhile, in a medium saucepan, cook artichoke hearts, covered, in ¼ cup boiling water for 6 minutes, or until tender. Drain and set aside.

3. Preheat broiler. Coat a cold broiler rack with cooking spray. Thread cooked artichoke hearts, yellow squash, and cherry tomatoes onto 4 long metal skewers, alternating vegetables attractively.

4. Remove chicken from marinade; reserve marinade. Place chicken and vegetable skewers on broiler rack. Brush vegetables with part of reserved marinade. Broil chicken and vegetables 3 to 4 inches from heat, turning once and basting with reserved marinade, until chicken is lightly golden and tender and vegetables are heated through, about 4 minutes for each side.

Per Serving: Calories: 224   Total fat: 5 g   Saturated fat: 1 g
Cholesterol: 82 mg   Percentage calories from fat: 19%

122 CHICKEN WITH DILLED DUMPLINGS
Prep: 25 minutes   Cook: 35 minutes   Serves: 4

This newer short-cut version of chicken and dumplings has all the flavor and taste of the old-fashioned kind without the work or the fat.

2½ cups homemade or canned reduced-sodium chicken broth
½ cup sliced leeks (white part only)
¼ teaspoon poultry seasoning or dried thyme leaves
¼ teaspoon pepper
4 chicken breast halves (1½ pounds), skinned and trimmed of all visible fat

¾ cup sliced carrots
¾ cup thawed frozen lima beans
½ cup sliced celery
Dilled Dumplings (recipe follows; prepared through step 1)
3 tablespoons flour
Salt

1. In a large skillet or flameproof casserole, place chicken broth, leeks, poultry seasoning, and pepper. Bring to a simmer over medium heat. Reduce heat to low, add chicken, cover, and simmer 10 minutes. Add carrots, lima beans, and celery. Cover and simmer 10 minutes longer.

2. Meanwhile, prepare dilled dumpling batter. Drop evenly in 4 large mounds directly onto chicken breasts. Cover and simmer 12 minutes, or until a wooden pick inserted into dumplings comes out clean. With a slotted spoon, place chicken, dumplings, and vegetables on a large platter; cover to keep warm.

3. Pour broth into a 2-cup glass measure; skim off any fat from top. You should have 1⅓ cups broth (add water or additional chicken broth, if necessary). Pour broth back into skillet.

4. In a small bowl, whisk together flour and ¼ cup water. Gradually stir into broth in skillet. Cook over medium heat, stirring, until slightly thickened and bubbly, 1 to 2 minutes. Season with salt and additional pepper to taste. Spoon gravy over chicken, dumplings, and vegetables.

DILLED DUMPLINGS

½ cup flour
1 tablespoon minced fresh dill or 1 teaspoon dried
¾ teaspoon baking powder

⅛ teaspoon salt
¼ cup skim milk
1 tablespoon canola oil

1. In a small bowl, stir together flour, dill, baking powder, and salt. In a small cup, combine milk and oil. Add to flour mixture and stir to blend.

2. Drop batter in 4 mounds on top of a hot stew or soup. Cook 12 minutes, or until done.

*Per Serving: Calories: 327 Total fat: 7 g Saturated fat: 1 g
Cholesterol: 76 mg Percentage calories from fat: 19%*

123   CHICKEN BREASTS PAPRIKASH

Prep: 5 minutes   Cook: 17 to 18 minutes   Serves: 4

Hungarian paprika gives a sharper flavor than domestic paprika, although you can substitute it in the recipe. The sauce uses nonfat sour cream, which does not curdle when heated as the regular high-fat sour cream does.

- 4 teaspoons Hungarian sweet paprika
- 4 skinless, boneless chicken breast halves (4 ounces each), trimmed of all visible fat
- Vegetable cooking spray
- 1 tablespoon butter
- ½ cup diced onion
- ⅛ cup dry white wine
- ¼ cup homemade or canned reduced-sodium chicken broth
- 8 ounces no-yolk noodles
- ¼ cup nonfat sour cream

1. Place paprika on a sheet of wax paper. Coat chicken breasts liberally on both sides with the paprika. Coat a large nonstick skillet with cooking spray and heat skillet over medium heat. Add butter. When melted, add chicken breasts and sauté over medium-high heat until lightly browned on both sides, about 4 minutes. Remove chicken breasts to a serving platter; cover and keep warm.

2. Add onion to skillet and sauté 1 minute. Add wine, stirring to scrape up any brown bits in pan. Increase heat to high and reduce wine to half. Stir in chicken broth and bring to a boil; lower heat. Add chicken breasts. Cover and simmer until chicken is tender, about 10 minutes.

3. Meanwhile, in a large saucepan of boiling salted water, cook noodles until tender but still firm, 3 to 5 minutes. Drain well.

4. Transfer noodles to a serving platter. Remove chicken breasts from sauce and arrange on top of noodles. Whisk sour cream into sauce in skillet until smooth. Cook and stir until sauce thickens slightly, 2 to 3 minutes. Spoon sauce over chicken.

Per Serving: Calories: 383   Total fat: 6 g   Saturated fat: 2 g
Cholesterol: 74 mg   Percentage calories from fat: 15%

124 SAUTÉED CHICKEN WITH TOMATO CAPER SAUCE

Prep: 8 minutes   Cook: 26 to 30 minutes   Serves: 4

Lemon peel and rosemary accent the flavors of this tasty dish. I like to serve it with a combination of small pasta shells and peas.

1 cup small shell pasta	2 teaspoons extra-virgin olive oil
1 cup frozen peas, thawed	
½ teaspoon dried rosemary leaves, crumbled	2 cups halved cherry tomatoes
	2 tablespoons drained capers
4 skinless, boneless chicken breast halves (1 pound), trimmed of fat	¼ cup homemade or canned reduced-sodium chicken broth
3 tablespoons flour	¼ cup chopped parsley
Vegetable cooking spray	4 lemon wedges

1. In a large saucepan filled with boiling water, cook pasta following package directions until tender but still firm, about 10 to 12 minutes. Drain and transfer to a deep serving platter. Add peas to hot pasta and toss to mix. Cover to keep warm.

2. While pasta is cooking, rub rosemary over chicken breasts. Coat well with flour. Coat a large nonstick skillet with cooking spray. Add olive oil and heat skillet over medium-high heat. Add chicken and cook, turning, until browned on both sides, about 4 minutes. Reduce heat to medium-low, cover, and cook until chicken is tender and white throughout, 8 to 10 minutes. Arrange chicken on top of pasta; cover to keep warm.

3. Coat same skillet with cooking spray. Add tomatoes and capers. Cook over medium-high heat, stirring, until tomatoes are hot and just softened, about 3 minutes. Add chicken stock and 3 tablespoons parsley. Cook, stirring, 1 minute longer.

4. Spoon sauce and tomatoes over chicken. Sprinkle remaining parsley on top. Garnish with lemon wedges to squeeze over each portion.

Per Serving: Calories: 297   Total fat: 5 g   Saturated fat: 1 g
Cholesterol: 66 mg   Percentage calories from fat: 16%

125 LEMON CHICKEN WITH GINGERED CONFETTI RICE

Prep: 15 minutes   Cook: 13 minutes   Serves: 4

The original recipe for this tangy Chinese lemon chicken called for frying the pieces. I stir-fried the chicken pieces without losing the great flavor of this dish. I give a range for the sugar depending upon whether you want a tangy or slightly sweeter chicken dish.

4 skinless, boneless chicken breast halves (1¼ to 1½ pounds), trimmed of all visible fat
2 lemons
1½ teaspoons canola oil
1 tablespoon finely chopped fresh ginger
1 teaspoon finely chopped garlic

½ cup homemade or canned reduced-sodium chicken broth
2 teaspoons cornstarch
2 to 3 teaspoons sugar
1 tablespoon reduced-sodium soy sauce
¼ cup diagonally cut (½-inch) scallions
Gingered Confetti Rice (recipe follows)

1. Cut chicken crosswise into ½-inch-wide strips. Grate zest from 1 lemon to equal 2 teaspoons. Squeeze juice from lemon to equal 2 tablespoons. Slice half of other lemon for garnish.

2. In a large nonstick skillet, heat oil over medium-high heat. Add half of chicken strips and stir-fry until browned, 3 to 5 minutes. Remove to a bowl with a slotted spoon. Repeat with remaining chicken strips. Transfer to bowl. Add ginger and garlic and toss to coat.

3. Pour chicken broth and reserved 2 tablespoons lemon juice into skillet. Bring to a boil. Reduce heat to low. Add chicken, cover, and simmer until chicken is cooked through, about 4 minutes.

4. In a small bowl, combine cornstarch, sugar, soy sauce, and 1 tablespoon water. Stir to dissolve cornstarch. Stir into skillet. Add reserved 2 teaspoons lemon zest. Bring to a boil over medium-high heat, stirring, until sauce thickens enough to coat chicken pieces, about 2 minutes. Spoon onto serving plates. Garnish with lemon slices. Serve with gingered confetti rice.

*Per Serving: Calories: 215   Total fat: 4 g   Saturated fat: 1 g
Cholesterol: 91 mg   Percentage calories from fat: 17%*

126   GINGERED CONFETTI RICE
Prep: 7 minutes   Cook: 15 to 20 minutes   Serves: 4 to 6

½ teaspoon salt
1 cup long-grain white rice
½ cup chopped scallions
½ cup diced jarred roasted red
   pepper   +slivered almonds

1 teaspoon finely chopped
   fresh ginger
2 teaspoons Asian sesame oil
½ teaspoon sugar

1. In a medium saucepan, bring 2 cups water and salt to a boil. Add rice and stir once. Quickly return to a boil. Reduce heat to low, cover, and simmer 15 to 20 minutes, until water is absorbed and rice is tender. Remove from heat; let stand 3 minutes.

2. Add scallions, roasted red pepper, ginger, oil, and sugar to rice. Stir with a fork to combine and fluff up rice.

Per Serving: Calories: 161   Total fat: 2 g   Saturated fat: 0 g
Cholesterol: 0 mg   Percentage calories from fat: 12%

127   CHICKEN PARMESAN WITH LINGUINE
Prep: 15 minutes   Cook: 17 to 22 minutes   Serves: 4

⅓ cup seasoned bread crumbs
3 tablespoons grated
   Parmesan or Asiago
   cheese
4 skinless, boneless chicken
   breast halves (4 ounces
   each), trimmed of all
   visible fat
2 tablespoons skim milk

8 ounces linguine
   Vegetable cooking spray
1 (14½-ounce) can Italian-style
   stewed tomatoes
½ teaspoon dried oregano
2 teaspoons cornstarch
   dissolved in 2
   tablespoons water

1. Combine bread crumbs and 2 tablespoons of Parmesan cheese on a sheet of wax paper. Using a pastry brush, brush chicken breasts with milk, then coat both sides with crumb mixture.

2. In a large saucepan of boiling salted water, cook linguine until tender but still firm, 8 to 10 minutes; drain. Transfer to a serving platter.

3. Meanwhile, coat a large nonstick skillet with cooking spray. Heat skillet over medium heat. Add chicken and cook, turning, until brown on both sides, about 8 to 10 minutes. Place chicken on top of linguine on platter; cover to keep warm.

4. In same skillet, combine stewed tomatoes and oregano. Stir in dissolved cornstarch and bring to a boil, stirring, until sauce is slightly thickened, 1 to 2 minutes. Spoon sauce over chicken and linguine. Sprinkle remaining 1 tablespoon cheese on top.

Per Serving: Calories: 439   Total fat: 4 g   Saturated fat: 2 g
Cholesterol: 70 mg   Percentage calories from fat: 9%

128   CHICKEN WITH RED GRAPES

Prep: 8 minutes   Cook: 13 to 15 minutes   Serves: 4

Serve this herb- and wine-flavored chicken dish with brown rice and steamed green beans.

1 tablespoon flour
½ teaspoon dried thyme leaves
½ teaspoon crumbled dried rosemary
¼ teaspoon salt
   Pinch of white pepper
4 skinless, boneless chicken breast halves (4 ounces each), trimmed of all visible fat

Vegetable cooking spray
2 teaspoons butter
½ cup dry white wine or canned reduced-sodium chicken broth
1½ cups halved seedless red grapes

1. On a sheet of wax paper, combine 2 teaspoons of flour with thyme, rosemary, salt, and white pepper. Rub liberally over surface of chicken.

2. Coat a large nonstick skillet with cooking spray and heat skillet over medium-high heat. Add butter. As soon as butter melts, add chicken breasts and cook, turning, until lightly browned on both sides, about 4 minutes total.

3. Pour in ¼ cup of wine. Reduce heat to low, cover, and simmer, basting once or twice with pan juices, 8 to 10 minutes, or until chicken is tender and white in center.

4. Remove chicken to a serving platter; cover to keep warm. In a small bowl, blend remaining 1 teaspoon flour with remaining ¼ cup wine. Gradually stir mixture into skillet. Bring to a boil, stirring until sauce thickens, 1 to 2 minutes. Add grapes and stir to heat and coat with sauce. Spoon sauce and grapes over chicken and serve at once.

Per Serving: Calories: 193   Total fat: 4 g   Saturated fat: 2 g
Cholesterol: 71 mg   Percentage calories from fat: 19%

129 CRUSTY OVEN "FRIED" CHICKEN
Prep: 12 minutes   Cook: 45 to 50 minutes   Serves: 6

I've always been disappointed with recipes I have tried for the "perfect" oven-fried chicken recipe. It wasn't juicy enough. Or crisp enough. You won't be disappointed with this fried chicken recipe. The chicken is first dipped in buttermilk, then a seasoned flour. It is dipped again in the buttermilk, lightly coated with cereal crumbs, and a little bit of oil is drizzled over the top. The results, a juicy, crispy "fried" chicken. You can serve it cold, although the crust will not be as crisp.

¾ cup buttermilk
1 (3-pound) broiler-fryer, cut up, skin and all visible fat removed
½ cup flour
1 teaspoon paprika

½ teaspoon salt
½ teaspoon pepper
4 cups cornflakes, slightly crushed (4 ounces)
Vegetable cooking spray
2 teaspoons canola oil

1. In a large bowl, place buttermilk. Add chicken pieces and turn to coat. On a sheet of wax paper, place flour, paprika, salt, and pepper. On another sheet of wax paper, place cornflakes.

2. Preheat oven to 400°F. Line a 10 x 15-inch jelly roll pan with aluminum foil. Coat foil with cooking spray (this makes for easier cleanup).

3. Lift chicken pieces, one at a time, from buttermilk; reserve buttermilk. Coat chicken thoroughly with seasoned flour and place on a wire rack until all the pieces have been coated with the flour. Redip chicken pieces, one at a time, into the reserved buttermilk. Place on cornflake crumbs. Using 2 forks, turn chicken pieces in crumbs to coat. Place on prepared pan; drizzle with oil.

4. Bake 30 minutes. Turn chicken pieces over and bake 15 to 20 minutes longer, until chicken is cooked through and the crust is crisp. Serve warm or cold.

Variation
Add 1 teaspoon herbs or spices, such as crushed rosemary, thyme, marjoram, sage, onion powder, or garlic powder to the seasoned flour mixture.

Per Serving: Calories: 269 Total fat: 5 g Saturated fat: 1 g
Cholesterol: 77 mg Percentage calories from fat: 19%

130   HONEY-MUSTARD CHICKEN THIGHS
Prep: 10 minutes   Cook: 35 minutes   Serves: 4

A barbecue-style chicken dish with a sweet flavor. Lining the baking pan with aluminum foil makes for easier cleanup.

2 **tablespoons honey**
1 **tablespoon Dijon mustard**
1 **tablespoon fresh lemon juice**
1 **garlic clove, crushed through a press**
¼ **teaspoon crumbled dried rosemary**

4 **chicken thighs (1¼ pounds total), skin removed, trimmed of all visible fat**
1 **pound small red potatoes, scrubbed**
1 **tablespoon chopped parsley**

1. In a small bowl, whisk together honey, mustard, lemon juice, garlic, and rosemary.

2. Line a shallow baking dish with aluminum foil. Arrange chicken in pan in a single layer. Set under cold broiler. Broil 4 to 5 inches from heat 10 minutes.

3. Brush thighs with about half of honey-mustard mixture. Turn chicken over and broil 10 minutes longer, or until chicken is tender and no longer pink near bone.

4. Meanwhile, in a large saucepan of boiling salted water, cook potatoes until tender in center, 12 to 15 minutes. Drain and quarter potatoes.

5. Arrange chicken on a large platter. Brush with remaining honey-mustard mixture. Spoon potatoes around chicken. Garnish with parsley.

Per Serving: Calories: 226   Total fat: 3 g   Saturated fat: 1 g
Cholesterol: 67 mg   Percentage calories from fat: 14%

131   CORNISH HENS WITH CILANTRO-LIME GREMOLATA AND MEXICAN RICE
Prep: 20 minutes   Cook: 45 to 60 minutes   Serves: 4

Cilantro, lime, and garlic are minced together and then tucked under the skin to flavor the hens. To keep the hens moist, roast with the skin on, then remove before serving to reduce fat and calories.

Vegetable cooking spray
1 **to 2 large limes**
2 **tablespoons chopped cilantro**
1 **tablespoon minced fresh garlic**

2 **small Cornish game hens (1 to 1¼ pounds each)**
¼ **teaspoon salt**
⅛ **teaspoon ground red pepper Mexican Rice (recipe follows)**

1. Preheat oven to 350°F. Coat a shallow roasting pan with cooking spray.

2. Remove thin peel from limes using a vegetable peeler (no white). Mince enough peel to make 1 tablespoon. Chop lime zest together finely with cilantro and garlic

3. With fingertips, gently loosen skin from hens over breast and legs, being careful not to break the skin. Spread cilantro mixture under skin. Sprinkle cavity and skin of hens with salt and pepper. Cut lime in half and place a half in each bird. Tie game hen legs with twine. Place hens, breast side down, in a shallow baking pan.

4. Roast 30 minutes. Turn hens breast side up; baste with pan juices. Roast until hens are tender, about 15 to 30 minutes longer. Remove hens to serving platter; remove twine from legs and lime halves from cavity and discard. Cut hens in half using poultry shears or a sharp knife. If there are any pan juices, pour into a cup measure; let fat rise to top and discard. Spoon pan juices over hen halves. Remove skin before eating. Serve with Mexican Rice.

NOTE: *If there are no pan juices, baste hens with a few tablespoons reduced-sodium chicken broth.*

Per Serving: Calories: 419 Total fat: 9 g Saturated fat: 2 g
Cholesterol: 82 mg Percentage calories from fat: 11%

---

132 MEXICAN RICE
Prep: 10 minutes   Cook: 22 to 28 minutes   Serves: 4 to 6

1 (16-ounce) can Mexican-style stewed tomatoes
About 1½ cups homemade or canned reduced-sodium chicken broth
1 teaspoon vegetable oil
1 cup long-grain white rice

½ cup chopped onion
1 garlic clove, minced
1 to 2 tablespoons chopped seeded ~~fresh jalapeño~~ *Canned chili* peppers
2 tablespoons minced cilantro or parsley

1. Drain liquid from stewed tomatoes into a 2-cup glass measure (there should be about ½ cup). Add enough chicken broth to equal 2 cups liquid. Coarsely chop tomatoes. Set tomatoes and broth mixture aside.

2. In a medium nonstick saucepan, heat oil over medium-high heat. Add rice and cook, stirring often, until it begins to turn opaque, 2 to 3 minutes. Stir in onion, garlic, jalapeño peppers, and ¼ cup water. Cook over medium-low heat, stirring constantly, until onions are translucent and rice is dry, about 5 minutes.

3. Add tomatoes and broth mixture to saucepan. Bring quickly to a boil. Reduce heat to low, cover, and simmer 15 to 20 minutes, until liquid is absorbed and rice is tender. Remove from heat; let stand 3 minutes. Add cilantro. Stir with a fork to combine and fluff up rice. Serve at once.

Per Serving: Calories: 159 Total fat: 2 g Saturated fat: 0 g
Cholesterol: 0 mg Percentage calories from fat: 4%

133 MOROCCAN-STYLE CHICKEN WITH COUSCOUS

Prep: 12 minutes   Cook: 45 to 50 minutes   Serves: 6

Putting part of the spices in the flour mixture to coat the bird, then adding the remaining spices to the sauce, flavors this dish fully.

1 (3- to 3½-pound) chicken, skin and all visible fat removed	2 teaspoons olive oil
¼ cup flour	½ cup chopped onion
¾ teaspoon salt	1 (16-ounce) can whole peeled tomatoes, liquid reserved
1 teaspoon ground cumin	2 garlic cloves, minced
½ teaspoon ground coriander	1 small lemon, thinly sliced
¼ teaspoon cayenne	2 cups couscous
Vegetable cooking spray	2 tablespoons chopped cilantro or parsley

1. Cut chicken into 8 serving pieces, then cut chicken breasts in half. In a plastic bag, combine flour, ¼ teaspoon salt, ½ teaspoon cumin, ¼ teaspoon coriander, and ⅛ teaspoon cayenne. Add chicken pieces a few at a time and shake to coat.

2. Coat a heavy nonstick skillet with cooking spray. Add olive oil and heat skillet over medium heat. Add chicken pieces in a single layer and cook, turning, until lightly browned on both sides, 5 to 7 minutes. Remove to plate. Pour off drippings from pan.

3. Add onion to skillet. Cook, stirring occasionally, until soft, about 3 minutes. Add tomatoes with their liquid, garlic, and remaining ½ teaspoon each salt and cumin, ¼ teaspoon coriander, and ⅛ teaspoon cayenne. Break up tomatoes with a wooden spoon. Arrange chicken pieces in sauce. Bring to a boil, reduce heat to low, cover, and simmer until chicken is done, about 25 minutes, spooning sauce over chicken a few times while cooking. Add lemon slices and simmer, uncovered, until heated through, about 5 minutes.

4. Meanwhile, in a small saucepan, bring 2 cups water to a boil. Add salt and couscous. Cover and remove from heat. Let stand 5 minutes.

5. Make a bed of couscous on a large platter. Arrange chicken pieces on couscous. Spoon sauce over chicken. Sprinkle cilantro on top and serve.

NOTE: *If preparing the chicken dish ahead of time, do not add lemon slices, as they will make the dish bitter. Add lemon slices after reheating.*

Per Serving: Calories: 430 Total fat: 6 g Saturated fat: 1 g
Cholesterol: 83 mg Percentage calories from fat: 13%

134 CHICKEN ENCHILADAS
Prep: 30 minutes   Cook: 50 minutes   Serves: 12

This is a perfect party dish for a crowd. You can make it up ahead of time, refrigerate, and bake as needed.

Vegetable cooking spray
12 (6-inch) light wheat flour tortillas with cracked wheatberries, or flour tortillas
½ cup chopped scallions
½ cup chopped red bell pepper
4 ounces Neufchâtel cheese, at room temperature
¾ teaspoon ground cumin
4 cups cooked chopped chicken or turkey (preferably white meat)

1 (10¾-ounce) can reduced-sodium cream of chicken soup
1 cup nonfat sour cream
1 cup skim milk
1 tablespoon finely chopped pickled jalapeño peppers (about 2 small)
½ cup coarsely shredded reduced-fat sharp Cheddar cheese

1. Preheat oven to 350°F. Coat a 9 x 13-inch baking dish with cooking spray. Stack tortillas and wrap in aluminum foil. Heat 10 minutes, or until hot.

2. Meanwhile, coat a small skillet with cooking spray. Add scallions and bell peppers and cook over medium heat until softened, about 2 minutes.

3. In a medium bowl, whisk together Neufchâtel cheese, cumin, and 1 tablespoon water until mixture is smooth. Stir in chopped chicken and cooked vegetables; set aside. In another bowl, whisk together chicken soup, sour cream, milk, and pickled jalapeño peppers. Stir 2 tablespoons into chicken mixture.

4. Remove tortillas from oven. Spoon a scant ⅓ cup chicken mixture onto each tortilla. Roll up and place seam side down in prepared dish. Pour remaining chicken soup mixture over enchiladas, covering completely. Cover securely with aluminum foil.

5. Bake 40 minutes, or until enchiladas are heated through and mixture is bubbly. Uncover, sprinkle with Cheddar cheese, and serve.

Per Serving: Calories: 232   Total fat: 6 g   Saturated fat: 3 g
Cholesterol: 53 mg   Percentage calories from fat: 26%

135   CHINESE-STYLE HOT CHICKEN SALAD
Prep: 25 minutes   Cook: 18 minutes   Serves: 6

2 whole chicken breasts on
   the bone (1¾ pounds),
   trimmed of all visible fat
6 cups shredded iceberg or
   romaine lettuce
1 (8-ounce) can sliced water
   chestnuts, drained
2 medium carrots, peeled and
   coarsely shredded
¼ cup reduced-sodium soy
   sauce
2 tablespoons honey
1 large garlic clove, minced
¼ teaspoon salt

3 tablespoons homemade or
   canned reduced-sodium
   chicken broth
2 teaspoons canola oil
¼ cup finely chopped scallions
1½ teaspoon finely chopped
   ginger
½ teaspoon crushed Szechuan
   peppercorns or
   ¼ teaspoon coarsely
   cracked black pepper
¼ teaspoon crushed hot
   pepper flakes

1. Split chicken breasts in half and place in a large saucepan. Pour in just enough water to cover the chicken. Bring to a simmer over medium heat. Reduce to low, cover, and simmer 15 minutes. Remove from heat and let stand, covered, 20 minutes.

2. Remove chicken from broth; discard broth or reserve for another use. Remove and discard skin, bones, and any visible fat. Cut chicken meat into 1-inch strips.

3. Toss together lettuce, water chestnuts, and carrots. Arrange on a large serving platter. Top with chicken shreds.

4. In a small bowl, combine soy sauce, honey, garlic, and salt. Stir to mix well. In a small saucepan, combine chicken broth, oil, scallions, ginger, Szechuan peppercorns, and hot pepper. Bring to a simmer over low heat, about 3 minutes. Stir sauce into soy mixture until blended. Pour sauce over chicken. Serve at once.

Per Serving: Calories: 192   Total fat: 4 g   Saturated fat: 1 g
Cholesterol: 53 mg   Percentage calories from fat: 19%

136 TURKEY TONNATO

Prep: 15 minutes   Cook: 20 to 30 minutes   Cool: 30 minutes
Chill: 3 to 4 hours   Serves: 6

One of the most elegant cold entrees I know—a takeoff on the classic vitello tonnato.

2 skinless, boneless turkey breast tenderloins (1½ pounds)	½ teaspoon salt Tonnato Sauce (recipe follows)
1 small onion, halved	1 tablespoon drained capers
1 celery rib, cut into 2-inch pieces	1 tablespoon chopped parsley
1 carrot, cut into 2-inch pieces	1 tablespoon thinly sliced lemon zest

1. In a medium skillet, place turkey, onion, celery, carrot, and salt. Pour enough water into skillet to cover turkey completely. Bring slowly to a boil. Reduce heat to low, cover, and simmer 20 to 30 minutes, or until turkey is tender. Let cool in broth 30 minutes. Remove turkey from broth and let cool slightly. Reserve 3 or 4 tablespoons of broth for tonnato sauce. Wrap turkey in plastic wrap and refrigerate 3 to 4 hours, or until very cold.

2. Cut turkey crosswise on an angle into ½-inch slices. Arrange slices, slightly overlapping, on a serving platter. Spoon part of the tonnato sauce over turkey to cover. Sprinkle with capers, parsley, and lemon zest. Pass remaining sauce at table. Serve at once or cover and refrigerate until ready to use.

Per Serving: Calories: 256 Total fat: 6 g Saturated fat: 1 g
Cholesterol: 86 mg Percentage calories from fat: 22%

137 TONNATO SAUCE

Prep: 5 minutes   Cook: none   Chill: 3 hours
Makes: 1⅓ cups, 6 servings

½ cup nonfat mayonnaise dressing	2 tablespoons fresh lemon juice
½ cup nonfat plain yogurt	1 tablespoon drained capers
1 (7-ounce) can albacore tuna in water, drained	3 to 4 tablespoons turkey or chicken broth or water (optional)
6 flat anchovies, patted dry between paper towels	

In a food processor, combine mayonnaise, yogurt, tuna, anchovies, lemon juice, and capers. Process until smooth. Transfer to a bowl, cover, and refrigerate 3 to 4 hours, or until very cold. If mixture is too thick, thin out with a few tablespoons broth or water.

Per Serving: Calories: 75 Total fat: 1 g Saturated fat: 0 g
Cholesterol: 15 mg Percentage calories from fat: 15%

138 TURKEY FAJITAS

Prep: 12 minutes   Cook: 15 minutes   Serves: 4

In my version of this popular Tex-Mex dish, strips of turkey are coated with a spiced orange yogurt, then tucked into large soft flour tortillas.

4 (6-inch) flour tortillas
¾ cup nonfat plain yogurt
2 tablespoons fresh orange juice
1 tablespoon thinly sliced orange zest (see Note)
2 teaspoons canola oil
2 teaspoons ground cumin
1 teaspoon ground coriander
¼ to ½ teaspoon cayenne, to taste

12 ounces turkey breast cutlets, cut into 3 x ¼-inch strips
1 medium green bell pepper, seeded and cut into thin strips
1 cup red onion slivers
2 garlic cloves, minced
Cilantro leaves (optional)

1. Preheat oven to 350°F. Stack tortillas, wrap in aluminum foil, and bake 10 minutes, until hot. Meanwhile, in a medium bowl, stir together yogurt, orange juice, and orange zest.

2. In a large nonstick skillet, heat oil over medium-high heat. Add cumin, coriander, and cayenne. Cook, stirring, 30 seconds. Add turkey strips, bell pepper, red onion, and garlic. Cook, stirring, until turkey is tender and white throughout and vegetables are tender, about 5 minutes. Add to yogurt mixture and toss to coat.

3. Divide turkey evenly on lower portion of warmed tortilla. Top with a few cilantro leaves. Bring bottom of tortilla up over filling, fold edges in, and leave top of tortilla open.

NOTE: *Use a zester to remove outer part of orange peel in thin strips or remove zest with a swivel-bladed vegetable peeler and cut into very thin strips with a sharp knife.*

*Per Serving: Calories: 236 Total fat: 5 g Saturated fat: 1 g
Cholesterol: 54 mg Percentage calories from fat: 18%*

139 SPICY TURKEY FINGERS WITH HONEY-MUSTARD DIP

Prep: 20 minutes   Cook: 10 minutes   Serves: 4

My son, Peter, loves spicy foods, "the hotta the betta"! I had him in mind when I developed this recipe. Then honey-mustard dip tempers the bite, but if you would prefer these turkey fingers a little milder, reduce the cayenne. These can also be served as a hot hors d'oeuvre.

Vegetable cooking spray	1½ teaspoons onion powder
2 skinless, boneless turkey breast tenderloins (1 pound)	1½ teaspoons dried basil
	1½ teaspoon dried thyme leaves
2 tablespoons buttermilk	1 teaspoon garlic powder
½ cup unseasoned fine dry bread crumbs	½ teaspoon pepper
	2 teaspoons canola oil
1 to 1½ teaspoons cayenne, or less to taste	⅓ cup honey
	2 tablespoons Dijon mustard

1. Preheat oven to 450°F. Coat a 10 x 15-inch jelly roll pan with cooking spray. Place turkey tenderloins, rounded side down, on work surface. Carefully cut in half lengthwise. Open tenderloin up and lay flat; cut at natural separation. Cut each half, crosswise, into 1-inch fingers. In a medium bowl, combine turkey with buttermilk; toss to coat thoroughly.

2. In a pie plate, combine bread crumbs, cayenne, onion powder, basil, thyme, garlic, and pepper; stir with a fork to mix. Stir in oil until crumbs are moistened. Coat turkey fingers thoroughly with seasoned crumb mixture (turning the meat with a fork helps). Place turkey in a single layer on prepared pan.

3. Bake, turning halfway through, 10 minutes, or until turkey fingers are lightly browned. Stir together honey and mustard and serve with hot turkey fingers as a dipping sauce.

*Per Serving: Calories: 307 Total fat: 4 g Saturated fat: 1 g
Cholesterol: 71 mg Percentage calories from fat: 12%*

140   TURKEY MARSALA WITH SWEET POTATO WEDGES

Prep: 10 minutes   Cook: 36 to 42 minutes   Serves: 4

You can substitute veal or thinly sliced chicken for this easy yet elegant dish flavored with marsala. Buy sweet potatoes all the same size and shape so they will cook in the allotted time.

4   **medium sweet potatoes (6 ounces each), peeled**
1   **tablespoon olive oil**
1   **teaspoon salt**
½   **teaspoon ground ginger**
3   **tablespoons flour**
¼   **teaspoon pepper**

4   **turkey breast cutlets (about 4 ounces each)**
   Vegetable cooking spray
½   **pound cremini or white button mushrooms, trimmed and thinly sliced**
½   **cup marsala**
2   **teaspoons chopped parsley**

1. Preheat oven to 375°F. Cut each sweet potato into 4 wedges. Place in a large bowl. Drizzle with 1 teaspoon olive oil, ½ teaspoon salt, and ginger. Toss to coat. Place on a large baking sheet. Bake 25 to 30 minutes, or until tender.

2. About 15 minutes before sweet potatoes are done, on a sheet of wax paper, mix together flour, remaining ½ teaspoon salt, and pepper. Dredge turkey slices in seasoned flour to coat both sides.

3. Coat a large nonstick skillet with cooking spray. Heat skillet over medium heat. Add turkey and cook, turning once, until cutlets are lightly browned on both sides and white in center, about 4 minutes. Place on a serving platter; cover to keep warm.

4. Add remaining 2 teaspoons olive oil to skillet. Add mushrooms and toss over high heat 2 minutes. Cover skillet, reduce heat to medium-low, and cook until mushrooms are tender, 3 to 4 minutes longer.

5. Add marsala to skillet and bring to a boil over high heat, scraping up any browned bits from bottom of pan. Cook, stirring, until sauce is slightly reduced, about 2 minutes. Spoon sauce over turkey and garnish with parsley. Arrange potato wedges alongside.

Per Serving: Calories: 399   Total fat: 8 g   Saturated fat: 1 g
Cholesterol: 70 mg   Percentage calories from fat: 21%

141   TURKEY MUSHROOM STROGANOFF

Prep: 15 minutes   Cook: 45 to 50 minutes   Serves: 4

It is preferable to use fresh dill for this saucy stroganoff, rather than dried, which does not give the same great flavor. I've paired the stroganoff with a basmati and wild rice blend. You can also serve it over egg-free wide noodles.

1 cup uncooked basmati and
    wild rice blend
1½ tablespoons butter
1 pound turkey cutlets, cut
    into ½-inch strips
½ cup sliced onion
1 teaspoon finely chopped
    garlic
¼ pound mushrooms, sliced
    ¼ inch thick (1½ cups)

1 tablespoon flour
½ teaspoon salt
¼ teaspoon pepper
3 tablespoons minced fresh
    dill
1 tablespoon ketchup
¾ cup homemade or canned
    reduced-sodium chicken
    broth
1 cup nonfat sour cream

1. In a medium saucepan, cook rice in 2 cups boiling water following package directions 45 to 50 minutes, or until water is absorbed and rice is tender.

2. Meanwhile, in a large nonstick skillet, melt butter over medium-high heat. Add turkey and cook, tossing, 2 minutes, or until turkey turns white. Add onion and garlic and cook, stirring, 2 minutes. Add mushrooms and cook until mushrooms soften and turkey is tender, about 2 minutes.

3. Sprinkle flour, salt, pepper, and 1 tablespoon dill over turkey. Cook, stirring, 1 minute. Add ketchup and chicken broth and bring to a boil, stirring, until sauce is smooth and thickened, 1 to 2 minutes.

4. Remove skillet from heat. Gradually stir in sour cream. Return to medium-low heat and cook just until hot, 1 to 2 minutes. Spoon turkey and sauce over rice. Sprinkle remaining 2 tablespoons dill on top and serve.

Per Serving: Calories: 372   Total fat: 6 g   Saturated fat: 3 g
Cholesterol: 82 mg   Percentage calories from fat: 13%

142   TURKEY CURRY
Prep: 15 minutes   Cook: 26 minutes   Serves: 4 to 6

This turkey curry contains the additional interest of eggplant and apple. Mango chutney stirred in gives the stew a tart-sweet note. Serve over rice or couscous.

Vegetable cooking spray
1 teaspoon canola oil
1 cup chopped onion
3 garlic cloves, minced
3 tablespoons curry powder
2 tablespoons finely chopped
    fresh ginger
1 teaspoon chili powder
2 large tomatoes, coarsely
    chopped (1 pound)
1 large Granny Smith apple
    (8 ounces), cored and
    coarsely chopped

1 to 1½ cups homemade or
    canned reduced-sodium
    chicken broth
2 skinless, boneless turkey
    breast tenderloins
    (1 pound), cut into
    1-inch cubes
1 cup diced (¾-inch)
    unpeeled eggplant
2 tablespoons currants
2 tablespoons chopped
    mango chutney
2 tablespoons sliced almonds

1. Coat a large nonstick skillet with cooking spray. Add oil and heat skillet over medium-high heat. Add onion and garlic and cook, stirring occasionally, until onion is golden, about 3 minutes. Add curry powder, ginger, and chili powder. Cook, stirring, 1 minute.

2. Add tomatoes, apple, and 1 cup chicken broth to skillet. Bring to a boil, reduce heat to low, cover, and simmer 10 minutes.

3. Stir in turkey and eggplant. Cover and simmer until turkey and eggplant are tender, about 12 minutes.

4. Stir in currants and chutney. Add remaining ½ cup chicken broth, if necessary, to thin sauce. Spoon into a serving bowl; sprinkle with almonds.

Per Serving: Calories: 244   Total fat: 5 g   Saturated fat: 1 g
Cholesterol: 56 mg   Percentage calories from fat: 18%

143   TURKEY MEATBALLS WITH SAUERKRAUT
Prep: 15 minutes   Cook: 1 hour   Serves: 6

This sweet-and-sour meatball dish is a family favorite. It is prepared as a main dish, but it can also be served as a hot hors d'oeuvre. Just make smaller meatballs and provide small plates and forks. The dish should be made a day in advance of serving for the flavors to mellow. I usually make a double recipe and freeze half.

2 slices of firm-textured whole wheat bread	1 (16-ounce) can sauerkraut, liquid reserved
1 pound lean ground turkey	1 (8-ounce) can tomato sauce
1½ cups finely chopped onions	¼ cup raisins
¼ cup plus 2 tablespoons firmly packed light brown sugar	

1. In a medium bowl, sprinkle 2 tablespoons water over bread; crumble with a fork. Add ground turkey, ½ cup of onion, and 2 tablespoons brown sugar; mix thoroughly. Shape into 18 meatballs about 1½ inches in diameter (2 level measuring tablespoons each). If you plan to serve as an appetizer, use 1 level measuring tablespoon for the meatballs.

2. In another medium bowl, combine remaining 1 cup onions and ¼ cup brown sugar. Add sauerkraut with liquid, tomato sauce, and raisins. Mix well.

3. In medium nonreactive saucepan, place one-third of sauerkraut mixture; top with half of meatballs. Top with half of remaining sauerkraut mixture and all of remaining meatballs. Cover with remaining sauerkraut. Bring to a boil, reduce heat to low, and simmer, covered, 1 hour. Let cool, then refrigerate overnight. To reheat, bring to a boil, reduce heat to low, cover, and simmer until heated through, about 15 minutes.

Per Serving: Calories: 243   Total fat: 6 g   Saturated fat: 2 g
Cholesterol: 55 mg   Percentage calories from fat: 23%

144   SOUTHWESTERN TURKEY TENDERLOIN WITH CRANBERRY SALSA

Prep: 5 minutes   Chill: 1 hour or more   Cook: 20 minutes   Serves: 4

Why just have turkey and cranberries on Thanksgiving Day? Here turkey tenderloin is marinated in Mexican spices, grilled, and served with a cranberry salsa for a dish that's a treat any day of the year.

¼ cup fresh lime juice
1 tablespoon balsamic
  vinegar
2 garlic cloves, minced
½ teaspoon sugar
¼ teaspoon ground cumin
¼ teaspoon ground coriander

¼ teaspoon hot Mexican chili
  powder
2 skinless, boneless turkey
  breast tenderloins
  (1 to 1½ pounds)
  Vegetable cooking spray
  Cranberry Salsa (recipe
  follows)

1. In a small bowl, combine lime juice, vinegar, garlic, sugar, cumin, coriander, and chili powder. Place turkey tenderloins in a large zip-top heavy-duty plastic bag. Pour over marinade. Squeeze bag to coat turkey with marinade; close bag. Refrigerate at least 1 hour or overnight.

2. Remove turkey from marinade; save marinade. Coat a top-of-the-stove grill with cooking spray. Heat grill over medium-high heat. Grill tenderloins 20 minutes, turning once and basting with reserved marinade. Cut turkey crosswise on an angle into ¼-inch slices and fan out on plate. Spoon 1 cup cranberry salsa alongside slices. Pass remaining salsa on the side.

*Per Serving: Calories: 246   Total fat: 1 g   Saturated fat: 0 g
            Cholesterol: 88 mg   Percentage calories from fat: 5%*

145   CRANBERRY SALSA

*Prep: 5 minutes   Cook: 5 to 7 minutes   Cool: 30 minutes
Chill: 2 hours   Makes: 2½ cups*

This savory cooked salsa will go well with any meat, poultry, or fish dish that has Southwestern flavors.

1 (12-ounce) bag fresh or
  frozen cranberries
¾ cup sugar
¼ cup finely diced red onion

2 tablespoons finely chopped
  cilantro
1 tablespoon minced seeded
  jalapeño pepper

1. In a nonreactive medium saucepan, combine cranberries, sugar, and ¾ cup water. Bring to a boil, stirring occasionally, until cranberries pop and mixture thickens slightly, 5 to 7 minutes.

2. Remove from heat and let stand 30 minutes, until cool. Stir in red onion, cilantro, and jalapeño pepper. Cover and refrigerate at least 2 hours for flavors to mellow. Serve slightly chilled.

*Per Serving: Calories: 77   Total fat: < 1 g   Saturated fat: 0 g
Cholesterol: 0 mg   Percentage calories from fat: 1%*

---

146   MEAT LOAF AND MASHED POTATOES
Prep: 20 minutes   Cook: 1 hour
Makes: 2 loaves, to serve 8 to 10 each

This recipe makes two meat loaves: one to eat and one to freeze. When cold, the meat loaf has the consistency of a paté. It makes a colorful addition to a buffet table. Slice into ¼-inch slices and arrange, overlapping slightly, on a large platter. Garnish with sprigs of fresh basil.

Vegetable cooking spray
2¼ pounds lean ground turkey
¼ pound hot or sweet turkey sausage, casings removed
1 (10-ounce) package frozen chopped spinach, thawed, drained, and squeezed dry
1¼ cups fresh bread crumbs
⅓ cup grated Asiago or Parmesan cheese
½ cup finely chopped onion

2 tablespoons chopped fresh basil or 2 teaspoons dried
3 egg whites
1 teaspoon salt
½ cup homemade or canned reduced-sodium chicken broth
1 (10-ounce) package frozen peas, thawed and drained
Buttermilk and Chive Mashed Potatoes (recipe follows)

1. Preheat oven to 350°F. Line a 10 x 15-inch jelly roll pan with aluminum foil; coat with cooking spray.

2. In a large bowl, combine ground turkey, turkey sausage, spinach, bread crumbs, cheese, onion, basil, egg, egg whites, salt, and ¼ cup of chicken broth. Mix lightly with hands or wooden spoon until combined. Fold in peas.

3. Divide meat mixture in half and lightly shape into 2 (10-inch-long) loaves on prepared pan. Bake meat loaves 1 hour, or until lightly browned and done, basting every 15 minutes with remaining ¼ cup chicken broth. Serve with mashed potatoes.

*Per Serving: Calories: 199   Total fat: 6 g   Saturated fat: 2 g
Cholesterol: 49 mg   Percentage calories from fat: 27%*

147 BUTTERMILK AND CHIVE MASHED POTATOES

Prep: 8 minutes   Cook: 10 minutes   Serves: 8

Buttermilk adds a rich and creamy taste, without the fat, to mashed potatoes.

2 **pounds all-purpose potatoes, peeled and cut into ½-inch cubes**
⅔ **to 1 cup buttermilk**

½ **teaspoon salt**
⅛ **teaspoon pepper**
1 **tablespoon chives or sliced scallions**

1. Place potatoes in a large saucepan with enough cold water to cover. Bring to a boil over high heat. Reduce heat to medium-low, cover, and cook 10 minutes, or until potatoes are tender. Drain potatoes and return to saucepan.

2. Shake pan over low heat to dry potatoes. Remove from heat. Mash potatoes with a fork or masher or put through a ricer. Add buttermilk, salt, and pepper. Whip until creamy smooth. Place in a serving bowl and top with chives.

Per Serving: Calories: 156   Total fat: 2 g   Saturated fat: 0 g
Cholesterol: 2 mg   Percentage calories from fat: 3%

Chapter 7

Svelte Fish and Shellfish

Growing up in Arizona, my encounters with fish were usually in a rectangular box from the supermarket freezer section or in the fish-and-chip fast-food chains that were so popular in my day. It wasn't until I moved to New York that I got hooked on fresh fish. The concern with reducing cholesterol and fat in our diet has spurred an increase in fish consumption. This trend has become apparent in the large selection of fish available in supermarkets, specialty food stores, and in local fish markets.

Eating fish just makes good sense. It is high in protein, low in fat, low in cholesterol, and rich in vitamins and minerals, especially A and D. Fish is also a natural source of Omega-3 fatty acids, which aid in the reduction of cholesterol. Omega-3 is a polyunsaturated fat found in almost all fish, though some varieties have more than others.

When buying fish, look for clear eyes, tight and shiny scales, and if the fish has gills they should be red. When purchasing fillets and steaks they should be translucent and shiny. Whether you buy fish whole or in parts it should be firm to the touch and should have no fishy smell. Fresh fish does not smell! And get to know your local fishmonger. He is a wealth of fish information.

Fish lends itself to a variety of flavors and preparations. Marinating it in a tangy marinade, then broiling or grilling the fish perks up the flavors. Steaming fish fillets with vegetables and herbs in parchment or a foil packet infuses the flavors, while whole fish can be steamed in a Chinese steamer basket, or you can improvise a steamer with a large skillet. Replacing part of the butter with olive oil or coating a skillet with cooking spray and a small amount of oil when sautéing fish reduces fat and calories.

Cornmeal-Crusted Codfish Cakes with Tomato Salsa is a homey type of dish with a slight Mexican flavor. Potato-Crusted Salmon Florentine and Orange-Sauced Flounder Roulades are elegant enough for company, and there's no need to order in when you can make Szechuan Shrimp or Chinese Sea Bass with Fermented Black Beans served with a bowl of rice. When you want to splurge, Cioppino, the fragrant fish stew, is a taste of the sea with clams, mussels, shrimp, and the catch of the day.

148 CORNMEAL-CRUSTED CODFISH CAKES WITH TOMATO SALSA

Prep: 1 hour (includes chilling time)   Cook: 26 to 34 minutes
Serves: 8

A light cornmeal crust coats these delicate codfish and potato cakes. You can make them up early in the day and cook them just before you are ready to serve. The salsa has pickled jalapeños and cilantro to complement the flavor of the fish cakes.

1 **pound potatoes, peeled and diced (about 2⅔ cups)**	½ **teaspoon cayenne**
1¼ **pounds fresh codfish, scrod, or halibut**	2 **to 3 tablespoons yellow cornmeal**
¼ **cup minced scallions**	**Vegetable cooking spray**
2 **tablespoons reduced-fat mayonnaise**	2 **teaspoons canola oil**
¾ **teaspoon salt**	**Tomato Salsa (recipe follows)**

1. In a medium saucepan, cook potatoes in boiling water (salted, if desired) until soft, about 10 to 12 minutes; drain. Meanwhile, in a large skillet, bring 1 inch of water to a boil. Add fish and bring water just to a simmer; lower heat. Simmer, uncovered, until fish flakes easily when tested with a fork, about 8 to 10 minutes. Remove fish to paper towels with a slotted spoon. Reserve ¼ cup poaching liquid. Remove skin and bones from fish.

2. In a food processor, place potatoes, fish, reserved ¼ cup poaching liquid, scallions, mayonnaise, salt, and cayenne. Process, using pulses, until mixture is fairly smooth. Spoon into a large bowl. Divide into 8 (½-cup) portions. Shape into 3 x ¾-inch fish cakes.

3. Place cornmeal on a sheet of wax paper. Coat fish cakes on both sides with the cornmeal. Reshape, if necessary. Place on a large baking sheet. Cover and refrigerate 30 minutes, or until firm.

4. In a large nonstick skillet, heat 1 teaspoon oil over medium heat. Add half of the fish cakes; cook 4 to 6 minutes, turning once, until they are brown and heated through. Place on a serving platter; cover and keep warm. Repeat with remaining 1 teaspoon oil and remaining fish cakes. Serve with Tomato Salsa.

Per Serving: Calories: 135   Total fat: 3 g   Saturated fat: 0 g
Cholesterol: 30 mg   Percentage calories from fat: 17%

149 TOMATO SALSA
Prep: 10 minutes   Cook: none   Chill: 1 hour   Makes: 2 cups

This all-purpose salsa has many uses, adding a fresh-tasting accent to almost any dish. Spoon over burgers as a relish; use as a dip with taco chips, the no-fried variety; or pair with meats or poultry.

1 **pound plum tomatoes, seeded and coarsely chopped**
2 **tablespoons finely chopped cilantro**
2 **tablespoons lemon or lime juice**

1 **tablespoon finely chopped seeded pickled jalapeño pepper**
1 **teaspoon grated lemon or lime zest**

In a medium bowl, combine tomatoes, cilantro, lemon or lime juice, pickled jalapeño pepper, and lemon or lime zest; stir to combine. Cover and refrigerate at least 1 hour for flavors to mellow.

*Per Serving: Calories: 12   Total fat: < 1 g   Saturated fat: 0 g
Cholesterol: 0 mg   Percentage calories from fat: 11%*

150 SZECHUAN SHRIMP
Prep: 20 minutes   Cook: 5 to 6 minutes   Serves: 4

¼ **cup ketchup, saltless if possible**
2 **tablespoons reduced-sodium soy sauce**
1 **tablespoon dry sherry**
½ **teaspoon sugar**
1½ **teaspoons minced fresh ginger**
¼ **teaspoon crushed hot pepper flakes**

2 **teaspoons canola oil**
1 **pound medium fresh shrimp, shelled and deveined (32)**
1½ **teaspoons finely chopped garlic**
½ **cup sliced (1-inch) scallions**
2 **cups hot cooked rice**

1. In a small bowl, combine ketchup, soy sauce, sherry, sugar, ginger, and hot pepper flakes.

2. In a large nonstick skillet, heat 1 teaspoon oil over medium-high heat. Add shrimp; stir-fry until pink and curled, about 3 minutes. Remove shrimp with a slotted spoon to a bowl.

3. Add remaining 1 teaspoon oil to skillet. Add garlic and scallions; stir-fry 1 minute. Add ketchup mixture. Cook, stirring constantly, until bubbly, about 30 seconds. Add shrimp and stir to combine with sauce; heat 1 minute. Serve over rice.

*Per Serving: Calories: 284   Total fat: 4 g   Saturated fat: 1 g
Cholesterol: 140 mg   Percentage calories from fat: 14%*

151 BAKED STUFFED CLAMS
Prep: 20 minutes   Cook: 7 to 10 minutes   Serves: 4

The hardest part of this recipe is shucking the clams. If you are not an expert at this, have your fishmonger do it for you when you purchase them. Or, place clams in freezer for 30 minutes. The cold relaxes the muscles and makes them easier to open.

Rock salt or coarse salt
12 large littleneck clams, scrubbed and opened on the half shell
1 cup fresh bread crumbs, preferably made with Italian bread
2 tablespoons finely chopped parsley

2 teaspoons minced fresh oregano or marjoram or ½ teaspoon dried
2 garlic cloves, minced
⅛ teaspoon pepper
2 teaspoons extra-virgin olive oil
2 teaspoons lemon juice
4 lemon wedges

1. Preheat oven to 425°F. Make a bed of the rock salt or coarse salt in a 9 x 13-inch baking pan (or use crumbled aluminum foil). Arrange the shucked clams on rock salt, nestling them in slightly so they won't tip over.

2. In a medium bowl, combine bread crumbs, parsley, oregano or marjoram, garlic, and pepper; mix with a fork to combine. Add olive oil and lemon juice; mix until crumbs are lightly moistened.

3. Sprinkle crumb mixture on top of each clam, covering clam completely. Bake 7 to 10 minutes, or until crumbs are golden. Serve with lemon wedges to squeeze over.

*Per Serving: Calories: 105   Total fat: 3 g   Saturated fat: 0 g
Cholesterol: 20 mg   Percentage calories from fat: 28%*

152 SWORDFISH AND NEW POTATOES WITH DILL SAUCE
Prep: 10 minutes   Chill: 1 hour   Cook: 18 to 24 minutes   Serves: 4

Grilled swordfish is topped with a creamy dill and mustard sauce. Try the sauce also with grilled salmon.

½ cup nonfat mayonnaise
½ cup nonfat plain yogurt
2 tablespoons white wine vinegar
4 teaspoons Dijon mustard
½ cup chopped fresh dill

1 pound new potatoes, scrubbed
4 swordfish steaks, cut ¾ inch thick (4 ounces each)
½ teaspoon salt
¼ teaspoon pepper
2 tablespoons fresh lime juice

1. In a small bowl, combine mayonnaise, yogurt, vinegar, mustard, and dill; stir to combine. Cover and refrigerate at least 1 hour for flavors to mellow.

2. In a large saucepan of boiling salted water, cook potatoes until tender, 15 to 20 minutes. Drain well.

3. Preheat broiler. Sprinkle steaks with salt and pepper; brush with lime juice. Broil 4 to 5 inches from heat 3 to 4 minutes on each side. Place on individual serving plates with boiled potatoes on the side. Spoon on dill sauce.

Per Serving: Calories: 262 Total fat: 4 g Saturated fat: 1 g
Cholesterol: 40 mg Percentage calories from fat: 16%

---

153   CIOPPINO
Prep: 45 minutes   Cook: 46 minutes   Serves: 8

Serve this elegant fish stew from San Francisco with crusty sourdough bread to sop up the juices. A green salad and fresh fruit are all you'll need to round out a perfect meal.

1 tablespoon olive oil
1 cup chopped onion
1 cup chopped green bell
   pepper
1 tablespoon minced garlic
1 (14½-ounce) can Italian
   peeled whole tomatoes,
   drained, juice reserved,
   and tomatoes coarsely
   chopped
1 cup tomato sauce
2 cups dry white wine

½ cup chopped parsley
½ teaspoon dried basil
½ teaspoon dried marjoram
½ teaspoon dried oregano
1 bay leaf
2 pounds firm-fleshed white
   fish (such as red snapper,
   sea bass, halibut, tilefish)
18 small hard-shelled clams
18 small mussels
1 pound medium shrimp

1. In a large saucepan, heat olive oil over high heat. Add onion, bell pepper, and garlic; sauté until vegetables are soft, about 5 minutes. Stir in tomatoes and reserved liquid, tomato sauce, wine, ¼ cup parsley, basil, marjoram, oregano, and bay leaf. Bring to a boil; lower heat. Simmer, with cover partially ajar, 30 minutes.

2. While sauce simmers, cut fish into 2-inch pieces. With a stiff brush, thoroughly scrub clams under cold water. Scrub and debeard mussels under cold water. Shell and devein shrimp.

3. Add fish to saucepan; simmer, uncovered, 5 minutes. Add clams and mussels; simmer, covered, 3 minutes. Add shrimp; simmer, covered, 3 minutes. Shrimp should be pink; clams and mussels fully opened. Discard any shellfish that do not open. Remove bay leaf.

4. Divide fish, clams, mussels, and shrimp among individual soup bowls. Ladle hot broth over seafood; sprinkle with remaining parsley.

Per Serving: Calories: 246 Total fat: 5 g Saturated fat: 1 g
Cholesterol: 124 mg Percentage calories from fat: 18%

154 MUSSELS IN SPICY BROTH
Prep: 12 minutes   Cook: 8 to 11 minutes   Serves: 4

Fresh basil accents this tomato and wine sauce for mussels. Do not substitute dried basil; it just does not have the flavor necessary for this shellfish dish.

1½ teaspoons olive oil
½ cup chopped onion
2 teaspoons finely chopped garlic
1 (16-ounce) can peeled tomatoes, juices reserved
1 cup dry white wine
¼ cup chopped basil leaves

2 tablespoons chopped parsley
¼ to ½ teaspoon crushed hot pepper flakes
32 mussels, scrubbed and beards removed (2 pounds)

1. In a large nonstick saucepan, heat olive oil over medium-low heat. Add onion and garlic. Cook, stirring occasionally, until onion is softened, 3 to 5 minutes. Stir in tomatoes with their juices and break up against side of saucepan with a wooden spoon. Add wine, basil, 1 tablespoon parsley, and hot pepper flakes. Bring to a boil; lower heat.

2. Add mussels to saucepan. Cover and steam 4 to 5 minutes until mussels have opened. (Discard any mussels that do not open.) Divide mussels among individual serving bowls. Spoon on sauce: sprinkle with remaining 1 tablespoon parsley.

*Per Serving: Calories: 148   Total fat: 3 g   Saturated fat: 1 g
Cholesterol: 18 mg   Percentage calories from fat: 28%*

155 ORANGE-SAUCED FLOUNDER ROULADES
Prep: 12 minutes   Cook: 22 to 27 minutes   Serves: 4

Scallions and orange zest are spread over the fish fillets, which are then rolled up and baked with an orange-wine sauce. It is a perfect dish for entertaining.

Butter-flavored cooking spray
2 teaspoons butter
¼ cup minced scallions
½ teaspoon grated orange zest
Pinch of thyme or tarragon
2 flounder fillets, halved lengthwise (8 ounces each)

½ teaspoon salt
⅛ teaspoon white pepper
¼ cup dry white wine
¼ cup orange juice
1 teaspoon cornstarch
1 tablespoon chopped parsley

1. Preheat oven to 350°F. Coat an 8-inch round shallow nonreactive baking dish with cooking spray. In a small skillet, melt butter over medium heat. Add scallions; cook and stir until soft, about 1 minute. Stir in orange zest and thyme or tarragon.

2. Sprinkle fish with salt and white pepper. Spread skinned side of fish lightly with half of the scallion mixture. Roll up fillets from wide end; secure each with a wooden pick. Place spiral side up in baking dish. Sprinkle with remaining scallion mixture. In a 1-cup glass measure, combine wine and orange juice; pour into baking dish.

3. Bake 20 to 25 minutes, or until fish flakes easily when tested with a fork. Carefully drain off cooking juices into a small saucepan. Bring to a simmer. In a small cup, combine cornstarch with 1 tablespoon water. Stir into saucepan. Cook and stir over medium-low heat until sauce thickens and boils, about 1 minute. Spoon sauce over fish. Remove wooden picks. Sprinkle with parsley.

Per Serving: Calories: 135   Total fat: 3 g   Saturated fat: 1 g
Cholesterol: 60 mg   Percentage calories from fat: 24%

---

156   FISH BONNE FEMME
Prep: 15 minutes   Cook: 15 to 18 minutes   Serves: 4

When you are in a hurry, this delicate fish dish with vegetables and wine is perfect for a light supper, and it's elegant enough for company. Serve with rice.

Vegetable cooking spray
2 teaspoons butter
4 medium carrots, peeled and cut into thin (2 x ⅛-inch) strips
2 cups sliced mushrooms (6 ounces)
2 medium leeks (white part only), cut into thin (2 x ⅛-inch) strips
2 teaspoons fresh lemon juice

2 teaspoons grated lemon zest
2 teaspoons minced fresh thyme or ¼ teaspoon dried
4 flounder, sole, orange roughy, or turbot fillets (4 to 5 ounces each)
½ teaspoon salt
⅛ teaspoon pepper
½ cup dry vermouth or white wine

1. Preheat oven to 450°F. Coat a large nonstick skillet with cooking spray. Add butter and melt over medium heat. Add carrots, mushrooms, and leeks. Cook, stirring occasionally, until vegetables are crisp-tender and mushrooms become limp, about 3 minutes. Add lemon juice, lemon zest, and thyme; toss to coat. Spread vegetable mixture in bottom of a 9-inch square glass or enameled baking dish.

2. Season fish fillets with salt and pepper. Fold fillets in half and arrange over vegetables. Pour on wine. Cover tightly with aluminum foil.

3. Bake 12 to 15 minutes, or until fish is opaque throughout. Transfer fish and vegetables to individual serving plates. Spoon some of wine sauce over each serving.

Per Serving: Calories: 250   Total fat: 4 g   Saturated fat: 2 g
Cholesterol: 66 mg   Percentage calories from fat: 17%

157   CURRIED SCALLOPS
Prep: 15 minutes   Cook: 11 to 12 minutes   Serves: 4

This is a very mild-flavored curry that does not overpower the delicate flavor of the scallops. Make sure the yogurt is at room temperature and that you add it slowly.

2 teaspoons butter
½ cup peeled and chopped tart apple, such as Granny Smith
½ cup chopped onion
2 teaspoons curry powder
2 tablespoons flour
½ teaspoon salt

¾ cup tomato juice
1 pound bay scallops, halved crosswise
1 cup peeled, halved, seeded, and sliced (¼-inch) cucumber
¼ cup nonfat plain yogurt, at room temperature

1. In a large nonstick skillet, melt butter over medium heat. Add apple and onion; sauté until soft, about 3 minutes. Stir in curry powder; cook and stir 1 minute. Blend in flour, salt, tomato juice, and ½ cup water. Bring to a boil; lower heat. Cover and simmer 5 minutes to blend flavors.

2. Add scallops and cucumber; stir to combine with sauce. Cover and simmer at low heat until scallops are firm and opaque in center, about 2 to 3 minutes. Remove from heat. Gradually stir in yogurt until combined.

Per Serving: Calories: 170   Total fat: 3 g   Saturated fat: 1 g
Cholesterol: 43 mg   Percentage calories from fat: 16%

158   LEMON-HERBED SCALLOPS
Prep: 8 minutes   Cook: 4 to 5 minutes   Serves: 4

One of my favorite seafood dishes is scampi. This scallop dish has all the flavor of a scampi with just a little bit of butter and olive oil.

1½ teaspoons butter
1½ teaspoons extra-virgin olive oil
1 tablespoon finely chopped garlic
1 pound bay scallops, shelled and deveined shrimp, or a combination, patted dry between paper towels
2 tablespoons finely chopped parsley

1 tablespoon finely chopped scallions
2 tablespoons fresh lemon juice
½ teaspoon grated lemon zest
⅛ teaspoon salt (optional) Pinch of white pepper
3 cups hot cooked rice or 8 ounces hot cooked linguine

1. In a large skillet, melt butter with olive oil over medium-high heat. Add garlic and sauté 30 seconds. Add scallops; cook and stir until scallops are firm and opaque in center, about 3 minutes.

2. Stir in parsley, scallions, lemon juice, lemon zest, salt, and pepper. Serve hot over rice or linguine.

Per Serving: Calories: 333 Total fat: 4 g Saturated fat: 1 g
Cholesterol: 41 mg Percentage calories from fat: 12%

---

159   POTATO-CRUSTED SALMON FLORENTINE
Prep: 20 minutes   Cook: 42 minutes   Serves: 4

In this contemporary recipe, salmon fillets are baked with a topping of shredded potatoes and carrots and served on a nest of spinach.

1 **pound baking potatoes**	¼ **teaspoon pepper**
Vegetable cooking spray	4 **small salmon steaks, 1 inch**
1 **medium onion, minced**	**thick (about 5 ounces**
1 **large carrot, peeled and**	**each)**
coarsely shredded	2 **teaspoons Dijon mustard**
1 **tablespoon chopped fresh**	1 **pound fresh spinach**
dill	**Lemon wedges**
½ **teaspoon salt**	

1. In a large pot of boiling water, cook potatoes until tender, about 20 minutes. Drain and let cool 15 minutes. When cool enough to handle, peel potatoes and shred on coarse holes of a hand grater.

2. Preheat oven to 400°F. Coat an 11 x 7-inch baking dish with cooking spray.

3. Coat a large nonstick skillet with vegetable spray and set over medium heat. Add onion and carrot; cook, stirring, 2 minutes, or until tender but not brown. Add potatoes, dill, salt, and pepper; mix with a fork to combine.

4. Cut salmon fillet into 4 equal pieces. Place fish skin side down in prepared baking dish. Spread ½ teaspoon mustard over each piece of salmon. Top each with ½ cup potato mixture, spreading evenly and pressing down gently to cover completely. Bake 15 minutes, or until fish flakes easily with a fork.

5. While fish is baking, trim and wash spinach well. Do not shake off water. Place in a large nonreactive saucepan. Cover and steam over high heat, 1 to 2 minutes, or until spinach is wilted but still bright green; drain well.

6. Divide spinach among 4 plates, making a nest in center. Remove skin from edges of salmon and place atop spinach nest. Place lemon wedge on each plate.

Per Serving: Calories: 303 Total fat: 9 g Saturated fat: 1 g
Cholesterol: 69 mg Percentage calories from fat: 26%

160   SHELLFISH IN TOMATO SAUCE WITH CILANTRO

Prep: 25 minutes   Cook: 20 to 22 minutes   Serves: 4

1¼ teaspoons olive oil
1 tablespoon minced garlic
1 tablespoon minced ginger
1 teaspoon minced seeded
    jalapeño pepper
½ teaspoon ground cumin
¼ teaspoon ground turmeric
2 medium tomatoes
    (12 ounces), peeled and
    coarsely chopped

16 mussels, scrubbed and
    beards removed
    (1 pound)
16 littleneck clams, scrubbed
    (1 pound)
1 tablespoon chopped cilantro

1. In a large nonstick skillet, heat olive oil over medium heat. Add garlic, ginger, and jalapeño pepper. Cook and stir 1 minute. Add cumin and turmeric; cook and stir 1 minute.

2. Add tomatoes and ½ cup water to skillet. Bring to a boil; lower heat. Cover and simmer 15 minutes, or until slightly thickened. Bring sauce back to a boil over high heat. Add mussels and clams; cover and steam 3 to 5 minutes, shaking pan occasionally, until shellfish have opened. Discard any shellfish that do not open.

3. Divide shellfish among individual serving bowls. Spoon on sauce; sprinkle with cilantro.

Per Serving: Calories: 74   Total fat: 2 g   Saturated fat: 0 g
Cholesterol: 15 mg   Percentage calories from fat: 28%

161   SEA BASS WITH FERMENTED BLACK BEANS

Prep: 10 minutes   Cook: 15 minutes   Serves: 4

    Sea bass is a mild-flavored dish that takes well to strong flavors. Fermented black beans can be purchased at Asian food stores and in the oriental food section of some supermarkets. You can also cook the fish in a steamer rather than by the method given below.

1 whole sea bass or red
    snapper, head and tail
    intact (1½ pounds)
1 teaspoon finely chopped
    fresh ginger
2 large scallions, cut into
    1-inch pieces
1 large garlic clove, minced

1 tablespoon fermented black
    beans, rinsed under cold
    water and drained
2 tablespoons reduced-
    sodium soy sauce
2 tablespoons dry sherry
1½ teaspoons canola oil

1. Make 3 diagonal slashes on both sides of fish. Place fish on a deep heatproof dish.

2. In a small bowl, combine ginger, scallion pieces, garlic, fermented black beans, soy sauce, sherry, and oil. Pour over fish.

3. In a skillet large enough to hold the plate, bring 1 inch of water to a boil. Place a round wire rack in skillet. (Make sure water is even with the rack.) Place dish with sea bass on rack. Cover tightly and steam 15 minutes over high heat, until fish flakes easily with a fork. Carefully remove dish with sea bass; spoon sauce in plate over fish.

Per Serving: Calories: 98   Total fat: 3 g   Saturated fat: 0 g
Cholesterol: 27 mg   Percentage calories from fat: 30%

---

162   CREOLE SCROD FILLETS
Prep: 12 minutes   Cook: 18 to 19 minutes   Serves: 4

Scrod is a name that is applied to baby cod and haddock. For this recipe, it doesn't matter which fish it is as long as it is fresh.

4   scrod fillets (5 ounces each) or 1⅓ pounds scrod, about 1 inch thick, cut into 4 equal pieces
1   tablespoon fresh lemon juice
   Salt and pepper
1   teaspoon olive oil
1   medium onion, chopped
1   small green bell pepper, finely diced

1   (14½-ounce) can Cajun-style stewed tomatoes, undrained
½   teaspoon crushed fennel seeds
¼   teaspoon crushed hot red pepper
⅛   teaspoon dried thyme leaves

1. Preheat oven to 350°F. Place scrod in a 9 x 11-inch baking dish. Drizzle lemon juice over fish. Season lightly with salt and pepper.

2. In a medium saucepan, combine olive oil, onion, bell pepper, and 1 tablespoon water. Cover and cook over medium heat 3 minutes. Uncover and cook, stirring often, until vegetables are softened, 2 to 3 minutes. Add tomatoes; break them up against side of saucepan with a wooden spoon. Add fennel seeds, hot pepper, and thyme. Bring to a boil and cook over medium heat, stirring, until sauce thickens slightly, about 3 minutes. Spoon sauce over fish, covering completely.

3. Cover dish loosely with aluminum foil. Bake 10 minutes, or until fish flakes easily with fork.

Per Serving: Calories: 168   Total fat: 1 g   Saturated fat: 0 g
Cholesterol: 61 mg   Percentage calories from fat: 6%

163 TROUT EN PAPILLOTE WITH LEMON HERBED RICE

Prep: 20 minutes   Cook: 10 to 12 minutes   Serves: 4

These mild-flavored trout fillets are cooked with a savory blend of herbs and julienne vegetables in foil packets.

Butter-flavored cooking
  spray
2 (9-ounce) dressed trout
  (head and tail removed),
  split in half
½ teaspoon salt
¼ teaspoon pepper
1 cup julienned carrot
1 cup julienned zucchini
½ cup julienned leek

2 tablespoons dry white wine
  or vermouth
2 teaspoons fresh lemon juice
1 teaspoon grated lemon zest
1 teaspoon chopped fresh
  thyme leaves or
  ½ teaspoon dried
Lemon Herbed Rice (recipe
  follows)

1. Preheat oven to 425°F. Coat four 15-inch-long pieces of aluminum foil with cooking spray. Place trout, skin side down, in center of foil. Sprinkle with salt and pepper.

2. Divide carrots, zucchini, and leeks evenly over trout. In a small cup, combine wine, lemon juice, and lemon zest. Drizzle over vegetables. Sprinkle with thyme.

3. Bring edges of foil together and crimp foil to seal tightly. Place on a large baking sheet. Bake 10 to 12 minutes, until trout is done and vegetables are crisp-tender. Pierce top of packets to release steam. Open packets and place trout and vegetables on individual serving plates alongside Lemon Herbed Rice. Drizzle liquid remaining in foil packets over all and serve at once.

*Per Serving: Calories: 320   Total fat: 6 g   Saturated fat: 1 g
Cholesterol: 43 mg   Percentage calories from fat: 18%*

164   LEMON HERBED RICE

Prep: 10 minutes   Cook: 18 minutes   Serves: 4 to 6

1 cup converted rice
1 teaspoon grated lemon zest
½ teaspoon salt
2 tablespoons chopped
  parsley

1 tablespoon minced fresh
  chives

1. In a medium saucepan, bring 2⅓ cups water to a boil. Stir in rice, lemon zest, and salt. Cover, reduce heat to low, and cook 18 minutes, or until liquid is absorbed and rice is tender. Remove from heat and let stand, covered, 5 minutes.

2. Fluff up rice with a fork. Add parsley and chives and toss lightly to mix.

Per Serving: Calories: 173   Total fat: < 1 g   Saturated fat: 0 g
Cholesterol: 0 mg   Percentage calories from fat: 1%

165   GRILLED SWORDFISH PROVENÇAL

Prep: 10 minutes   Cook: 11 to 13 minutes   Serves: 4

2 swordfish steaks, ¾ inch
  thick (8 ounces each)
1½ teaspoons extra-virgin olive
  oil
2 tablespoons finely chopped
  garlic
1 medium onion, cut into
  8 wedges

¼ teaspoon fennel seeds,
  crushed
1 (16-ounce) can peeled plum
  tomatoes, liquid reserved
¼ cup slivered fresh basil
  leaves
1 tablespoon slivered
  Kalamata olives

1. Cut each fish steak in equal halves. In a small cup, combine olive oil with 1 tablespoon garlic. Rub over top of the steaks; let stand at room temperature about 15 minutes.

2. Meanwhile, preheat broiler. In a medium saucepan, place remaining 1 tablespoon garlic, onion, fennel seeds, and 2 tablespoons water; cook and stir over medium heat until onion has softened, about 3 to 4 minutes. Add undrained tomatoes, breaking them up against the side of the saucepan with a wooden spoon. Cook, uncovered, over medium heat, until sauce begins to thicken but is still saucy, about 5 to 6 minutes. Keep warm.

3. Broil fish 5 to 6 inches from heat 3 minutes, or until fish begins to brown slightly and flakes easily when tested with a fork. Place on a platter, using a wide spatula. Top with sauce. Sprinkle with basil slivers and olives.

Per Serving: Calories: 183   Total fat: 6 g   Saturated fat: 1 g
Cholesterol: 39 mg   Percentage calories from fat: 30%

166 FRESH TUNA STEAKS WITH PINEAPPLE SALSA

Prep: 5 minutes   Stand: 30 minutes   Cook: 8 minutes   Serves: 4

Aniseed and ginger perk up the flavor of these grilled fish steaks. You can substitute tilefish, salmon steaks, or swordfish for the tuna.

1¼ teaspoons canola oil
1 tablespoon rice wine
   vinegar
2 teaspoons reduced-sodium
   soy sauce
2 teaspoons finely chopped
   ginger

1 teaspoon crushed aniseed
1 teaspoon sugar
2 tuna steaks, cut ¾ inch thick
   (10 to 12 ounces each)
   Pineapple Salsa (recipe
   follows)

1. In a 9 x 11-inch dish, place oil, vinegar, soy sauce, ginger, aniseed, and sugar. Cut each fish steak into 2 equal pieces. Add fish steaks to marinade; turn to coat. Let stand at room temperature 30 minutes, turning once.

2. Preheat broiler. Broil fish 4 inches from heat 4 minutes. With a wide spatula, turn fish over and broil 4 minutes longer, or until fish flakes easily when tested with a fork. Serve topped with pineapple salsa.

*Per Serving: Calories: 264 Total fat: 9 g Saturated fat: 2 g
        Cholesterol: 53 mg Percentage calories from fat: 30%*

167 PINEAPPLE SALSA

Prep: 15 minutes   Cook: none   Chill: 1 hour   Makes: 2 cups

I prefer to make this refreshing salsa with fresh pineapple. You can substitute 2 cups canned pineapple chunks in unsweetened pineapple juice. Drain and reserve 2 tablespoons juice and cut the chunks in half.

2 cups cut up (½-inch cubes)
   fresh pineapple
½ cup chopped red bell
   pepper
2 tablespoons chopped
   scallions

1 tablespoon finely chopped
   cilantro
2 teaspoons finely chopped
   seeded jalapeño pepper
   (optional)
2 teaspoons finely chopped
   fresh ginger

In a medium bowl, combine pineapple, bell pepper, scallions, cilantro, jalapeño pepper, and ginger. Cover and refrigerate at least 1 hour for flavors to mellow.

*Per Serving: Calories: 43 Total fat: < 1 g Saturated fat: 0 g
        Cholesterol: 0 mg Percentage calories from fat: 6%*

Chapter 8

Meatless Main Dishes

One summer, after a hiking trip, long before vegetarianism was in vogue, my younger son announced he was a vegetarian. Being a single parent with a pressure-packed job, I was not too enthusiastic about cooking an additional meal at the end of the day. His decision to eliminate meat and poultry products, but not fish, eggs, and dairy products made meatless cooking doable. I would prepare meals in my usual fashion, but add more complex carbohydrates, such as beans and legumes, grains and pasta. Since our daily diet always included fresh vegetables and fruits and followed a well-balanced diet, I had the situation well under control. Six months after his teenage conversion, he succumbed to the aroma of a roasting chicken, but even today meatless meals are still very much a part of our diet.

This nutritious, low-fat way of eating less meat and more vegetables, beans, grains, and pasta has become more mainstream. And it lends itself to the adventurous tastes of contemporary cooking, which incorporates ingredients from all over the world. Asia, Latin America, and the Middle East all have cuisines with an abundance of meatless dishes. There are as many vegetarian stir-fries as you can imagine. Spicy Vegetables with Tofu served over brown rice is one of them. Italian dishes abound with vegetables, as in my Vegetable Lasagne and Spinach Basil Calzones. Indian cuisine is represented with Curried Sweet Potatoes, Cauliflower, and Green Beans, to be served on a bed of couscous or rice. And Mexican food is full of meatless main dishes that can be assembled in minutes; Cheesy Bean Burritos and Chiles Rellenos Casserole are just two.

A visit to the health food store can be an awesome experience. New fresh foods and frozen ingredients are abundantly displayed. Stock up on a few or shop for ideas. Vegetable Burgers with Sesame Yogurt Sauce is a takeoff on a frozen vegetable burger product. Gather ideas from vegetarian restaurants, vegetarian cookbooks, and magazines. The Grilled Portobello Mushrooms with Papaya Salsa was a recipe idea I gleaned from an upscale vegetarian restaurant in my neighborhood.

Check out other chapters in this book for meatless ideas, and don't skip the desserts. A baked apple, fruit compote, or orzo or tapioca pudding with their fruit sauce toppings add the perfect ending to a meatless low-fat meal.

168 CHEESY BEAN BURRITOS
Prep: 20 minutes   Cook: 20 minutes   Serves: 4

These burritos are quite savory and go together quickly. Check your supermarket or health food store for flavored soft tortillas, such as jalapeño and cilantro or mild chile, which are 98 percent fat-free. You can substitute them for the regular or whole wheat tortillas in this recipe. I like to add a few fresh cilantro leaves to each burrito before rolling them up, as they give a burst of flavor when bitten into.

8 (6-inch) soft regular or whole wheat flour tortillas
1 cup chopped onion
1 (16-ounce) can nonfat refried beans
2 to 3 teaspoons minced seeded jalapeño pepper

1 cup coarsely shredded reduced-fat sharp Cheddar cheese
Cilantro leaves (optional)
3 cups shredded iceberg or romaine lettuce
½ cup bottled chunky medium or hot salsa

1. Preheat oven to 350°F. Stack tortillas and wrap in aluminum foil. Heat 10 minutes, or until hot.

2. Meanwhile, in a medium saucepan, place onion with 2 tablespoons water. Cover and cook over medium-low heat until onion is tender, about 5 minutes. Stir in refried beans and jalapeño pepper. Cook, stirring often, until heated through, 2 to 3 minutes.

3. Spoon a slightly heaping ¼ cup of bean mixture onto lower third of each tortilla. Sprinkle with 2 tablespoons cheese and top with 2 to 3 cilantro leaves. Bring lower edge of tortilla up over filling. Fold ends in and roll up like a jelly roll. Place burritos seam side down on a large baking sheet; cover loosely with foil.

4. Bake burritos 10 minutes, or until heated through. To serve, place ¾ cup lettuce on each serving plate. Top with 2 burritos. Spoon 1 tablespoon salsa over each burrito.

Per Serving: Calories: 334   Total fat: 8 g   Saturated fat: 4 g
Cholesterol: 20 mg   Percentage calories from fat: 21%

169   VEGETABLE BURGERS WITH SESAME YOGURT SAUCE

Prep: 25 minutes (includes cooling time)   Cook: 15 to 16 minutes
Serves: 4

I'm particularly fond of vegetable burgers and will usually order them in vegetarian restaurants. Here is my version, made savory and satisfying with loads of vegetables and black-eyed peas, topped with a lightly spiced sauce.

Vegetable cooking spray
1 teaspoon canola oil
½ pound mushrooms, minced
½ cup shredded carrot
¼ cup minced scallions
1 (16-ounce) can black-eyed peas, drained and mashed well
⅓ cup unseasoned bread crumbs
¼ cup chopped parsley

¼ cup frozen egg substitute, thawed, or 1 egg
¾ teaspoon salt
½ teaspoon dried thyme leaves
¼ teaspoon pepper
4 whole wheat sandwich buns
4 large leaves of lettuce
1 large tomato, sliced
½ cup alfalfa or radish sprouts
Sesame Yogurt Sauce (recipe follows)

1. Coat a large nonstick skillet with cooking spray. Add oil and heat skillet over medium heat. Add mushrooms, carrot, scallions, and 2 tablespoons water. Cook, stirring often, until vegetables are soft and liquid has evaporated, about 7 to 8 minutes. Place vegetables in a large bowl; let cool.

2. Add mashed black-eyed peas, bread crumbs, parsley, egg substitute, salt, thyme, and pepper to vegetables. Mix to blend well. Shape into four 3½-inch patties on a sheet of wax paper.

3. Coat a large nonstick skillet or griddle with cooking spray and heat until hot. Lift patties with a large spatula and place in skillet or on griddle. Cook over medium heat, turning once, until browned on both sides and heated through, about 8 minutes.

4. To serve, slice rolls in half. Place a lettuce leaf on bottom of bun; top with burger, slices of tomato, some sprouts, sesame yogurt sauce, and top of bun.

SESAME YOGURT SAUCE
Makes: about ¾ cup

½ cup nonfat plain yogurt
3 tablespoons tahini (Middle Eastern sesame paste)

2 teaspoons fresh lemon juice
⅛ to ¼ teaspoon cayenne, to taste

In a small bowl, combine yogurt, tahini, lemon juice, and cayenne; stir to combine.

Per Serving: Calories: 401 Total fat: 11 g Saturated fat: 2 g
Cholesterol: 1 mg Percentage calories from fat: 24%

170   BLACK BEAN STEW WITH BUTTERNUT SQUASH AND YELLOW RICE

Prep: 10 minutes   Cook: 17 minutes   Serves: 4

2 teaspoons canola oil
½ cup chopped onion
1 garlic clove, minced
2 cups peeled, diced (½-inch) butternut squash (8 ounces)
½ cup dry sherry
½ cup vegetable or chicken broth
¾ teaspoon ground cumin

¾ teaspoon ground coriander
1 (19-ounce) can black beans, drained and rinsed
2 teaspoons sherry wine vinegar or red wine vinegar
2 tablespoons chopped cilantro
Yellow Rice (page 212)

1. In a large nonstick skillet, heat oil over medium heat. Add onion, garlic, and squash. Cook, stirring occasionally, until onion is golden, about 5 minutes. Add sherry, broth, cumin, and coriander. Reduce heat to medium-low, cover, and simmer 10 minutes, or until squash is tender.

2. Add black beans and sherry wine vinegar to skillet; stir to combine. Cover and simmer 2 minutes longer, or until heated through. Stir in cilantro. Serve over yellow rice.

*Per Serving: Calories: 171   Total fat: 3 g   Saturated fat: 0 g
Cholesterol: 0 mg   Percentage calories from fat: 20%*

171   MEXICAN-STYLE CHILI WITH POLENTA SQUARES

Prep: 15 minutes   Cook: 20 minutes   Serves: 8

There is nothing more welcome than a hot bowl of chili on a blustery evening. This quick-and-easy chili is topped with sautéed polenta squares and Monterey Jack cheese. You can serve the chili over rice if you prefer.

1 teaspoon canola oil
3 cups chopped onions
1 tablespoon minced garlic
2 (16-ounce) cans pinto or kidney beans, liquid reserved
2 (14½-ounce) cans chunky Mexican-style tomato sauce

1½ tablespoons hot Mexican chili powder
2 teaspoons ground cumin
Polenta Squares (recipe follows)
½ cup coarsely shredded reduced-fat Monterey Jack cheese

1. In a large saucepan, heat oil over medium heat. Add onions and garlic. Cook, stirring occasionally, until softened and slightly golden, about 5 minutes.

2. Add beans with their liquid, chunky tomato sauce, chili powder, and cumin; stir to combine. Bring slowly to a boil, reduce heat, and simmer, uncovered, 15 minutes, stirring frequently.

3. To serve, spoon into 8 individual bowls. Top with polenta squares and sprinkle each with 2 tablespoons cheese.

Per Serving: Calories: 258 Total fat: 3 g Saturated fat: 1 g Cholesterol: 5 mg Percentage calories from fat: 11%

---

172 POLENTA SQUARES
Prep: 3 minutes Chill: 30 minutes Cook: 7 minutes Serves: 8

These quickly sautéed polenta squares can be served with chili or as a change of pace from potatoes or rice.

Vegetable cooking spray 1¼ cups yellow cornmeal
½ teaspoon salt

1. Coat a 9-inch square baking pan with cooking spray. In a medium saucepan, bring 2 cups water to a boil with salt. In a small bowl, whisk together 1 cup cold water and cornmeal; gradually stir into boiling water until mixture is smooth. Cook, stirring, until mixture thickens, about 1 minute. Pour into prepared pan and spread evenly. Place in refrigerator to firm up, at least 30 minutes.

2. Remove polenta from refrigerator and cut into 16 squares. Coat a large griddle with cooking spray and heat over medium heat until hot. Add polenta squares, in batches if necessary, and cook, turning, until lightly browned on both sides, about 6 minutes total.

Per Serving: Calories: 80 Total Fat: < 1 g Saturated fat: 0 g Cholesterol: 0 mg Percentage calories from fat: 5%

173   CHILES RELLENOS CASSEROLE   *Make 1/2*
Prep: 12 minutes   Cook: 45 minutes   Serves: 8

Chiles rellenos are large fresh poblano peppers stuffed with cheese, dipped in a batter, and fried. This savory casserole has many of the same flavors, but without all the fat and calories.

Vegetable cooking spray
2 (4-ounce) cans chopped green chiles, drained
1 (8-ounce) can whole-kernel corn, drained
¼ cup finely chopped scallions
1½ cups coarsely shredded reduced-fat sharp Cheddar cheese (6 ounces)

1 ← 2 cups skim milk
1 (8-ounce) container frozen egg substitute, thawed (1 cup) o.- 4 eggs
¼ teaspoon hot Mexican chili powder
1 cup buttermilk baking mix
1 cup 1% low-fat cottage cheese

Loaf Pan.

1. Preheat oven to 350°F. Coat a 9-inch square baking pan with cooking spray. Place green chiles, corn, scallions, and cheese in prepared pan; stir to mix.

2. In a medium bowl, whisk together milk, egg substitute, and chili powder. Add baking mix and whisk just until smooth. Stir in cottage cheese. Spoon over chili-corn mixture in pan.

3. Bake 45 minutes, or until casserole is puffed and a knife inserted near center comes out clean. Serve hot.

*Per Serving: Calories: 198   Total fat: 5 g   Saturated fat: 3 g
Cholesterol: 17 mg   Percentage calories from fat: 24%*

174   GNOCCHI WITH BROCCOLI RABE AND BROWNED GARLIC SLICES
Prep: 5 minutes   Cook: 10 to 12 minutes   Serves: 4

Gnocchi is an Italian dumpling made with flour or semolina and is somewhat oval in shape. I've teamed it with browned garlic slices and broccoli's more assertive cousin, broccoli rabe.

1 bunch (1 pound) of broccoli rabe, tough stems removed, cut into 1-inch lengths
1 (16-ounce) package frozen gnocchi
1 tablespoon extra-virgin olive oil

2 tablespoons thinly sliced garlic
½ teaspoon salt
⅛ to ¼ teaspoon crushed hot red pepper
2 tablespoons grated fresh Parmesan cheese

1. In a large saucepan filled with boiling water, cook broccoli rabe until tender, 8 to 10 minutes. Drain into a colander.

2. Meanwhile, in another large saucepan filled with boiling water, cook gnocchi, without salt or oil, until just tender, about 5 minutes. Ladle out and reserve ⅓ cup cooking water. Drain gnocchi. In a large bowl, combine broccoli rabe and gnocchi; cover to keep warm.

3. In a small skillet, heat olive oil over medium heat. Add garlic and sauté until it is soft and slices begin to brown at the edges, about 2 minutes. Pour mixture over broccoli rabe and gnocchi. Add reserved cooking water, salt, and hot pepper flakes; toss to coat. Sprinkle with Parmesan cheese. Serve at once.

Per Serving: Calories: 315 Total fat: 6 g Saturated fat: 2 g
Cholesterol: 19 mg Percentage calories from fat: 17%

175 SPICY EGGPLANT WITH RICE SPAGHETTI
Prep: 10 minutes   Cook: 30 minutes Serves: 4

Chinese flavors accent this zippy pasta dish. Rice spaghetti and hoisin sauce can be bought in health food stores, in the Asian food section of a supermarket, or in Asian markets. Vermicelli or spaghettini can be substituted for the rice spaghetti.

Vegetable cooking spray
1 medium eggplant ~~Tofu~~
   (1 pound), cut into
   1-inch cubes
2 teaspoons Asian sesame oil
3 tablespoons hoisin sauce
1½ tablespoons reduced-
   sodium soy sauce
2 tablespoons red wine
   vinegar

½ teaspoon sugar
¼ to ½ teaspoon crushed hot
   red pepper
1 garlic clove, minced
2 teaspoons minced fresh
   ginger
2 tablespoons sliced scallions
8 ounces rice spaghetti,
   vermicelli, or spaghettini
   → Use ½.

1. Preheat oven to 450°F. Coat a 10 x 15-inch jelly roll pan with cooking spray. In a large bowl, toss eggplant with sesame oil. Place eggplant in a single layer in prepared pan. Bake 30 minutes, or until eggplant is tender and browned, stirring to turn every 10 minutes.

2. Meanwhile, in a small bowl, combine hoisin sauce, soy sauce, vinegar, sugar, hot pepper, garlic, ginger, and scallions. Stir to mix well.

3. In a large saucepan filled with boiling water, cook pasta, without salt or oil, until tender but still firm, about 15 minutes, 9 to 11 minutes for the vermicelli or spaghettini. Drain and transfer to a large bowl. Add eggplant and sauce to pasta and toss to coat.

Per Serving: Calories: 299 Total fat: 3 g Saturated fat: 0 g
Cholesterol: 0 mg Percentage calories from fat: 8%

176 VEGETABLE LASAGNE

Prep:30 minutes   Cook: 52 minutes   Stand: 10 minutes   Serves: 9

There are many versions of vegetable lasagne. This one uses an oven-ready lasagna noodle, which doesn't have to be cooked before using, and the sauce has spinach added to it.

Vegetable cooking spray
2 teaspoons extra-virgin olive oil
2 cups chopped fresh broccoli
1 cup thinly sliced carrots
1 cup sliced scallions
½ cup chopped red bell pepper
1 tablespoon finely chopped garlic
1 teaspoon dried oregano
1 teaspoon dried basil

1 (16-ounce) container 1% low-fat cottage cheese
1½ cups coarsely shredded part-skim mozzarella cheese
Creamy Spinach Sauce (recipe follows)
12 oven-ready lasagne noodles (from an 8-ounce package)
3 tablespoons grated fresh Parmesan cheese

1. Coat a large nonstick skillet or flameproof casserole with cooking spray. Add olive oil and heat skillet over medium heat. Add broccoli, carrots, scallions, bell pepper, and garlic. Cook, stirring occasionally, until vegetables are softened, about 6 minutes. Add oregano and basil; set aside.

2. Preheat oven to 375°F. Coat a 9 x 13-inch baking pan with cooking spray. Stir cottage cheese and mozzarella into cooled vegetable mixture.

3. Spread ½ cup of spinach sauce on bottom of prepared pan. Place 3 uncooked lasagne noodles over sauce. Top with ¾ cup of sauce, then one-third of vegetable mixture. Repeat layering 2 more times. Cover with remaining pasta. Spread remaining 1 cup spinach sauce over top. Sprinkle with Parmesan cheese. Cover tightly with foil.

4. Bake 45 minutes, or until bubbly hot. Let stand 10 minutes before serving.

*Per Serving: Calories: 272   Total fat: 7 g   Saturated fat: 4 g
Cholesterol: 20 mg   Percentage calories from fat: 24%*

---

177 CREAMY SPINACH SAUCE

Prep: 2 minutes   Cook: 6 minutes   Makes: 4 cups

½ cup flour
3 cups 1% low-fat milk
¼ cup grated Parmesan cheese
½ teaspoon salt
¼ teaspoon pepper
⅛ teaspoon ground nutmeg

1 (10-ounce) package frozen chopped spinach, thawed to room temperature and drained (do not squeeze out liquid)

1. Place flour in a medium saucepan. Gradually stir in milk until mixture is smooth. Cook over medium heat, stirring, until mixture comes to a boil and thickens slightly, about 5 minutes.

2. Add Parmesan cheese, salt, pepper, and nutmeg. Cook, stirring, 1 minute longer. Blend in spinach.

*Per Serving: Calories: 87   Total fat: 2 g   Saturated fat: 1 g
                Cholesterol: 6 mg   Percentage calories from fat: 19%*

---

178   INDIVIDUAL EGGPLANT PARMESAN CASSEROLES

Prep: 26 minutes   Cook: 40 to 45 minutes   Serves: 4

½ cup defatted vegetable or
   chicken broth
½ cup chopped onion
1 garlic clove, minced
1 (1-pound) can whole
   tomatoes, drained, ¼ cup
   juice reserved, tomatoes
   chopped
⅓ cup tomato paste
1 teaspoon dried oregano
1 teaspoon dried basil
1 medium eggplant (1 pound)

1 medium zucchini
   (5 ounces), cut into
   ¼-inch slices
1 cup sliced mushrooms
   (3 ounces)
1 cup 1% low-fat cottage
   cheese, drained
½ cup coarsely shredded part-
   skim mozzarella cheese
¼ cup finely shredded
   Parmesan or Asiago
   cheese

1. In a medium saucepan, place broth, onion, and garlic. Bring to a boil over high heat. Reduce heat to medium-low and simmer, uncovered, until onion is soft, about 5 minutes. Add chopped tomatoes with reserved ¼ cup juice, tomato paste, oregano, and basil. Bring to a boil, reduce heat, and simmer, uncovered, 15 minutes, or until slightly thick but not runny.

2. While sauce cooks, cut eggplant in half lengthwise, then cut crosswise into ½-inch-thick slices. In a large skillet, bring ½ cup water to a boil. Add eggplant, zucchini, and mushrooms. Cover and simmer 10 to 12 minutes, or until vegetables have softened. With a slotted spoon, remove vegetables to paper towels; pat dry.

3. Preheat oven to 350°F. Divide vegetables evenly among individual shallow casseroles or gratin dishes. Spoon ¼ cup cottage cheese over each serving of vegetables. Top each with ¼ cup sauce. Sprinkle 2 tablespoons mozzarella and 1 tablespoon Parmesan cheese over each casserole.

4. Bake 20 to 25 minutes, or until casseroles are heated through and cheese is melted. Serve hot.

*Per Serving: Calories: 202   Total fat: 6 g   Saturated fat: 3 g
                Cholesterol: 15 mg   Percentage calories from fat: 24%*

179 MEATLESS MOUSSAKA

Prep: 20 minutes   Cook: 1 hour 27 minutes to 1 hour 37 minutes
Stand: 10 minutes   Serves: 9

Moussaka is a Greek specialty consisting of eggplant, meat (usually lamb), and a sauce poured over the top, which forms a custardy layer. I've substituted brown rice for the meat and used low-fat substitutes to reduce the fat and calorie counts.

2 teaspoons olive oil	2 medium eggplants (about
1 cup chopped onion	1 pound each), cut
1 garlic clove, minced	crosswise into ½-inch-
1 cup brown rice	thick slices
1 cup tomato sauce	Low-Fat Cheese Sauce
¼ cup chopped parsley	(recipe follows)
1 teaspoon cinnamon	3 tablespoons grated fresh
¾ teaspoon salt	Parmesan cheese
Vegetable cooking spray	

1. In a large nonstick skillet, heat olive oil over medium heat. Add onion and garlic and cook, stirring occasionally, until slightly golden, 4 to 6 minutes. Add rice and cook, stirring, 1 minute. Pour in 2½ cups water. Bring to a boil over high heat. Reduce heat to low, cover, and simmer 35 to 45 minutes, or until water is absorbed and rice is tender. Add tomato sauce, parsley, cinnamon, and salt; mix with a fork to combine.

2. While rice is cooking, preheat broiler. Coat a 10 x 15-inch jelly roll pan with cooking spray. Place eggplant slices on prepared pan; lightly coat with cooking spray. Broil eggplant about 4 inches from heat just until brown, about 3 to 4 minutes. Turn slices over and lightly coat with cooking spray. Continue to broil until brown on second side, 3 to 4 minutes. You may have to do this in two batches. Reduce oven temperature to 375°F.

3. To assemble, coat a 9 x 13-inch baking pan with cooking spray. Place half of eggplant slices in pan. Spread rice mixture evenly over top. Sprinkle with 1 tablespoon Parmesan cheese. Top with remaining eggplant slices. Pour cheese sauce on top and sprinkle with remaining 2 tablespoons Parmesan cheese.

4. Bake 45 minutes, or until bubbly and lightly brown. Let stand 10 minutes before serving.

Per Serving: Calories: 208   Total fat: 4 g   Saturated fat: 1 g
Cholesterol: 5 mg   Percentage calories from fat: 16%

180   LOW-FAT CHEESE SAUCE
Prep: 5 minutes   Cook: 5 minutes   Makes: 4 cups

2 tablespoons flour
1½ cups 1% low-fat milk
½ cup frozen egg substitute,
    thawed

1 (16-ounce) container 1%
    low-fat cottage cheese
¼ teaspoon ground nutmeg
    Salt and freshly ground
    pepper

1. Place flour in a medium saucepan. Gradually stir in milk until mixture is smooth. Cook over medium-low heat, stirring often, until mixture boils and thickens slightly, about 5 minutes. Remove from heat; let cool.

2. Sieve cottage cheese into a medium bowl. Beat in egg substitute until well blended. Stir cottage cheese mixture into cooled milk sauce. Season with nutmeg and salt and pepper to taste.

*Per Serving: Calories: 75 Total fat: 1 g Saturated fat: 1 g
          Cholesterol: 4 mg Percentage calories from fat: 13%*

---

181   VEGETARIAN PICADILLO
Prep: 12 minutes   Cook: 16 to 18 minutes   Serves: 4 to 5

Picadillo is a Latin American meat hash. I've substituted kidney beans for the meat and the combination of sweet and savory flavors is delicious. Although you can serve the picadillo right away, I have found that it mellows upon standing. Make it early in the day or the night before if you prefer. Serve over rice or wrap like a burrito in a large heated flour tortilla.

2 teaspoons vegetable oil
1 cup diced green bell pepper
1 cup diced red bell pepper
½ cup coarsely chopped onion
1 large garlic clove, minced
2 (16-ounce) cans red kidney
    beans, drained and
    rinsed

1 cup tomato sauce
¼ cup currants
½ teaspoon ground cumin
½ teaspoon ground coriander
¼ teaspoon cinnamon
2 tablespoons slivered toasted
    almonds

1. In a large nonstick skillet, heat oil over medium-high heat. Add green and red bell peppers, onion, and garlic. Cook, stirring occasionally, until vegetables are soft, about 8 minutes.

2. Stir in kidney beans, tomato sauce, currants, cumin, coriander, cinnamon, and ½ cup water. Cook over medium heat, stirring occasionally, until heated through and saucy, 8 to 10 minutes. Stir in almonds just before serving.

*Per Serving: Calories: 218 Total fat: 5 g Saturated fat: 0 g
          Cholesterol: 0 mg Percentage calories from fat: 19%*

182 CURRIED SWEET POTATOES, CAULIFLOWER, AND GREEN BEANS

Prep: 20 minutes   Cook: 24 minutes   Serves: 6

As a main course, serve these tasty vegetables with white or brown rice, couscous, or kasha. Top with a dollop of plain nonfat yogurt.

2 teaspoons vegetable oil	¼ teaspoon pepper
½ cup chopped onion	2 cups peeled chunked
½ cup chopped red bell	(1-inch) sweet potatoes
pepper	(12 ounces)
3 tablespoons flour	2 cups cauliflorets (10 ounces)
1 teaspoon curry powder	2 cups sliced (1-inch) fresh
½ teaspoon ground cumin	green beans (8 ounces)
½ teaspoon salt	

1. In a large nonstick skillet, heat oil over medium heat. Add onion and bell pepper. Cook, stirring occasionally, until tender, about 3 minutes. Sprinkle on flour, curry powder, cumin, salt, and pepper. Cook, stirring, 30 seconds.

2. Add sweet potatoes and 2½ cups water to skillet. Reduce heat to medium-low, cover, and simmer 10 minutes. Add cauliflower and green beans, cover, and cook until potatoes are tender and cauliflower and beans are crisp-tender, about 10 minutes.

*Per Serving: Calories: 119   Total fat: 2 g   Saturated fat: 0 g
Cholesterol: 0 mg   Percentage calories from fat: 14%*

---

183 GRILLED PORTOBELLO MUSHROOMS WITH PAPAYA SALSA

Prep: 10 minutes   Cook: 5 minutes   Serves: 4

Portobello mushrooms have a very meaty flavor, and upon occasion, I like to serve them as a main course. You can broil them, grill them on a barbecue, or, as I do, roast them on a stove-top grill.

4 (3- to 4-inch) portobello	1 tablespoon minced fresh
mushrooms, about	garlic
¼ pound each	⅛ teaspoon salt
Olive oil cooking spray	Freshly ground pepper
2 tablespoons balsamic	2 cups mixed salad greens,
vinegar	such as frisée, red oak
2 tablespoons vegetable or	leaf, or mizuna
chicken broth or water	Papaya Salsa (recipe
2 teaspoons extra-virgin olive	follows)
oil	

1. Wipe mushrooms with a damp paper towel. Remove stems and save for another use. Lightly coat a stove-top grill with cooking spray and heat over high heat, or preheat broiler.

2. In a small bowl, combine vinegar, broth, olive oil, garlic, salt, and a generous grinding of pepper. Using a pastry brush, brush both sides of mushrooms liberally with vinaigrette.

3. Grill or broil mushrooms over high heat, turning once, until tender, about 5 minutes. Place mushrooms on a cutting board and cut each into thick diagonal slices, keeping each mushroom together.

4. To serve, place ½ cup greens on each dinner plate. Top with a mushroom, slightly overlapping slices, and spoon ½ cup papaya salsa over each mushroom.

Per Serving: Calories: 117   Total fat: 4 g   Saturated fat: 0 g
Cholesterol: 0 mg   Percentage calories from fat: 25%

---

184   PAPAYA SALSA
Prep: 10 minutes   Cook: none   Chill: 30 minutes   Makes: 2 cups

1½ cups coarsely chopped fresh
    papaya (about ½ large)
¼ cup coarsely chopped red
    onion
¼ cup coarsely chopped red
    bell pepper

1 tablespoon minced seeded
    jalapeño pepper
3 tablespoons minced fresh
    cilantro
1 tablespoon fresh lime juice

In a medium bowl, combine papaya, red onion, bell pepper, jalapeño pepper, cilantro, and lime juice. Stir to mix. Cover and refrigerate at least 30 minutes for flavors to mellow. Drain off liquid before serving.

Per Serving: Calories: 28   Total fat: 0 g   Saturated fat: 0 g
Cholesterol: 0 mg   Percentage calories from fat: 2%

185   TOSTADAS GRANDES
Prep: 15 minutes   Cook: 10 minutes   Serves: 4

Instead of being fried, these tortillas are baked in the oven until crisp. This is somewhat like an open-faced sandwich and salad combination.

4 (8-inch) reduced-fat soft whole wheat flour tortillas
1 (16-ounce) can nonfat refried beans
1 (4-ounce) can chopped jalapeño peppers, drained
½ teaspoon ground cumin

3 cups shredded romaine or iceberg lettuce
½ cup coarsely shredded reduced-fat Monterey Jack cheese
½ cup nonfat sour cream
½ cup diced seeded tomatoes
2 tablespoons sliced scallions

1. Preheat oven to 375°F. Place tortillas on a baking sheet. Bake, turning once, 10 minutes, or until tortillas are dry and crisp.

2. Just before tortillas are done, in a medium nonstick saucepan, place refried beans, jalapeño peppers, and cumin. Heat over low heat, stirring frequently, until hot, 2 to 3 minutes.

3. Divide bean mixture equally and spread over tortillas. Top each with ¾ cup shredded lettuce, 2 tablespoons each of Monterey Jack cheese and sour cream, 2 tablespoons tomato, and a sprinkling of scallions. Serve at once.

Per Serving: Calories: 244   Total fat: 5 g   Saturated fat: 2 g
Cholesterol: 10 mg   Percentage calories from fat: 18%

---

186   BAKED POTATO TOPPED WITH TOMATO, FETA CHEESE, AND RED ONION
Prep: 5 minutes   Cook: 45 minutes   Serves: 4

Here is a hot baked potato with a cool topping that makes a satisfying meatless meal. If time is a problem, you can microwave the potatoes, though neither the flavor nor the texture will be the same.

4 medium-large baking potatoes (about 8 ounces each), scrubbed
½ cup halved small cherry tomatoes
¼ cup finely diced red onion
1 tablespoon coarsely chopped Kalamata olives
1 teaspoon balsamic vinegar

1½ teaspoons extra-virgin olive oil
1 tablespoon chopped parsley
1½ teaspoons finely chopped fresh oregano or ½ teaspoon dried
¼ cup crumbled feta cheese (1½ ounces)

1. Preheat oven to 425°F. Pierce top of potatoes a few times with a fork. Bake 45 minutes, or until soft.

2. In a small bowl, combine cherry tomatoes, red onion, olives, vinegar, olive oil, parsley, and oregano.

3. When potatoes are done, cut an X on top of each. Hold ends with pot holders and squeeze gently toward center to pop open. Fluff with a fork. Top each potato with ¼ cup tomato topping and 1 tablespoon feta cheese. Serve hot.

*Per Serving: Calories: 223   Total fat: 5 g   Saturated fat: 2 g
              Cholesterol: 9 mg   Percentage calories from fat: 19%*

---

187   POTATO TORTILLA
Prep: 15 minutes   Cook: 21 to 24 minutes   Serves: 6

   I first tasted this rustic potato omelet on a trip to Portugal. It was in a picnic basket supplied by the food staff at the posada, or inn, where I was staying. I loved every bite! In Portugal and Spain a *tortilla* is a thick egg omelet, much like a frittata. I've reduced the fat content by using 3 egg whites instead of adding additional whole eggs. The potatoes must be cut paper-thin to cook in the allotted time.

1 tablespoon extra-virgin olive oil	1 small red onion, thinly sliced
1½ pounds all-purpose potatoes, peeled and cut into ⅛-inch slices (3½ cups)	1 teaspoon salt
	⅛ teaspoon pepper
	3 whole eggs
1 large Italian sweet frying pepper, seeded and thinly sliced into rings	3 egg whites

1. In a large cast-iron or heavy nonstick skillet, heat 1½ teaspoons olive oil over medium-low heat. Place half of potatoes in skillet. Top with frying pepper and red onion. Season with ¼ teaspoon salt and half of pepper. Top with remaining potatoes, ¼ teaspoon salt, and remaining pepper. Cover and cook over medium-low heat, turning vegetables occasionally, until potatoes are tender and lightly browned, about 15 minutes.

2. In a large bowl, beat eggs, egg whites, and remaining ½ teaspoon salt. Add potato mixture and mix thoroughly to coat. Wipe out skillet.

3. Add remaining 1½ teaspoons oil to skillet and heat over medium heat. Pour potato-egg mixture into skillet and press potatoes down firmly and evenly. Cook over medium-low heat until bottom of tortilla is brown and top is somewhat set, 3 to 5 minutes. Loosen tortilla from edge of pan. Place a large platter on top and carefully flip over. Slide tortilla back into pan and cook until bottom is brown and eggs are cooked, about 3 to 4 minutes. Cut into wedges to serve. Serve warm or at room temperature.

*Per Serving: Calories: 154   Total fat: 5 g   Saturated fat: 1 g
              Cholesterol: 109 mg   Percentage calories from fat: 28%*

188   GINGERED BROWN RICE PATTIES WITH SWEET-AND-SOUR PINEAPPLE SAUCE

Prep: 12 minutes   Cook: 12 minutes   Serves: 6

This is a good way to use leftover rice. You can purchase raw sunflower seeds at health food stores or use dry-roasted sunflower seeds and add the lesser amount of salt called for in the recipe.

1½ cups cold cooked brown
    rice (without salt or fat)
    (see Note)
½ cup coarsely shredded
    zucchini, squeezed of
    liquid
½ cup coarsely shredded carrot
¼ cup whole wheat flour
1 egg white
1 tablespoon raw or dry-
    roasted sunflower seeds

1 teaspoon minced fresh
    ginger
¼ to ½ teaspoon salt
⅛ teaspoon cayenne
    Vegetable cooking spray
2 teaspoons canola oil
    Sweet-and-Sour Pineapple
    Sauce (recipe follows)
2 tablespoons sliced scallions

1. In a large bowl, combine brown rice, zucchini, carrot, whole wheat flour, egg white, sunflower seeds, ginger, salt, and cayenne. Mix until well blended. Shape into 6 (3 x ¼-inch) patties (⅓ cup each).

2. Coat a large griddle with cooking spray. Using a pastry brush, brush griddle with half of oil and heat over medium heat until hot. Lift half of patties onto griddle with a wide spatula. Cook, turning once, until golden on both sides, about 6 minutes. Remove patties to a serving platter; cover to keep warm. Repeat with remaining oil and patties.

3. Serve patties topped with a spoonful of sweet-and-sour pineapple sauce and a sprinkling of scallions. Place remaining sauce in a sauce boat and pass at the table.

NOTE: *If you don't have cooked rice, cook ½ cup brown rice in 1¼ cups boiling water 35 to 40 minutes, or until water is absorbed and rice is tender; cool.*

Per Serving: Calories: 164   Total fat: 3 g   Saturated fat: 0 g
Cholesterol: 0 mg   Percentage calories from fat: 17%

189   SWEET-AND-SOUR PINEAPPLE SAUCE
Prep: 2 minutes   Cook: 2 minutes   Makes: about 1 cup

¼ cup sugar
4 teaspoons cornstarch
⅔ cup unsweetened pineapple
   juice

¼ cup apple cider vinegar

In a small skillet, combine sugar and cornstarch. Stir in pineapple juice and vinegar. Cook over medium heat, stirring, until sauce boils and thickens, about 2 minutes. Serve warm.

Per Serving: Calories: 21   Total fat: 0 g   Saturated fat: 0 g
Cholesterol: 0 mg   Percentage calories from fat: 0%

190   TOFU BURGERS WITH SPAGHETTI SAUCE
Prep: 15 minutes   Cook: 11 minutes   Serves: 8

You won't miss the meat with this savvy tofu burger. You can also serve this burger in a crusty roll, topped with spaghetti sauce, or with all the trimmings—spinach, tomato slices, shredded carrots, and sprouts.

1 pound soft tofu, finely
   mashed (3 cups)
1 cup seasoned bread crumbs
¼ cup grated fresh Parmesan
   cheese
½ cup finely chopped red bell
   pepper
½ cup finely chopped scallions
1 large garlic clove, minced

¼ cup homemade or canned
   vegetable broth or
   reduced-sodium chicken
   broth
2 to 3 tablespoons yellow
   cornmeal
   Olive oil cooking spray
2 teaspoons olive oil
2 cups jarred low-fat spaghetti
   sauce

1. In a medium bowl, blend together tofu, bread crumbs, and Parmesan cheese with a fork until mixture is crumbly.

2. In a large skillet, place bell pepper, scallions, garlic, and vegetable or chicken broth. Cook and stir over high heat until vegetables are tender and liquid has evaporated, about 3 minutes. Stir into tofu mixture. Shape into 8 (3 x ½-inch-thick) patties. Coat well with cornmeal.

3. Coat a large skillet with cooking spray. Add 1 teaspoon olive oil and heat skillet over medium heat. Sauté half the patties until golden brown and heated through, about 2 minutes on each side. Remove to a serving platter; cover and keep warm. Add remaining teaspoon oil to skillet and sauté remaining patties. In a medium saucepan, heat spaghetti sauce until hot. Spoon sauce over burgers and serve.

Per Serving: Calories: 150   Total fat: 4 g   Saturated fat: 1 g
Cholesterol: 2 mg   Percentage calories from fat: 26%

191   SPINACH BASIL CALZONES
Prep: 22 to 25 minutes   Cook: 16 minutes   Serves: 8

These calzones are hearty and relatively easy to prepare. You will need to make a double recipe of pizza crust. It is important to seal the calzone tightly and coat them thoroughly with the egg substitute to prevent the filling from seeping out during baking.

1 teaspoon extra-virgin
    olive oil
1 large garlic clove, minced
4 cups washed, trimmed, and
    lightly packed spinach
    leaves (6 ounces)
    Olive oil cooking spray
1 (15-ounce) container low-fat
    ricotta cheese
½ cup shredded provolone
    cheese

2 tablespoons finely chopped
    fresh basil leaves or
    2 teaspoons dried
¼ teaspoon salt
¼ teaspoon cayenne
    Double recipe Low-Fat
    Pizza Crust (page 61)
3 to 4 tablespoons egg
    substitute, thawed

1. In a large nonstick skillet, heat olive oil over medium-high heat. Add garlic and cook 30 seconds. Add spinach and cook, stirring often, until spinach is wilted and liquid has evaporated, about 3 minutes; drain. Let cool slightly, then chop.

2. Preheat oven to 425°F. Lightly coat 2 large baking sheets with cooking spray. In a large bowl, combine ricotta, provolone, basil, salt, and cayenne. Stir in spinach; set aside.

3. Cut pizza dough into 8 equal wedges. Working with 1 piece of dough at a time (keep remaining dough covered with a clean kitchen towel to prevent drying out), roll out to a 7-inch round with a lightly floured rolling pin on a lightly floured work surface.

4. Place about ½ cup ricotta filling on lower third of dough. Brush edge of dough lightly with water. Bring top of round over filling to meet edge of dough. Press with fingertips to seal, then press again with tines of a floured fork. Repeat with remaining dough and filling. Lift calzones with a wide spatula and place on prepared baking sheet.

5. Cut 3 small ½-inch slits on top of each calzone to allow steam to escape. Brush thoroughly with egg substitute. Bake 12 minutes, or until lightly golden. Serve warm or at room temperature.

Per Serving: Calories: 356 Total fat: 9 g Saturated fat: 3 g
*   Cholesterol: 14 mg Percentage calories from fat: 21%*

192 SPICY VEGETABLES WITH TOFU
Prep: 20 minutes   Cook: 6 to 7 minutes   Serves: 4

For a milder version of this dish, eliminate the hot pepper flakes. Make sure you have all the ingredients measured out before you begin the recipe, as it takes just minutes to prepare.

¼ cup dry sherry
4 teaspoons cornstarch
2 tablespoons reduced-sodium soy sauce
2 tablespoons cider vinegar
2 teaspoons minced fresh ginger
1 teaspoon sugar
¼ teaspoon crushed hot red pepper
2 teaspoons canola oil
1 cup thinly sliced carrots

1 cup yellow or red bell pepper strips
3 ounces snow peas, trimmed, or 1 cup broccoli florets
½ cup (1-inch) scallion pieces
1 garlic clove, minced
1 (10½-ounce) package 1% fat firm tofu, drained and cut into ¾-inch cubes
½ cup halved water chestnuts
4 cups hot cooked white or brown rice

1. In a small bowl, stir together sherry, cornstarch, soy sauce, vinegar, ginger, sugar, and hot pepper until cornstarch is dissolved and mixture is smooth. Blend in ½ cup water.

2. Heat a large nonstick skillet or wok over high heat. Add oil and swirl to coat pan. Add carrots, bell pepper, snow peas, scallions, and garlic. Stir-fry until vegetables are crisp-tender, 3 to 4 minutes. Push vegetables to one side.

3. Stir soy sauce mixture and add to pan. Cook over medium heat, stirring, until sauce is thickened and bubbly, about 1 minute. Add tofu and water chestnuts. Cook, stirring gently, until heated through, about 2 minutes. Serve over rice.

Per Serving: Calories: 405   Total fat: 4 g   Saturated fat: 0 g
Cholesterol: 0 mg   Percentage calories from fat: 9%

Chapter 9

All Sorts of Salads

When it comes to healthier, lighter eating, salads take center stage. High in fiber, vitamins, and minerals, they can star in any course of the meal—as appetizers, first courses, or accompaniments to lunch or dinner. Made with fish or fowl, beans, pasta, grains, or small amounts of red meat, they become savory satisfying meals in themselves. Laden with fruit, they can double as dessert to satisfy a sweet tooth. This eat-it-anytime, anything-goes food is so versatile, you can serve a salad a day for weeks without repeating the same green, vegetable, or fruit.

The displays of various greens in supermarkets and in open-air markets make for a cast of thousands. Choose from crisp varieties by the head or pound, wrapped in transparent bags or see-through trays, packaged ready-to-use salad mixes, and seasonal fresh herbs—chives, basil, thyme, oregano, tarragon, sage, dill—all fresh for the picking. For variety and interest, look for regional and seasonal favorites—radicchio, red leaf and oak leaf lettuce, arugula, frisée (often called chicory), mâche, and mesclun (a mix of small salad greens and herbs) are just a few. Swiss chard, kale, dandelion, mustard, and beet greens add an unusual flavor touch to salads and provide more calcium, iron, vitamins C and A than their paler varieties.

When creating salads, color and texture become as important as taste. Remember when a tomato was just red and a bell pepper green? Today tomatoes come in red and yellow rounds, oval plums, yellow and red pear-shaped, and tiny rounds. A profusion of colorful peppers—red, green, yellow, orange, and black—offer the potential of an artist's palate. And uncommon fruits, blood orange, Asian pear, carambola (star fruit) share shelf space with kiwi, mango, and papaya.

The salads in this chapter, though, go beyond vegetables. They include pasta, rice, beans, and nutritionally rich whole grains, such as quinoa and barley, which not only add flavor and fiber, but are packed with complex carbohydrates. Broiled and grilled fish, turkey, chicken, and meat add variety, as do canned water-packed seafood, such as tuna and salmon. No wonder these days salads are so exciting to eat.

And here is where you can splurge, providing you don't drench those salads in fatty dressings. Choose flavorful, low-fat salad dressings and add toppings such as cheese, nuts, and seeds sparingly to keep calorie and fat counts down. Buttermilk, low- or nonfat yogurt, skim milk, low-fat tofu, nonfat mayonnaise, and cottage cheese whirled in a blender all provide tastier and healthier substitutes for high-fat creamy dressings.

Chef's Salad is made lighter in fat and calories with fat-free turkey bacon, reduced-fat Swiss cheese, and a yogurt and low-fat mayonnaise-based salad dressing. Creamy Chicken and Apple Salad has a cumin- and coriander-spiked yogurt dressing. Up your fiber and complex carbohydrate intake with bean and grain salads: Bean Salad Olé, Couscous, Zucchini, and Raisin Salad, Quinoa Salad with Lemon and Mint, and Barley Tabbouleh use only one tablespoon of olive oil in their dressings. Creamy Cole Slaw and Herbed New Potato Salad are perfect low-fat accompaniments to any outdoor barbecue.

The array of salad dressings used in specific salads can be mixed and matched with other salads to help you create your own healthier, tasty salad. All you have to do is take a bow.

193   SCALLOP, ORANGE, AND PEPPER SALAD
Prep: 10 minutes   Cook: 4 minutes   Chill: 1 hour   Serves: 4

The subtle flavor of ginger adds just the right touch to this light seafood salad. For a dramatic presentation, serve in barrel-shaped wine goblets.

2 **large navel oranges**
2 **teaspoons canola oil**
1 **tablespoon minced fresh ginger**
1 **pound sea scallops, halved if large**

1 **medium green bell pepper, cut into 1-inch chunks (1 cup)**
4 **large radicchio leaves**

1. With a vegetable peeler, remove thin colored zest from one orange, being careful not to include any white pith. Cut zest into 2 x ⅛-inch strips to equal 2 tablespoons. With a small sharp knife, remove peel and white pith from both oranges; section oranges.

2. In a large nonstick skillet, heat oil over high heat. Add ginger and cook 1 minute. Add scallops and cook 1 minute. Add julienned orange zest and cook, stirring often, until scallops are opaque in center, about 2 minutes. Transfer to a bowl; let cool slightly. Cover and refrigerate scallops and orange sections separately until well chilled, about 1 hour.

3. When ready to serve, add scallops and bell pepper to orange sections. Place a radicchio leaf on each of 4 chilled salad plates or in wine goblets. Mound scallop salad in center of leaf.

Per Serving: Calories: 170   Total fat: 3 g   Saturated fat: 0 g
Cholesterol: 37 mg   Percentage calories from fat: 17%

194   CHEF'S SALAD
Prep: 30 minutes   Cook: 3 to 5 minutes   Serves: 4

An up-to-date version of this classic salad. I've substituted a low-fat turkey bacon and Swiss cheese, added a sweet apple to complement the salad, and used a combination of spinach, romaine, and radicchio for texture and color.

3 slices of French or Italian bread, cut ½ inch thick
1 garlic clove, cut in half
   Vegetable cooking spray
4 slices 95% fat-free turkey bacon, cut in 4 x ¼-inch pieces (½ cup)
6 cups assorted torn greens, such as spinach, romaine, and radicchio

1 small red Delicious apple, cored and cut into chunks
1 cup sliced mushrooms
½ cup slivered red onion
2 ounces reduced-fat Swiss cheese, cut into thin strips (½ cup)
   Lemon Buttermilk Dressing (page 167) or Light Blue Cheese Dressing (recipe follows)

1. Toast bread slices in a toaster or under broiler until lightly browned. Rub both sides with cut garlic. Cut into ½-inch croutons.

2. Coat a nonstick skillet with cooking spray. Add bacon and cook just until curly and lightly browned, 3 to 5 minutes. Drain on a paper towel.

3. Place salad greens in a large bowl. Add apple, mushrooms, red onion, Swiss cheese, and cooked turkey bacon; toss to coat. Sprinkle garlic croutons on top. Use 2 tablespoons salad dressing for each serving.

*Per Serving: Calories: 218   Total fat: 7 g   Saturated fat: 1 g
        Cholesterol: 13 mg   Percentage calories from fat: 27%*

195   LIGHT BLUE CHEESE DRESSING
Prep: 5 minutes   Cook: none   Chill: 1 hour   Makes: about 2¼ cups

Blue cheese dressing is my favorite. This low-fat version is close to the real thing. Silken tofu has a smooth rather than a grainy texture or mouth feel. You can find 1 percent silken tofu at a health food store.

1 cup buttermilk
½ cup nonfat mayonnaise dressing
½ cup nonfat plain yogurt

1½ to 2 ounces crumbled blue cheese (about ½ cup)
1½ teaspoons fresh lemon juice
1 garlic clove, crushed

In a blender, combine buttermilk, mayonnaise, yogurt, blue cheese, lemon juice, and garlic. Whirl until smooth. Place in a bowl. Cover and refrigerate at least 1 hour for flavors to mellow.

*Per Serving: Calories: 16   Total fat: < 1 g   Saturated fat: 0 g
        Cholesterol: 1 mg   Percentage calories from fat: 19%*

196 WARM BEEF AND RICE SALAD WITH WILTED SPINACH AND FETA CHEESE

Prep: 15 minutes   Cook: 21 to 24 minutes   Serves: 4

To make it easier to slice the meat paper-thin here, place the steak in the freezer for about 30 minutes, until it is partially frozen, before cutting it into strips.

1 cup uncooked long-grain rice
1 tablespoon extra-virgin olive oil
1 tablespoon red wine vinegar
½ teaspoon dried oregano
½ teaspoon dried basil
¼ teaspoon pepper
  Olive oil cooking spray
8 ounces boneless top round steak, trimmed and cut crosswise into paper-thin strips

½ cup red onion slivers
1 garlic clove, minced
4 cups slightly packed torn fresh spinach leaves (4 ounces)
2 small ripe tomatoes (8 ounces), each cut in 8 wedges
½ cup halved, seeded cucumber slices (¼-inch)
2 tablespoons crumbled low-fat feta cheese (1 ounce)

1. In a medium saucepan, bring 2 cups water to a boil. Add rice; stir once. Cover and simmer over low heat 18 to 20 minutes, or until water is absorbed and rice is tender.

2. In a small bowl, combine olive oil, vinegar, oregano, basil, and pepper.

3. Coat a large nonstick skillet with cooking spray. Heat skillet over medium-high heat. Add beef, red onion, and garlic; stir-fry until meat turns color and is done, about 2 to 3 minutes. Add herbed vinegar mixture, spinach, tomatoes, and cucumber to skillet. Cook, stirring, just until spinach is slightly wilted and vegetables are warmed, about 1 minute. Remove from heat.

4. To serve, spoon rice on large serving platter. Top with beef mixture; sprinkle with feta cheese. Serve at once.

Per Serving: Calories: 454 Total fat: 8 g Saturated fat: 2 g
Cholesterol: 39 mg Percentage calories from fat: 16%

197 SMOKED CHICKEN AND PEAR SALAD WITH ROSEMARY LIME DRESSING

Prep: 10 minutes   Cook: none   Serves: 4

2 medium pears
2 teaspoons lemon juice
½ pound smoked chicken or
   turkey breast, cut into
   ½-inch dice
2 large celery ribs, finely
   diced
¼ teaspoon salt

⅛ teaspoon pepper
   Rosemary Lime Dressing
   (recipe follows)
¼ pound mesclun (mixed
   baby lettuces) or torn
   Boston lettuce
2 tablespoons coarsely
   chopped walnuts

1. Quarter pears and scoop out cores. Cut pears into ½-inch dice. In a large bowl, toss pears with lemon juice to prevent discoloration.

2. Add chicken and celery to pears. Season with salt and pepper. Add dressing and toss to coat evenly.

3. On a serving platter, make a bed of mesclun. Top with chicken and pear salad. Sprinkle walnuts on top.

*Per Serving: Calories: 163   Total fat: 3 g   Saturated fat: 0 g
Cholesterol: 25 mg   Percentage calories from fat: 18%*

198 ROSEMARY LIME DRESSING

Prep: 5 minutes   Cook: none   Makes: about ⅔ cup

This assertive dressing is delicious with a mixture of greens and fresh fruit, such as pears or apples.

½ cup nonfat plain yogurt
2 tablespoons minced
   scallions
1 tablespoon fresh lime juice
¼ teaspoon grated lime zest

1½ teaspoons chopped fresh
   rosemary or ½ teaspoon
   dried
1 teaspoon honey

In a medium bowl, whisk together yogurt, scallions, lime juice, lime zest, rosemary, and honey. Cover and refrigerate until ready to use.

*Per Tablespoon: Calories: 9   Total fat: < 1g   Saturated fat: 0 g
Cholesterol: 0 mg   Percentage calories from fat: 2%*

199   SALMON AND ASPARAGUS SALAD

Prep: 20 minutes   Cook: 7 to 10 minutes   Serves: 4

You can serve this salmon and asparagus combination warm, at room temperature, or cold, depending upon your taste. Another firm-fleshed fish, such as swordfish or tuna, can be substituted for the salmon.

1 **pound salmon fillet, cut 1 inch thick, or 4 (4-ounce) salmon steaks**
1¼ **pounds fresh asparagus, trimmed**

1 **bunch of watercress, tough stems removed**
Lemon Dill Sauce (recipe follows)

1. Preheat broiler. Broil salmon 4 inches from heat 7 to 10 minutes, just until fish is opaque in center; let cool. If using a salmon fillet, cut into 4 equal pieces.

2. Meanwhile, in a large skillet filled with 1 inch of boiling water, cook asparagus, uncovered, until crisp-tender, 3 to 5 minutes, depending upon thickness of asparagus. Drain and let cool slightly.

3. On 4 dinner plates, arrange salmon and asparagus. Tuck in watercress decoratively. Drizzle some of Lemon Dill Sauce over salads. Serve with remaining sauce on the side.

Per Serving: Calories: 222 Total fat: 7 g Saturated fat: 1 g
Cholesterol: 64 mg Percentage calories from fat: 30%

200   LEMON DILL SAUCE

Prep: 5 minutes   Cook: none   Makes: ½ cup

This sauce is also good over tossed greens, fresh cooked vegetables, or drizzled over a baked potato.

½ **cup nonfat plain yogurt**
¼ **cup nonfat dry skim milk powder**
2 **tablespoons minced fresh dill**
2 **tablespoons fresh lemon juice**

1 **teaspoon finely chopped lemon zest**
1 **tablespoon finely chopped scallions**
Pinch of cayenne

In a small bowl, whisk together yogurt, skim milk, dill, lemon juice, lemon zest, scallions, and cayenne. Cover and refrigerate until serving time.

Per Tablespoon: Calories: 18 Total fat: < 1 g Saturated fat: 0 g
Cholesterol: 1 mg Percentage calories from fat: 2%

201   STEAK AND PEPPER SALAD WITH HORSERADISH ONION SAUCE

Prep: 15 minutes   Cook: 21 minutes   Serves: 4

For year-round preparation, I've given directions for broiling the steak and vegetables here, but, of course, the dish will taste better if you cook them on an outdoor grill. The cooking time will be about the same.

2 teaspoons cracked black pepper	2 large green bell peppers, cut into 3-inch-wide wedges (1 pound)
12 ounces top beef round steak (London broil), cut 1 inch thick, trimmed of all fat	1 large yellow or red onion, cut into 1-inch wedges
¼ teaspoon salt	1 teaspoon olive oil
2 large red bell peppers, cut into 3-inch-wide wedges (1 pound)	Curly endive (frisée) or watercress
	Horseradish Onion Sauce (recipe follows)

1. Preheat broiler. While broiler is preheating, press pepper onto steak; let stand at room temperature 15 minutes. Broil steak 4 inches from heat, turning once, 5 minutes per side for rare or longer to desired doneness. Place steak on a cutting board. Season with salt. Leave broiler on.

2. Place red and green peppers and onion in a large bowl. Add olive oil and toss to coat. Place vegetables on a large baking sheet. Broil 4 inches from heat 6 minutes; turn over. Broil until peppers are soft and slightly blackened, about 5 minutes longer.

3. Slice cooled steak across grain into thin diagonal slices. Arrange steak, peppers, and onion on 4 large dinner plates. Tuck in greens. Serve with Horseradish Onion Sauce or Horseradish Mustard Cream (page 165).

Per Serving: Calories 212   Total fat: 4 g   Saturated fat: 1 g
Cholesterol: 49 mg   Percentage calories from fat: 18%

202   HORSERADISH ONION SAUCE

Prep: 3 minutes   Cook: none   Makes: ½ cup

Try this sauce with grilled chicken or to perk up a mild-flavored fish.

½ cup nonfat plain yogurt	1 tablespoon minced red onion
1½ tablespoons prepared red horseradish	

In a small bowl, whisk together yogurt, horseradish, and red onion. Cover and refrigerate until ready to use.

Per Tablespoon: Calories: 10   Total fat: < 1 g   Saturated fat: 0 g
Cholesterol: 1 mg   Percentage calories from fat: 3%

203 BARLEY TABBOULEH
Prep: 30 minutes   Cook: 12 minutes   Chill: 2 hours   Serves: 4

Nutty grains of pearl barley along with tomatoes, cucumber, and fresh herbs are tossed with tabbouleh dressing to form this refreshing salad.

½ teaspoon salt
1 cup quick-cooking pearl barley
2 large ripe plum tomatoes, cut into large chunks
1 large unpeeled Kirby cucumber, cut into ½-inch dice
⅓ cup finely chopped fresh mint leaves

⅓ cup finely chopped scallions
⅓ cup finely chopped parsley
¼ cup fresh lemon juice
1 tablespoon extra-virgin olive oil
1 tablespoon Dijon mustard
1 teaspoon garlic, crushed through a press

1. In a large saucepan, bring 2 cups water to a boil with salt. Add barley; return to a boil. Reduce heat, cover, and simmer until barley is tender, about 12 minutes. Drain off excess water and rinse briefly under cold water to stop cooking; drain again.

2. In a large bowl, combine cooked barley, tomatoes, cucumber, mint, scallions, parsley, lemon juice, olive oil, mustard, and garlic. Toss to mix. Cover and refrigerate at least 2 hours for flavors to mellow, stirring occasionally. Serve cold.

Per Serving: Calories: 185   Total fat: 4 g   Saturated fat: 1 g
Cholesterol: 0 mg   Percentage calories from fat: 19%

204 CREAMY CHICKEN AND APPLE SALAD
Prep: 10 minutes   Cook: 20 minutes   Chill: 1 hour   Serves: 6

I like to poach chicken with its skin and bones, as they help flavor the meat. Both are then removed, and the broth is frozen for another use. This salad is refreshing and is best eaten the same day it is made.

2 pounds chicken breast halves or chicken thighs, or a combination
1 celery rib with leafy top
1 carrot, chunked
1 thick slice of onion
Pinch of salt and pepper
1 cup nonfat plain yogurt

¼ teaspoon ground cumin
¼ teaspoon ground coriander
1 large flavorful apple, such as Empire or Granny Smith
2 scallions, cut into thin diagonal slices
Red leaf lettuce

1. In a large deep skillet, place chicken, celery, carrot, onion, salt, and pepper. Add water just to cover. Bring to a simmer over medium heat. Reduce heat to low, cover, and simmer until chicken is tender with no trace of pink near bone, about 20 minutes. Let chicken cool in broth until cool enough to handle.

2. Remove skin and bones from chicken and discard. Slice chicken into pieces about ½ inch wide and 2 to 3 inches long. There should be about 3 cups. Strain broth and freeze in containers for another use.

3. In a large bowl, combine yogurt, cumin, and coriander. Mix well. Add chicken, apple, and scallions; toss lightly to coat. Cover and refrigerate at least 1 hour for flavors to mellow. To serve, line 6 large chilled dinner plates with lettuce leaves. Mound salad in center.

Per Serving: Calories: 159   Total fat: 3 g   Saturated fat: 1 g
Cholesterol: 62 mg   Percentage calories from fat: 16%

---

205   PAPAYA GRAPEFRUIT CRAB SALAD
Prep: 30 minutes   Cook: none   Serves: 4

Don't be concerned about the amount of cayenne in the crab salad mixture. Its bite is tempered with the sweet and tart taste of the fruit.

2　medium pink grapefruits	2　tablespoons white wine vinegar
1　large papaya	
¾　pound fresh lump crabmeat, excess liquid squeezed out, or 2 (6-ounce) cans lump crabmeat, drained, rinsed, and squeezed dry	1　tablespoon extra-virgin olive oil
	1½　teaspoons chopped fresh sage or ½ teaspoon dried, crumbled
½　cup chopped celery	¼　teaspoon cayenne
¼　cup minced red onion	Boston lettuce leaves

1. With small sharp knife, remove peel and white pith from grapefruits. Section grapefruit over a bowl to catch juices (reserve grapefruit juice). Peel, halve, seed, and slice papaya. In another bowl, combine crabmeat, celery, and red onion.

2. In a small bowl, whisk together 2 tablespoons of reserved grapefruit juice with vinegar, olive oil, sage, and cayenne. Pour over crabmeat; toss gently to combine.

3. Line a large platter or 4 large chilled dinner plates with lettuce leaves. Arrange papaya slices and grapefruit sections in clusters. Mound crabmeat mixture in center.

Per Serving: Calories: 202   Total fat: 5 g   Saturated fat: 1 g
Cholesterol: 85 mg   Percentage calories from fat: 23%

206   ITALIAN BREAD SALAD
Prep: 15 minutes   Cook: 25 minutes   Serves: 2 to 4

There are many versions of this classic, called *panzanella* in Italy. The salad usually contains old bread that has been softened, usually with tomato and oil. This version uses pita bread and herbs. It will serve 2 as a main course or 4 as a first course.

2 (6-inch) nonfat whole wheat pita rounds
1 garlic clove, halved
1 pound tomatoes, cut into 1-inch chunks
¼ teaspoon salt
½ cup thinly sliced Kirby cucumber

½ cup red onion slivers
1 tablespoon extra-virgin olive oil
1 tablespoon red wine vinegar
1 tablespoon chopped parsley
1 tablespoon thinly shredded fresh mint or basil

1. Preheat oven to 300°F. Split each pita bread horizontally into 2 rounds. Rub each cut side with garlic. Cut each half into 8 wedges. Place pita triangles on a large baking sheet. Bake, turning occasionally, 25 minutes, or until crisp.

2. Place tomatoes in a medium bowl. Season with salt. Add pita triangles and toss to mix. Let stand 10 minutes for bread to soften. Add cucumber and red onion.

3. In a small bowl, whisk together olive oil, vinegar, 1 tablespoon water, parsley, and mint. Pour over salad and toss to coat. Serve immediately.

Per Serving: Calories: 151   Total fat: 5 g   Saturated fat: 1 g
Cholesterol: 0 mg   Percentage calories from fat: 26%

207   SHRIMP AND BEAN SALAD WITH GREEN GODDESS SALAD DRESSING
Prep: 15 minutes   Cook: 5 to 7 minutes   Serves: 6

½ pound green beans, cut into 2-inch lengths
¾ pound large shrimp, shelled and deveined
1 (15-ounce) can cannellini or small white beans, rinsed and drained
1 garlic clove, crushed through a press
¼ teaspoon freshly ground pepper

2 tablespoons fresh lemon juice
2 teaspoons extra-virgin olive oil
Low-Fat Green Goddess Salad Dressing (recipe follows)
Salt
1 large tomato, cut into 6 wedges

1. In a large saucepan of boiling salted water, cook green beans until tender but still firm and bright green, 5 to 7 minutes. Drain and rinse under cold running water; drain well.

2. Meanwhile, bring another saucepan of water to a boil over high heat. Add shrimp and cook until loosely curled, pink, and just opaque throughout, 2 to 3 minutes; drain.

3. In a medium bowl, combine shrimp, white beans, garlic, ⅛ teaspoon pepper, 1 tablespoon lemon juice, and 1 teaspoon olive oil. Toss lightly to mix. Add ½ cup dressing and toss to coat. Mound shrimp and beans in center of a large platter.

4. Toss green beans with remaining lemon juice, olive oil, pepper, and salt to taste. Arrange around shrimp. Garnish platter with tomato wedges and pass remaining Green Goddess Salad Dressing on the side.

Per Serving: Calories: 144   Total fat: 3 g   Saturated fat: 0 g
Cholesterol: 71 mg   Percentage calories from fat: 19%

---

208   LOW-FAT GREEN GODDESS SALAD DRESSING

Prep: 7 minutes   Cook: none   Makes: 1 cup

This dressing is especially good over a seafood salad.

½ **cup nonfat mayonnaise dressing**
½ **cup lightly packed parsley leaves**
2 **tablespoons sliced scallions**

3 **tablespoons tarragon white wine vinegar**
2 **teaspoons anchovy paste**
1 **garlic clove, smashed**
½ **teaspoon dry mustard**

In a food processor or blender, combine mayonnaise, parsley, scallions, vinegar, anchovy paste, garlic, and mustard. Puree until smooth. Transfer to a small bowl. Cover and refrigerate at least 1 hour for flavors to mellow.

Per Tablespoon: Calories: 9   Total fat: < 1 g   Saturated fat: 0 g
Cholesterol: 1 mg   Percentage calories from fat: 10%

209 HOT SPICY TURKEY AND CORN SALAD WITH MARINATED CARROT STRIPS

Prep: 20 minutes   Cook: 4 to 7 minutes   Serves: 4

Thai food is in! This interesting combination of hot and cold flavors uses lean ground turkey instead of beef. Prepare the marinated carrot strips first.

Marinated Carrot Strips
(recipe follows)
6 cups shredded romaine or
iceberg lettuce
1 tablespoon cornstarch
3 tablespoons reduced-
sodium soy sauce
½ cup red wine vinegar

1 teaspoon canola oil
1 tablespoon minced seeded
fresh jalapeño pepper
¼ cup slivered fresh ginger
(1 x ⅛-inch)
1 pound lean ground turkey
1½ cups canned or thawed
frozen corn kernels

1. Prepare marinated carrot strips. Place salad greens on a large platter. Cover and refrigerate.

2. In a small bowl, dissolve cornstarch in soy sauce. Stir in vinegar and set aside.

3. In a large nonstick skillet, heat oil over medium-high heat. Add jalapeño pepper, ginger, and ground turkey. Cook, stirring often, until turkey is no longer pink, 3 to 5 minutes.

4. Stir cornstarch mixture again and add to skillet. Cook, stirring, until sauce boils and thickens slightly, 1 to 2 minutes. Add corn and heat through, about 1 minute. Spoon over greens. Surround with marinated carrot strips. Serve at once.

*Per Serving: Calories: 320   Total fat: 11 g   Saturated fat: 3 g
Cholesterol: 83 mg   Percentage calories from fat: 29%*

210 MARINATED CARROT STRIPS

Prep: 5 minutes   Cook: 2 to 3 minutes   Makes: about 2 cups

You can increase this recipe and serve it as a cold side salad or as part of a vegetable platter.

4 large carrots
½ cup red wine vinegar

2 teaspoons sugar

1. With a vegetable peeler, peel carrots, halve lengthwise, then cut into 2 x ¼-inch strips. In a medium saucepan of boiling salted water, cook carrots 2 to 3 minutes, until bright orange and just slightly softened. Drain and rinse briefly under cold running water.

2. Place warm carrot strips in a small bowl. Add vinegar and sugar; toss to combine. Cover and refrigerate until ready to serve. Drain before serving.

*Per ¼-Cup Serving: Calories: 22   Total fat: < 1 g   Saturated fat: 0 g
Cholesterol: 0 mg   Percentage calories from fat: 3%*

211   SMOKED TURKEY AND SPINACH SALAD WITH HORSERADISH MUSTARD CREAM

Prep: 20 minutes   Cook: none   Serves: 4

This composed salad is the perfect meal for those sultry summer days. To save time, buy shredded red cabbage in the produce section of your supermarket.

6 cups lightly packed torn fresh spinach leaves (about ½ pound)	12 ounces thinly sliced deli-style smoked turkey
2 cups shredded red cabbage	Horseradish Mustard Cream (recipe follows)
1 medium zucchini, thinly sliced	Cracked black pepper

Line 4 chilled dinner pates with spinach. Arrange cabbage and zucchini at opposite ends of plates. Place turkey slices in center. Drizzle on Horseradish Mustard Cream and top with a few grindings of pepper.

Per Serving: Calories: 153   Total fat: 3 g   Saturated fat: 1 g
Cholesterol: 45 mg   Percentage calories from fat: 19%

212   HORSERADISH MUSTARD CREAM

Prep: 3 minutes   Cook: none   Makes: ½ cup

You can also use this dressing as a spread over bread for a meat or poultry sandwich, or as a dip for vegetables.

¼ cup nonfat mayonnaise dressing	2 tablespoons Dijon-style horseradish mustard
¼ cup nonfat plain yogurt	2 to 3 tablespoons skim milk

In a small bowl, whisk together mayonnaise, yogurt, mustard, and milk. Cover and refrigerate until ready to use.

Per Tablespoon: Calories: 14   Total fat: < 0 g   Saturated fat: 0 g
Cholesterol: 0 mg   Percentage calories from fat: 1%

213   BEAN SALAD OLÉ
Prep: 10 minutes   Cook: none   Chill: 1 hour   Serves: 6

1   tablespoon canola oil
1½ tablespoons distilled white
     vinegar
½   teaspoon hot Mexican chili
     powder
½   teaspoon ground cumin
¼   teaspoon salt
⅛   teaspoon cayenne

1   (16-ounce) can red kidney
     beans, rinsed and
     drained
½   cup thinly sliced celery
½   cup diced (½-inch) orange or
     red bell pepper
⅓   cup diced onion

In a large bowl, whisk together oil, vinegar, chili powder, cumin, salt, and cayenne. Add kidney beans, celery, bell pepper, and onion. Toss lightly to mix. Cover and refrigerate at least 1 hour for flavors to mellow. Serve cold or at room temperature.

Per Serving: Calories: 82   Total fat: 3 g   Saturated fat: 0 g
Cholesterol: 0 mg   Percentage calories from fat: 30%

214   BLACK BEAN AND RICE SALAD
Prep: 18 minutes   Cook: 20 minutes   Chill: 2 hours   Serves: 8

As a side salad, this zesty mélange can turn a simple piece of grilled chicken or fish into a complete meal. As a main course for four, serve with corn on the cob and a tomato and avocado salad.

1   cup long-grain white rice
1   (16-ounce) can black beans,
     drained and rinsed
½   cup diced red bell pepper
¼   cup diced red onion
2   tablespoons finely chopped
     cilantro
1   tablespoon minced seeded
     fresh jalapeño pepper

2   tablespoons extra-virgin
     olive oil
1½ teaspoons white wine
     vinegar
1   garlic clove, minced
¼   teaspoon hot Mexican chili
     powder
⅛   teaspoon cayenne

1. In a medium saucepan, bring 2 cups water to a boil over high heat. Add rice and bring back to a boil. Reduce heat to low, cover, and simmer until water is absorbed, about 20 minutes. Place rice in a large wire mesh strainer and rinse briefly under cold water; drain well.

2. Place rice in a serving bowl. Add black beans, bell pepper, red onion, cilantro, and jalapeño pepper. Toss gently to mix.

3. In a small bowl, whisk together olive oil, vinegar, garlic, chili powder, and cayenne. Pour over salad; toss to coat. Cover and refrigerate at least 2 hours for flavors to mellow. Serve cold or at room temperature.

Per Serving: Calories: 151   Total fat: 4 g   Saturated fat: 1 g
Cholesterol: 0 mg   Percentage calories from fat: 23%

215 BROCCOLI JICAMA SLAW WITH LEMON BUTTERMILK DRESSING

Prep: 10 minutes   Cook: none   Serves: 4 to 6

Tangy dressing perks up the flavors of this unusual slaw, flecked with crisp strips of jicama.

3 cups packaged broccoli slaw (8 ounces)	¼ cup chopped fresh dill Lemon Buttermilk Dressing (recipe follows)
1 cup thin strips of jícama (4 ounces)	

1. In a large salad bowl, combine broccoli slaw, jícama, and dill. Toss to mix.

2. Pour dressing over salad and toss until vegetables are evenly coated. Serve at once or cover and refrigerate up to 2 hours before serving.

Per Serving: Calories: 55 Total fat: < 1 g Saturated fat: 0 g
Cholesterol: 2 mg Percentage calories from fat: 9%

216 LEMON BUTTERMILK DRESSING

Prep: 5 minutes   Chill: 1 hour   Makes: ¾ cup

Nonfat dry milk gives this dressing a thicker, creamier consistency than liquid milk would.

½ cup buttermilk	1 tablespoon finely chopped onion
¼ cup nonfat dry skim milk powder	¼ teaspoon sugar
2 tablespoons fresh lemon juice	Pinch of cayenne

In a small bowl, whisk together buttermilk and dry skim milk powder until blended. Stir in lemon juice, onion, sugar, and cayenne. Cover and refrigerate at least 1 hour for flavors to mellow.

Per Tablespoon: Calories: 21 Total fat: < 1 g Saturated fat: 0 g
Cholesterol: 1 mg Percentage calories from fat: 8%

217   GARBANZO BEAN SALAD WITH CREAMY LEMON SPICE DRESSING

Prep: 14 minutes   Cook: none   Chill: 1 hour   Serves: 8

1 (19-ounce) can garbanzo
    beans (chickpeas),
    drained and rinsed
2 large plum tomatoes,
    seeded and diced
1 medium red bell pepper,
    diced (1 cup)
2 tablespoons sliced scallions

2 tablespoons minced parsley
2 tablespoons currants or
    raisins
1 garlic clove, minced
1 teaspoon finely chopped
    fresh ginger
    Creamy Lemon Spice
    Dressing (recipe follows)

In a large bowl, combine garbanzo beans, tomatoes, bell pepper, scallions, parsley, currants, garlic, and ginger. Add dressing and toss to coat. Cover and refrigerate at least 1 hour for flavors to mellow. Serve cold.

CREAMY LEMON SPICE DRESSING
Makes: 1/3 cup

This salad dressing is also great over steamed vegetables, such as artichokes, green beans, and asparagus.

3 tablespoons nonfat plain
    yogurt
2 tablespoons fresh lemon
    juice

2 teaspoons olive oil
½ teaspoon ground turmeric
½ teaspoon ground cumin
½ teaspoon ground coriander

In a small bowl, whisk together yogurt, lemon juice, olive oil, turmeric, cumin, coriander, and 1 tablespoon water. Cover and refrigerate at least 1 hour for flavors to mellow.

*Per Serving: Calories: 82   Total fat: 3 g   Saturated fat: 0 g
                Cholesterol: 0 mg   Percentage calories from fat: 30%*

218   CREAMY COLE SLAW

Prep: 20 minutes   Cook: none   Serves: 8 to 12

You can use half green and half red cabbage for the slaw. You can also substitute Savoy cabbage, which has a slightly nuttier flavor. To save time, buy shredded cabbage in the produce section of the supermarket.

1 pound green or red cabbage or a combination, shredded (about 8 cups)	1 cup nonfat plain yogurt
	2 tablespoons cider vinegar
	2 tablespoons skim milk
½ cup sliced scallions	1 teaspoon celery seeds
½ cup chopped parsley	½ teaspoon salt
½ cup nonfat mayonnaise dressing	⅛ teaspoon white pepper

In a large bowl, combine cabbage, scallions, and parsley. In a small bowl, mix together mayonnaise, yogurt, vinegar, milk, celery seeds, salt, and pepper. Add to cabbage; toss to mix well. Cover and refrigerate until ready to serve. Best if used within 2 days.

Per Serving: Calories: 37   Total fat: < 1 g   Saturated fat: 0 g
Cholesterol: 1 mg   Percentage calories from fat: 4%

219   COUSCOUS, ZUCCHINI, AND RAISIN SALAD

Prep: 15 minutes   Cook: none   Chill: 1 hour   Serves: 6

½ teaspoon salt	¼ cup currants or raisins
1 cup couscous	1 teaspoon finely chopped lemon zest
1 medium (8-ounce) zucchini, quartered lengthwise, then cut crosswise into ¼-inch slices	¼ cup red wine vinegar
	1 tablespoon extra-virgin olive oil
½ cup sliced scallions	¼ teaspoon cayenne
½ cup coarsely chopped red bell pepper	¼ teaspoon ground cardamom
	¼ teaspoon ground coriander

1. In a medium saucepan, bring 1½ cups water to a boil with salt. Stir in couscous. Cover and remove from heat. Let stand until water is absorbed, about 5 minutes.

2. Place couscous in a large bowl. Add zucchini, scallions, bell pepper, currants, and lemon zest. Stir with a fork to mix.

3. In a small bowl, whisk together vinegar, oil, cayenne, cardamom, and coriander. Pour over couscous; stir with a fork to moisten. Cover and refrigerate at least 1 hour for flavors to mellow. Serve cold.

Per Serving: Calories: 165   Total fat: 3 g   Saturated fat: 0 g
Cholesterol: 0 mg   Percentage calories from fat: 14%

220   THAI-STYLE CUCUMBER SALAD ~Kim Chee

Prep: 15 minutes   Cook: 5 minutes   Chill: 3 hours   Serves: 6 to 8

With this spicy side dish, a little goes a long way. It is really more of a fresh pickle than a salad.

2 teaspoons sugar	1 garlic clove, minced
1 teaspoon crushed hot red pepper	2 large (1-pound) cucumbers, preferably European seedless
½ teaspoon salt	
½ teaspoon paprika	1½ teaspoons Asian sesame oil
¼ teaspoon black and red pepper blend or ⅛ teaspoon *each* ground black pepper and cayenne	1 small red onion, cut into thin slivers (1 cup)
	1 tablespoon fresh lime juice

1. In a small bowl, combine sugar, hot pepper, salt, paprika, black and red pepper blend, and garlic. Mix well.

2. Cut cucumbers in half lengthwise, then crosswise into ¼-inch slices, enough to make 4 cups. (If using waxed cucumbers, peel cucumber, cut lengthwise in half, and scoop out seeds before cutting into ¼-inch slices.)

3. In a large nonstick skillet, heat sesame oil over medium-high heat. Add cucumbers and red onion. Cook, stirring often, 2 minutes. Add spice mixture and cook 1 minute. Add lime juice and cook, stirring, until most of liquid is absorbed, about 1 minute. Transfer to a bowl and let cool. Cover and refrigerate at least 3 hours for flavors to mellow. Serve at room temperature.

Per Serving: Calories: 34   Total fat: 1 g   Saturated fat: 0 g
Cholesterol: 0 mg   Percentage calories from fat: 28%

221 POTATO SALAD WITH CHIVE GOAT CHEESE DRESSING

Prep: 10 minutes   Stand: 30 minutes   Cook: 15 to 25 minutes
Serves: 8 to 10

Here is a potato salad that's great as a side dish or part of a buffet table. During the summer months I like to use the walnut-size new potatoes, which I steam, then cut the unpeeled potatoes in quarters.

1¼ **pounds red potatoes or walnut-size red new potatoes**
2 **tablespoons white wine vinegar**
¼ ~~**cup nonfat mayonnaise dressing**~~

¼ **teaspoon salt**
¼ **teaspoon coarsely cracked black pepper**
Chive Goat Cheese Dressing (recipe follows)

Don't need all –
Green onions

1. In a large saucepan of boiling salted water, cook potatoes until tender, 15 to 25 minutes, depending on size. Drain and rinse under cold running water. As soon as potatoes are cool enough to handle, peel off skins. Cut larger potatoes into ¾-inch dice; quarter small new potatoes.

2. Place warm potatoes in a medium bowl. Drizzle with vinegar and toss lightly to coat. Let stand until cool.

3. Add mayonnaise, salt, and pepper and toss lightly to coat. Pour goat cheese dressing over potatoes and toss again to coat. Cover and refrigerate at least 1 hour for flavors to mellow, mixing occasionally. Serve slightly chilled.

CHIVE GOAT CHEESE DRESSING
Makes: ¾ cup

Try this dressing over mesclun (mixed baby lettuces) or sliced ripe tomatoes, or drizzle onto an open-face turkey sandwich.

¼ **cup (2 ounces) fresh goat cheese, such as montrachet**
¼ **cup nonfat or reduced fat (Neufchâtel) cream cheese**
¼ **cup nonfat mayonnaise dressing**

⅓ **cup skim milk**
2 **tablespoons minced chives**
1 **tablespoon minced fresh dill or 1 teaspoon dried**

In a small food processor or blender, place goat cheese, cream cheese, mayonnaise, milk, chives, and dill. Process until smooth. Place in a small bowl. Cover and refrigerate until ready to use.

Per Tablespoon: Calories: 86 Total fat: 1 g Saturated fat: 1 g
Cholesterol: 4 mg Percentage calories from fat: 15%

222 RAVIOLI SALAD WITH SQUASH

Prep: 30 minutes (includes standing time)   Cook: 10 minutes
Chill: 2 hours   Serves: 4 to 6

You can blanch the zucchini and yellow squash if you wish, or leave them raw for the salad. The addition of sun-dried tomatoes adds to the flavor.

⅔ cup sun-dried tomatoes (not packed in oil)
1 (16-ounce) package frozen mini cheese ravioli
1 medium zucchini (8 ounces), cut lengthwise, then crosswise into ¼-inch slices
1 medium yellow squash (8 ounces), cut lengthwise, then crosswise into ¼-inch slices

2 tablespoons finely chopped scallions
2 tablespoons finely chopped parsley
2 teaspoons extra-virgin olive oil
1 tablespoon fresh lemon juice
2 teaspoons white wine vinegar
2 teaspoons Dijon mustard
1 garlic clove, minced
¼ teaspoon salt

1. Bring a large saucepan filled with water to a boil. Remove ½ cup water and place it in a small bowl with sun-dried tomatoes. Let stand 10 minutes to soften tomatoes. Add ravioli to boiling water and cook 8 minutes. Add zucchini and yellow squash. Cook until ravioli are just done and vegetables are crisp-tender, about 2 minutes; drain. Rinse ravioli and vegetables briefly under cold water to stop cooking; drain well. Place in a large bowl.

2. Drain sun-dried tomatoes; pat dry and cut in half. Place in bowl with pasta and vegetables. Add scallions and parsley.

3. In a small bowl, whisk together olive oil, lemon juice, 1 tablespoon water, vinegar, mustard, garlic, and salt. Pour over pasta and toss gently. Cover and refrigerate at least 2 hours for flavors to mellow. Serve cold.

Per Serving: Calories: 363 Total fat: 10 g Saturated fat: 4 g
Cholesterol: 30 mg Percentage calories from fat: 24%

223 TWO-TOMATO PASTA SALAD WITH LOW-FAT PESTO DRESSING

Prep: 10 minutes   Stand: 15 minutes   Cook: 10 to 12 minutes
Serves: 6

6 sun-dried tomato halves
   (not oil-packed)
8 ounces penne, ziti, or elbow
   macaroni

4 large plum tomatoes,
   seeded and cut into
   ½-inch dice
   Low-Fat Pesto Dressing
   (recipe follows)

1. Place sun-dried tomatoes in a small heatproof bowl and cover with boiling water. Let stand 15 minutes, or until soft. Drain and pat dry on paper towels. With kitchen scissors or a sharp knife, cut sun-dried tomato halves into ¼-inch dice.

2. Meanwhile, in a large pot of boiling salted water, cook pasta until tender but still firm, 10 to 12 minutes. Drain and rinse under cold running water until cool. Drain well.

3. In a large bowl, combine pasta with sun-dried tomatoes and fresh plum tomatoes. Toss lightly to mix. Pour dressing over salad and toss until evenly coated. Serve at room temperature.

Per Serving: Calories: 202 Total fat: 1 g Saturated fat: 0 g
Cholesterol: 2 mg Percentage calories from fat: 7%

224 LOW-FAT PESTO DRESSING

Prep: 10 minutes   Cook: none   Makes: 1½ cups

This variation of a pesto sauce uses no oil. Serve it over salad greens as well as over pasta or in a pasta-based salad.

¾ cup nonfat skim ricotta
   cheese
½ cup packed fresh basil
2 tablespoons sliced scallions
1 garlic clove, smashed

¼ cup skim milk
2 tablespoons grated fresh
   Parmesan cheese

In a food processor or blender, combine ricotta cheese, basil, scallions, garlic, milk, and Parmesan cheese. Process until smooth. Place in a small bowl. Cover and refrigerate until ready to use.

Per Tablespoon: Calories: 12 Total fat: < 1 g Saturated fat: 0 g
Cholesterol: 1 mg Percentage calories from fat: 14%

225 QUINOA SALAD WITH LEMON AND MINT

Prep: 10 minutes   Cook: 18 minutes   Chill: 2 hours   Serves: 8 to 9

Quinoa (pronounced *KEEN-wah*), a high-protein, calcium-rich grain, has a crunchy texture and nutty taste. You'll find it in health food stores and in the rice and grain section of many supermarkets. Cook it just like rice.

1   cup quinoa
½   cup finely chopped parsley
¼   cup finely chopped fresh
      mint
⅓   cup sliced scallions
¼   cup currants or raisins
2   tablespoons pine nuts
1   garlic clove, minced

2   teaspoons finely chopped
      lemon zest
2   tablespoons fresh lemon
      juice
¼   teaspoon salt
⅛   teaspoon pepper
1   tablespoon extra-virgin
      olive oil

1. In a medium saucepan, bring 2 cups water to a boil. Add quinoa and bring back to a boil. Reduce heat to low, cover, and simmer until water is absorbed, about 15 minutes. Let cool.

2. Place quinoa in a medium bowl. Add parsley, mint, scallions, currants, pine nuts, garlic, lemon zest, lemon juice, salt, pepper, and olive oil. Toss lightly with a fork to combine. Cover and refrigerate at least 2 hours for flavors to mellow. Serve cold.

*Per Serving: Calories: 110   Total fat: 4 g   Saturated fat: 0 g
                    Cholesterol: 0 mg   Percentage calories from fat: 29%*

226 SOUTHWESTERN GAZPACHO PASTA SALAD

*Prep: 30 minutes   Cook: 7 to 9 minutes   Chill: 2 hours
Serves: 6 to 8*

I'm one of those people who loves gazpacho all year round. Here I've teamed it up with another of my favorite foods—pasta.

8   ounces rotelle, rotini, or
      other spiral pasta
4   medium tomatoes
      (1¼ pounds), seeded and
      coarsely chopped
1   cup peeled, seeded, and
      diced cucumber
½   cup diced green bell pepper

¼   cup diced red onion
¼   cup chopped cilantro
2   tablespoons fresh lime juice
2   tablespoons extra-virgin
      olive oil
1   tablespoon minced seeded
      fresh jalapeño pepper
½   teaspoon salt
¼   teaspoon cayenne

1. In a large saucepan of boiling salted water, cook pasta following package directions until tender but still firm, 7 to 9 minutes. Drain and rinse briefly under cold water; drain again.

2. Place pasta in a large bowl. Add tomatoes, cucumber, bell pepper, red onion, cilantro, lime juice, olive oil, jalapeño pepper, salt, and cayenne. Toss lightly to coat. Cover and refrigerate at least 2 hours for flavors to mellow. Serve cold.

Per Serving: Calories: 179   Total fat: 5 g   Saturated fat: 1 g
Cholesterol: 0 mg   Percentage calories from fat: 24%

---

227   EASY RICE SALAD WITH ZIPPY TOMATO DRESSING

Prep: 10 minutes   Cook: 18 to 20 minutes   Serves: 6

1¼ cups converted white rice
½ teaspoon salt
   Zippy Tomato Dressing
   (recipe follows)
1 medium green bell pepper,
   cut into ¼-inch dice

1 medium red bell pepper, cut
   into ¼-inch dice
1 medium cucumber, peeled,
   seeded, and cut into
   ¼-inch dice

1. In a medium saucepan, bring 2½ cups of water to a boil. Add rice and salt. Cover, reduce heat to low, and cook 18 to 20 minutes, until water is absorbed and rice is tender. Transfer to a large bowl.

2. Pour dressing over hot rice and toss to coat. Let stand about 10 minutes to cool slightly.

3. Add green and red peppers and cucumber to salad and toss to mix. Serve at room temperature or cover and refrigerate until chilled.

ZIPPY TOMATO DRESSING

Makes: about 1 cup

Serve this dressing over mixed greens, or try it with pasta.

1 (6-ounce) can tomato juice
1½ tablespoons red wine
   vinegar
1 tablespoon extra-virgin
   olive oil

1 garlic clove, minced
¼ teaspoon dry mustard
½ teaspoon dried oregano
1 tablespoon minced parsley

In a medium bowl, whisk together tomato juice, vinegar, oil garlic, mustard, and oregano. Stir in parsley. Cover and refrigerate until ready to use.

Per Serving: Calories: 182   Total fat: 3 g   Saturated fat: 0 g
Cholesterol: 0 mg   Percentage calories from fat: 13%

228   SWEET POTATO APPLE RAISIN SLAW

Prep: 15 minutes   Cook: none   Chill: 1 hour   Serves: 8

When I was a kid I adored shredded carrot salad with raisins and walnuts. Here is my version of the same, using shredded raw sweet potatoes. You will be surprised how delicious this salad tastes, and how nutritious it is. Shred the sweet potatoes in a food processor or through the larger holes of a hand grater.

3 cups peeled, coarsely shredded sweet potatoes (about ¾ pound)
2 cups cubed (¾-inch) crisp red apples, such as Empire or red Delicious
¾ cup diagonally sliced celery
½ cup raisins

¼ cup reduced-fat mayonnaise dressing
¼ cup nonfat plain yogurt
1 tablespoon fresh lemon juice
2 tablespoons toasted chopped walnuts (optional)

1. In a large bowl, combine sweet potatoes, apples, celery, and raisins.

2. In a small bowl, blend together mayonnaise, yogurt, and lemon juice; fold into sweet potato mixture. Cover and refrigerate at least 1 hour for flavors to mellow. Just before serving, stir in walnuts, if using. Serve cold.

Per Serving: Calories: 126   Total fat: 3 g   Saturated fat: 0 g
Cholesterol: 0 mg   Percentage calories from fat: 20%

229   MEXICAN FRUIT SALAD WITH CILANTRO DRESSING

Prep: 15 minutes   Cook: none   Serves: 6

This beautiful mélange of fruits with a honey and lime-laced cilantro dressing makes a cool, refreshing first course or an unusual side salad, especially appropriate with spicy foods.

Soft leaf or romaine lettuce leaves
1 large ripe papaya, peeled, halved, seeded, and sliced
2 large pink grapefruits, peeled (no white) and sectioned

2 large kiwi, peeled and sliced
½ pound seedless red or green grapes, or a combination, cut in clusters
Cilantro Dressing (recipe follows)

Line a large chilled platter with lettuce leaves. Arrange papaya, grapefruit, kiwi, and grapes in clusters over lettuce. Drizzle with Cilantro Dressing.

Per Serving: Calories: 135   Total fat: 2 g   Saturated fat: 0 g
Cholesterol: 0 mg   Percentage calories from fat: 12%

230 CILANTRO DRESSING
Prep: 5 minutes   Cook: none   Makes: ½ cup

Try this dressing drizzled over fresh melon wedges, such as honeydew, Crenshaw, or Persian.

2½ tablespoons fresh lime juice
2 tablespoons white wine
    vinegar
3 tablespoons honey

2 teaspoons olive oil
1 tablespoon finely chopped
    cilantro

In a small bowl, whisk together lime juice, vinegar, honey, and olive oil. Stir in cilantro just before serving.

*Per Tablespoon: Calories: 36   Total fat: 1 g   Saturated fat: 0 g
              Cholesterol: 0 mg   Percentage calories from fat: 26%*

231 ORANGE, KIWI, AND JICAMA SALAD
Prep: 20 minutes   Cook: none   Serves: 6

A citrus vinaigrette flavors this delectable salad. I like to serve it with cold chicken, turkey, or seafood. To cut the mint leaves, place in a stack and cut into thin shreds with a knife.

1 small head of leafy green or
    red leaf lettuce, or a
    combination, cleaned and
    separated
3 large navel oranges, peeled
    and cut into ¼-inch slices
3 large kiwi, peeled and cut
    into ¼-inch slices
1 small red onion, thinly
    sliced (1 cup)

1 cup thin strips of jicama
    (2 x ¼-inch)
½ cup orange juice
1½ tablespoons olive oil
1 tablespoon fresh lemon
    juice
2 teaspoons honey
2 tablespoons thinly
    shredded mint leaves

1. On a large platter, arrange lettuce leaves. Arrange oranges, kiwi, red onion, and jicama attractively over greens.

2. In a small bowl, whisk together orange juice, olive oil, lemon juice, and honey. Drizzle some dressing over salad. Sprinkle with mint. Pass remaining dressing on the side.

*Per Serving: Calories: 137   Total fat: 4 g   Saturated fat: 0 g
           Cholesterol: 0 mg   Percentage calories from fat: 23%*

☆232   HERBED NEW POTATO SALAD

Prep: 10 minutes   Cook: 15 to 20 minutes   Chill: 2 hours   Serves: 8

Yogurt takes the place of sour cream in this traditional potato salad laced with herbs.

2 **pounds small new potatoes**
2 **tablespoons red wine vinegar**
1 **cup diagonally sliced celery**
½ **cup scallions**
2 **tablespoons chopped parsley**

⅔ **cup nonfat plain yogurt**
⅔ **cup nonfat mayonnaise dressing**
1 **teaspoon dry mustard**
½ **teaspoon salt**

Add: fresh mint

1. Scrub potatoes well. Place in a large saucepan. Add just enough water to cover. Bring to a boil. Reduce heat and cook at a low boil until potatoes are tender, 15 to 20 minutes. (Test with a skewer to prevent potatoes from splitting.) Drain well.

2. When potatoes are cool enough to handle, cut in halves or quarters, if large. Place in a large bowl. Sprinkle with vinegar; toss to combine. Let stand 10 minutes for potatoes to absorb vinegar, tossing once or twice. Add celery, scallions, and parsley.

3. In a small bowl, mix together yogurt, mayonnaise, dry mustard, and salt. Add to potatoes and toss to coat well. Cover and refrigerate at least 2 hours for flavors to mellow. Serve cold.

*Per Serving: Calories: 122   Total fat: < 1 g   Saturated fat: 0 g
Cholesterol: 0 mg   Percentage calories from fat: 3%*

Chapter 10

Vibrant Vegetables

Vegetables make good nutritional sense. They have little or no fat, are low in calories and sodium and high in fiber, are rich sources of vitamins and other nutrients, and contain no cholesterol. Leading health authorities recommend that everyone should eat three to five servings of vegetables a day as part of a healthy and nutritious diet. A serving consists of one cup of raw leafy vegetables, ½ cup cooked or raw, cut-up vegetables, or ¾ cup vegetable juice. Best of all, as so many of us have discovered, in the trendiest of restaurants, vegetables can be delicious.

The variety of colors, flavors, and textures in the recipes in this chapter should tempt even the most reluctant of vegetable eaters. Low-fat starters like Artichokes with Basil Hollandaise, made with no eggs, could begin the most elegant of meals. And versatile side dishes, such as Glazed Lemon Carrots, Broccoli with Garlic Slivers, and Corn Fritters would pair well with almost any simple chicken or fish.

And who can resist potatoes! This excellent source of complex carbohydrates—the body's best energy source—is perfect eating for any occasion. Old-fashioned favorites with a new twist include Scalloped Potatoes, Buttermilk and Chive Mashed Potatoes, and Chili-"Fried" French Fries. Indian-Spiced Sweet Potato Cakes, Potato Knishes, and Sautéed Plantains with Sweet Spices sample three different ethnic cuisines.

If you are a vegetarian, look closely at this chapter for a mix of recipes that could make up most of a meatless meal.

233 ASPARAGUS WITH LEMON AND TARRAGON

Prep: 15 minutes   Cook: 3 to 5 minutes   Serves: 4

At the height of the asparagus season, this is one of the first recipes I make.

1¼ **pounds fresh asparagus, trimmed**
1½ **teaspoons extra-virgin olive oil**
1 **tablespoon grated lemon zest**

1 **tablespoon minced fresh tarragon or 1 teaspoon dried**
1 **tablespoon fresh lemon juice**
Pinch of sugar

1. In a large skillet, cook asparagus with tips facing one way in 1 inch of boiling water just until crisp-tender, about 3 to 5 minutes; drain. Place asparagus on a serving plate; keep warm.

2. In a small skillet, heat olive oil. Stir in lemon zest, tarragon, lemon juice, and sugar. Spoon over asparagus. Serve warm or at room temperature.

Per Serving: Calories: 27 Total fat: 1 g Saturated fat: 0 g
Cholesterol: 0 mg Percentage calories from fat: 30%

234 GLAZED FRESH BEETS

Prep: 5 minutes   Cook: 38 to 48 minutes   Serves: 4

The sharpness of the vinegar cuts the sweetness of the marmalade in this sweet-sour preparation. If you wish, you can make this with canned beets. Use 2 (16-ounce) cans sliced beets, drained, and eliminate the first step of the recipe.

1 **pound fresh beets, preferably small**
2 **tablespoons orange marmalade fruit spread**

1 **tablespoon cider vinegar**
2 **teaspoons butter**
¼ **teaspoon salt**

1. Cut off all but 1 inch of stems and roots from beets; rinse well. Do not peel. Place beets in a medium saucepan and add water to cover. Bring to a boil, reduce to low, cover, and cook until beets can be pierced easily with a fork, 35 to 45 minutes; drain. When beets are cool enough to handle, slip off skins. Slice beets with a crinkle vegetable cutter or small sharp knife.

2. In same saucepan, place marmalade, vinegar, butter and salt. Cook over medium-low heat, stirring, until marmalade melts, about 1 minute. Add beets and toss to coat. Cook until beets are glazed and hot, about 2 minutes.

Per Serving: Calories: 72 Total fat: 2 g Saturated fat: 1 g
Cholesterol: 5 mg Percentage calories from fat: 24%

235 BRUSSELS SPROUTS WITH LEMON AND DILL

Prep: 15 minutes   Cook: 15 minutes   Serves: 6

1¼ pounds brussels sprouts
2 teaspoons butter
1 to 1½ tablespoons fresh
    lemon juice
2 tablespoons minced fresh
    dill or 1½ teaspoons dried

¼ teaspoon finely chopped
    garlic
¼ teaspoon salt
    Pinch of pepper

1. Cut off bottom stems of sprouts; trim off tough outer leaves and make a tiny crosswise incision at base of each to speed up cooking. Cut large sprouts in half; rinse well.

2. In a steamer basket, place sprouts and steam until tender, about 15 minutes. Transfer to a serving bowl.

3. Add butter, lemon juice, dill, garlic, salt, and pepper to hot brussels sprouts. Toss until butter is melted.

Per Serving: Calories: 49   Total fat: 2 g   Saturated fat: 1 g
Cholesterol: 3 mg   Percentage calories from fat: 24%

236 BROCCOLI WITH GARLIC SLIVERS

Prep: 10 minutes   Cook: 3 to 5 minutes   Serves: 4

Tender broccoli florets heightened with the flavor of browned garlic slices make this a vegetable dish that is sure to be a hit.

1 large bunch of broccoli
    (about 2 pounds)
1½ teaspoons olive oil
2 large garlic cloves, thinly
    sliced

1 tablespoon minced parsley
1 tablespoon chopped fresh
    basil or 1 teaspoon dried
    Lemon wedges

1. Rinse broccoli; remove outer leaves and stalks (save for another use); cut broccoli into 1½-inch florets. Place florets in a steamer basket and steam until crisp-tender, 3 to 5 minutes. Transfer to a serving dish.

2. Meanwhile, in a small nonstick skillet, heat olive oil over medium heat. Add garlic slices and cook just until edges of garlic begin to brown, 1 to 2 minutes. Immediately drizzle over broccoli. Add parsley and basil and toss to mix. Serve hot, with lemon wedges on the side.

Per Serving: Calories: 58   Total fat: 2 g   Saturated fat: 0 g
Cholesterol: 0 mg   Percentage calories from fat: 28%

237   ARTICHOKES WITH BASIL HOLLANDAISE

Prep: 20 minutes   Cook: 22 to 32 minutes   Serves: 6

This mock hollandaise tastes almost like the real thing. You can also refrigerate the sauce and reheat it over simmering water. Try it with asparagus or broccoli as well.

6 **medium artichokes** **Lemon slice** ½ **cup nonfat mayonnaise** **dressing** ½ **teaspoon grated lemon zest**	2 **tablespoons fresh lemon** **juice** **Pinch of cayenne** 1 **tablespoon chopped fresh** **basil or 1 teaspoon dried**

1. Rinse artichokes, trim stems, and remove loose outer leaves. Cut off 1 inch of tops; snip off sharp leaf tips. Brush cut sides with lemon slice. Place in a large saucepan of boiling salted water and cook over medium heat until a leaf pulls out easily, 20 to 30 minutes. Drain artichokes in a colander upside down.

2. In top of a double boiler, whisk 2 tablespoons hot water into mayonnaise. Set over simmering water and cook, stirring, until heated through, about 2 minutes. Stir in lemon zest, lemon juice, cayenne, and basil.

3. To eat: Pull off a leaf and dip base of leaf in sauce. Draw through teeth, eating only tender flesh. Discard rest of leaf. Continue until a cone of young leaves appears. Pull away cone, eating little bits of soft flesh; then scoop out and discard fuzzy white "choke." Eat remaining artichoke heart with a fork and knife, dipping each piece in sauce.

Per Serving: Calories: 45   Total fat: < 1 g   Saturated fat: 0 g
Cholesterol: 0 mg   Percentage calories from fat: 2%

238   SWEET-AND-SOUR RED CABBAGE

Prep: 15 minutes   Cook: 1 hour 5 minutes   Serves: 4 to 6

2 **teaspoons butter** ¾ **cup coarsely chopped onion** 2 **tart green apples, halved,** **cored, and coarsely** **chopped** 6 **cups shredded red cabbage** **(about 1 pound)**	¾ **teaspoon salt** ⅛ **teaspoon pepper** ¼ **cup cider vinegar** 2 **tablespoons firmly packed** **light brown sugar**

1. In a large nonstick saucepan, melt butter over medium heat. Add onion and apples. Cook, stirring occasionally, until apples are tender and onion is lightly browned, about 10 minutes.

2. Add red cabbage, salt, and pepper; toss to combine. Cover and cook over low heat, stirring occasionally, until cabbage is wilted, about 20 minutes.

3. In a small bowl, stir together vinegar and brown sugar until sugar is dissolved. Add to cabbage. Cover and cook over low heat, stirring occasionally, until cabbage is just tender, about 35 minutes.

Per Serving: Calories: 96 Total fat: 2 g Saturated fat: 1 g
Cholesterol: 4 mg Percentage calories from fat: 17%

---

239 INDIVIDUAL CARROT SOUFFLÉS
Prep: 30 minutes   Cook: 1 hour 5 minutes   Serves: 6

For these soufflés, it is preferable to mash the carrots with a fork rather than puree in a food processor as they become too airy. As with all soufflés these should be served as soon as they are removed from the oven, or they will deflate. Serve as a first course or side dish.

8 large carrots (about
   1¼ pounds), peeled
   and thinly sliced
1 small baking potato (about
   6 ounces), peeled and cut
   into ½-inch dice
   Vegetable cooking spray
3 tablespoons flour
1 teaspoon sugar

½ teaspoon salt
¼ teaspoon ground cinnamon
¼ teaspoon grated nutmeg
¼ teaspoon ground ginger
¾ cup 1% low-fat milk
1 tablespoon butter, melted
1 whole egg, separated
1 or 2 egg whites
¼ teaspoon cream of tartar

1. In a large saucepan of boiling water, cook carrots and potato, covered, until very tender, about 20 minutes; drain. Return carrots to saucepan and shake pan over low heat to remove excess moisture, about 30 seconds. Transfer carrots and potato to a bowl and mash well with a fork.

2. Preheat oven to 350°F. Coat six (6-ounce) straight-sided ramekins or custard cups with cooking spray. Place ramekins or custard cups on a 10 x 15-inch jelly roll pan.

3. In a small bowl, whisk together flour, sugar, salt, cinnamon, nutmeg, ginger, and milk until smooth. In a medium saucepan, melt butter over low heat. Gradually whisk milk mixture into butter. Bring to a boil over medium heat, whisking until mixture is thickened and smooth, 2 to 3 minutes. Remove from heat.

4. In a small bowl, beat egg yolk until well blended. Whisk in a small amount of hot milk mixture, then gradually stir yolk mixture back into saucepan. Blend in mashed carrots and potato.

5. In a large bowl with an electric mixer on high speed, beat egg whites with cream of tartar until stiff but not dry, about 2 minutes. Fold into carrot mixture. Spoon mixture into ramekins or custard cups, filling to top. Bake 40 minutes, or until centers are set and soufflés are puffy. Serve at once.

Per Serving: Calories: 121 Total fat: 4 g Saturated fat: 2 g
Cholesterol: 42 mg Percentage calories from fat: 28%

240 CORN FRITTERS
Prep: 15 minutes   Cook: 8 to 12 minutes   Makes: 20

Tempt your family with these tiny no-fry fritters chock-full of corn and scallions. They make a great hot appetizer, dipped in maple syrup, or a fine side dish.

2 **eggs or ½ cup frozen egg substitute, thawed**	¼ **cup finely chopped scallions**
½ **teaspoon salt**	2 **tablespoons flour**
¼ **teaspoon cayenne**	1 **teaspoon baking powder**
2 **cups fresh corn kernels or frozen whole-kernel corn, thawed and drained**	**Vegetable cooking spray**
	Maple syrup (optional)

1. In a medium bowl, beat eggs with salt and cayenne. Stir in corn and scallions. Blend in flour and baking powder.

2. Coat a large nonstick griddle with cooking spray. Heat griddle until a few drops of water dance about. Drop level tablespoons of batter onto griddle. Cook until little holes appear on top and edges of fritter seem set, 2 to 3 minutes. Turn over and cook until brown on second side, 2 to 3 minutes. Remove to a serving platter and cover with foil to keep warm. Repeat with remaining batter, stirring often. Serve drizzled with maple syrup, if desired.

Per Fritter: Calories: 26 Total fat: 1 g Saturated fat: 0 g
Cholesterol: 21 mg Percentage calories from fat: 29%

---

241 GLAZED LEMON CARROTS
Prep: 15 minutes   Cook: 11 to 13 minutes   Serves: 6

This carrot dish is a family favorite. Be sure to remove the lemon slices immediately after cooking to prevent the carrots from becoming bitter.

1 **package (1 pound) baby carrots or 1 pound carrots, peeled and cut into ¼-inch diagonal slices**	2 **teaspoons butter**
	2 **thin slices lemon**
	2 **tablespoons firmly packed light brown sugar**

1. In a large nonstick skillet, bring 2 cups water to a boil over high heat. Add carrots and return to a boil. Reduce heat to medium-low and cook, uncovered, until carrots are firm-tender, about 8 minutes; drain well.

2. In same skillet, melt butter over medium heat. Return carrots to pan. Add lemon slices. Sprinkle with brown sugar and toss to coat. Cover, reduce heat to low, and cook, stirring once or twice, until carrots are lightly glazed, about 3 to 5 minutes. Remove lemon slices and serve while hot.

Per Serving: Calories: 60 Total fat: 1 g Saturated fat: 1 g
Cholesterol: 3 mg Percentage calories from fat: 20%

242   SAUTÉED PLANTAINS WITH SWEET SPICES
Prep: 5 minutes   Cook: 7 to 9 minutes   Serves: 4

Use plantains that are yellow and speckled with brown spots; you want the sweetness, not the starch of green plantains. Serve as a side dish with poultry or meat, as part of a vegetarian meal, or as a hot hors d'oeuvre.

2 **yellow plantains (about**	¼ **teaspoon ground cloves**
12 ounces)	2 **teaspoons butter**
½ **teaspoon grated nutmeg**	1 **teaspoon canola oil**
½ **teaspoon cinnamon**	

1. Peel plantains and slice into ¼-inch diagonal slices. Place plantain slices in a large plastic bag with nutmeg, cinnamon, and cloves. Shake well to coat.

2. In a large nonstick skillet, melt 1 teaspoon butter with ½ teaspoon oil over medium-high heat. Add half of the plantains (preferably in a single layer) and cook until golden brown and tender, turning once, about 3 to 4 minutes. Remove to a serving plate; cover and keep warm. Repeat with remaining butter, oil, and plantain slices. Serve hot.

Per Serving: Calories: 97   Total fat: 3 g   Saturated fat: 1 g
Cholesterol: 5 mg   Percentage calories from fat: 29%

243   GREEN BEANS WITH WATER CHESTNUTS
Prep: 20 minutes   Cook: 11 to 15 minutes   Serves: 6

For a change, try green beans with an oriental flavor. If you like spicy food, use the higher amount of hot pepper flakes, or more to your taste.

2 **teaspoons canola oil**	1½ **pounds fresh green beans,**
1 **teaspoon minced fresh**	**trimmed and cut into**
ginger	**2-inch lengths**
1 **teaspoon minced garlic**	¼ **teaspoon salt**
¼ **cup slivered red onion**	⅛ **to ¼ teaspoon crushed hot**
1 **(8-ounce) can sliced water**	**red pepper, to taste**
chestnuts, drained and	
rinsed well	

1. In a wok or large skillet, heat oil. Add ginger and garlic; stir-fry 1 minute. Add red onion and water chestnuts; stir-fry 2 to 3 minutes. Remove to a bowl.

2. Add green beans, salt, hot pepper, and ¼ cup water to same wok or skillet. Cover and cook over medium-high heat until crisp-tender, 7 to 10 minutes. Return onion and water chestnuts to pan. Stir-fry 1 minute longer, or until all liquid has evaporated.

Per Serving: Calories: 58   Total fat: 2 g   Saturated fat: 0 g
Cholesterol: 0 mg   Percentage calories from fat: 24%

244 SZECHUAN EGGPLANT
Prep: 15 minutes   Cook: 10 to 11 minutes   Serves: 4

Eggplant has an affinity for oil, sopping it up like a sponge, so stir-fried Szechuan eggplant is ordinarily beyond low-fat eating. But tossing the vegetable with just a little bit of oil and then cooking it in a nonstick skillet coated with vegetable cooking spray retains the flavor while it reduces the amount of fat.

1 medium eggplant (about 1¼ pounds)	⅛ teaspoon crushed hot red pepper
2 teaspoons canola oil	Vegetable cooking spray
1½ tablespoons reduced-sodium tamari or soy sauce	2 teaspoons minced fresh ginger
½ teaspoon sugar	1 garlic clove, minced
	1½ teaspoons cornstarch mixed with 1 tablespoon water

1. Cut unpeeled eggplant into 2 x ½ x ½-inch strips. Place in a large bowl. Add oil and toss gently to coat. In a small bowl, combine tamari, sugar, hot pepper, and ¼ cup water.

2. Coat a large nonstick skillet with cooking spray; heat skillet. Add ginger and garlic and cook until garlic is softened and fragrant, about 1 minute. Add eggplant. Cook, tossing, until eggplant softens, 3 to 4 minutes.

3. Sir in tamari mixture. Cover and cook over low heat until eggplant is tender, about 5 minutes. Stir cornstarch mixture and stir into skillet. Raise heat to medium and bring to a boil, stirring until sauce is smooth and thickened, about 1 minute.

Per Serving: Calories: 67 Total fat: 2 g Saturated fat: 0 g
Cholesterol: 0 mg Percentage calories from fat: 30%

245 LEMON CRUMBED PARSNIPS
Prep: 15 minutes   Cook: 10 to 13 minutes   Serves: 4

This root vegetable is almost always overlooked. It has a natural sweetness when fresh, but can get woody if too old.

2 tablespoons fresh bread crumbs	2 teaspoons butter
1 pound parsnips, trimmed, peeled, and cut into 2 x ¼-inch strips	1 tablespoon fresh lemon juice
	1 tablespoon minced cilantro, parsley, or mint

1. In a small dry skillet, toast bread crumbs over medium-low heat, stirring often, until lightly browned and crisp, 2 to 3 minutes.

2. In a steamer basket, steam parsnips until crisp-tender, about 3 minutes.

3. In a large nonstick skillet, melt butter over medium heat and cook until butter begins to turn nut brown in color, about 2 minutes. Add the cooked parsnips and toss to coat. Cook, stirring once or twice, until parsnips begin to brown slightly, 3 to 5 minutes. Add lemon juice, bread crumbs, and cilantro, toss, and serve.

Per Serving: Calories: 94   Total fat: 2 g   Saturated fat: 1 g   Cholesterol: 5 mg   Percentage calories from fat: 20%

246   CARROT-STUFFED TWICE-BAKED POTATOES
Prep: 30 minutes   Cook: 60 to 67 minutes   Serves: 4

Carrots are whipped into mashed baked potatoes, mounded into the potato shells, and baked again. You can make these up ahead of time and refrigerate them. Just add 10 minutes more to the second baking, or heat in a microwave. Make sure the carrots are very tender when cooked, so they will mash up smoothly with the potatoes.

4 medium baking potatoes (about 6 ounces each)	1 teaspoon salt
1½ cups peeled and thinly sliced carrots	¼ teaspoon pepper
¼ cup nonfat sour cream	Pinch of grated nutmeg
	2 teaspoons butter, melted

1. Preheat oven to 450°F. Scrub potatoes well and dry. Pierce with a fork in several places. Place potatoes directly on oven rack. Bake 50 to 55 minutes, or until tender.

2. Meanwhile, in a large saucepan, cook carrots in boiling water to cover until tender, 15 to 20 minutes. Drain, reserving cooking water.

3. Cut a thin lengthwise slice off top of each potato. Scoop out pulp, leaving a ¼-inch-thick shell. Place potatoes and carrots in a bowl and mash until smooth. Add sour cream, salt, pepper, and nutmeg. Whip until light and fluffy, adding 1 to 2 tablespoons of reserved cooking water.

4. Spoon potato-carrot mixture into potato shells, mounding generously, or use a large pastry bag fitted with a rosette tip. Place potatoes in a shallow baking dish just large enough to hold them. Drizzle with melted butter. Bake 10 to 12 minutes, or until potatoes are heated through.

Per Serving: Calories: 183   Total fat: 2 g   Saturated fat: 1 g   Cholesterol: 5 mg   Percentage calories from fat: 11%

247 DOUBLE CRANBERRY ROASTED ONIONS

Prep: 15 minutes   Cook: 2¼ to 2¾ hours   Serves: 6

The caramelized onion halves with a tart cranberry topping are fabulous with roast turkey or pork.

Vegetable cooking spray
3 large red onions (10 ounces each and about 3½ inches in diameter)
¾ cup fresh or frozen cranberries
¼ cup dried cranberries
⅓ cup sugar

1 tablespoon balsamic vinegar
⅛ teaspoon salt
⅛ teaspoon pepper
2 teaspoons butter, melted
2 tablespoons coarsely chopped pecans

1. Preheat oven to 350°F. Coat a 10 x 15-inch jelly roll pan with cooking spray.

2. Cut unpeeled onions lengthwise in half. Arrange cut sides down in a single layer in baking pan. Roast, uncovered, 2 to 2½ hours, or until onions are soft to the touch and nicely browned on bottom.

3. Meanwhile, in a small bowl, combine fresh and dried cranberries, sugar, and vinegar; let stand, stirring occasionally, 2 to 2½ hours.

4. Turn onions cut sides up. Season with salt and pepper. Drizzle each onion half with ½ teaspoon melted butter. Add pecans to cranberry mixture and spoon with juices over caramelized onions. Cover loosely with foil and return to oven. Bake 15 minutes longer, or until cranberry mixture is hot.

*Per Serving: Calories: 151   Total fat: 3 g   Saturated fat: 1 g
            Cholesterol: 3 mg   Percentage calories from fat: 19%*

248 POTATO VEGETABLE LATKES
Prep: 18 minutes   Cook: 42 minutes   Serves: 8

Latkes is a Yiddish word for pancakes. These potato pancakes have zucchini and carrots added to them, along with a touch of rosemary. Serve as an accompaniment to meat, poultry, or fish. A food processor is a great help in shredding the vegetables. To save cooking time, use two skillets. The above time reflects the use of one cooking pan.

2 large all-purpose potatoes (1 pound), peeled, coarsely shredded, and squeezed dry (see Note)
1 medium zucchini, coarsely shredded
2 large carrots, peeled and coarsely shredded
½ cup chopped scallions or onion

1 tablespoon finely chopped garlic
2 eggs
⅓ cup flour
1½ teaspoon salt
¼ teaspoon pepper
¼ teaspoon crumbled rosemary
Vegetable cooking spray
1 tablespoon olive oil

1. Preheat oven to 250°F. In a large bowl, place shredded potatoes, zucchini, carrots, chopped scallions, garlic, eggs, flour, salt, pepper, and rosemary. Mix until thoroughly combined.

2. Coat a large griddle or skillet with cooking spray. Heat griddle until a few drops of water dance about. Brush griddle lightly with olive oil. Drop vegetable mixture by measuring tablespoonfuls onto griddle and flatten to 2½-inch rounds. Cook over medium heat until golden on both sides, about 6 minutes total, turning once. Place on a large baking sheet and keep warm in oven. Repeat with remaining vegetable mixture, lightly brushing griddle with olive oil each time.

NOTE: *To prevent potatoes from discoloring, place in a bowl filled with cold water until ready to use; squeeze dry before adding to remaining ingredients.*

Per Serving: Calories: 100 Total fat: 4 g Saturated fat: 0 g
Cholesterol: 52 mg Percentage calories from fat: 29%

249   CHILI-"FRIED" FRENCH FRIES
Prep: 15 minutes   Cook: 40 minutes   Serves: 4

If you love French fries the way I do, this alternative to "frying" by baking the potatoes in the oven with a tiny bit of oil is a satisfying substitute.

1½ **pounds large baking**
   potatoes, scrubbed well
2 **teaspoons Mexican-style**
   chili powder

2 **teaspoons olive oil**
½ **teaspoon coarse (kosher) salt**

1. Preheat oven to 475°F. Place a 10 x 15-inch jelly roll pan in oven while preheating.

2. Cut unpeeled potatoes lengthwise into ½-inch slices; then cut each slice lengthwise into ½-inch-thick strips. Place potatoes in a large bowl and toss with chili powder. Add olive oil and toss again. Place in a single layer on hot baking sheet.

3. Bake 20 minutes. Turn potatoes over and continue baking 20 minutes longer, or until crisp and brown. Sprinkle with salt and serve hot.

Per Serving: Calories: 157 Total fat: 3 g Saturated fat: 0 g
Cholesterol: 0 mg Percentage calories from fat: 15%

250   LEMON PARSLEYED NEW POTATOES
Prep: 5 minutes   Cook: 10 to 20 minutes   Serves: 6

New potatoes can be found during the spring and summer months. I usually get them at the farmers' market. If you can find baby yellow potatoes, substitute them for the red ones. The potatoes can also be steamed.

1½ **pounds small new red**
   potatoes or baby yellow
   potatoes, scrubbed
2 **teaspoons butter**
1 **tablespoon lemon juice**

½ **teaspoon grated lemon zest**
1 **tablespoon chopped parsley**
½ **teaspoon salt**
⅛ **teaspoon pepper**

1. Place potatoes in a large saucepan with enough cold water just to cover. Bring to a boil over high heat. Reduce heat to medium-low, cover, and cook until tender, 15 to 20 minutes for red potatoes or 10 to 15 minutes for baby yellow potatoes; drain. Place in a serving bowl.

2. In a small skillet, melt butter. Stir in lemon juice, lemon zest, parsley, salt, and pepper. Pour over potatoes and toss gently to coat. Serve hot.

Per Serving: Calories: 104 Total fat: 1 g Saturated fat: 1 g
Cholesterol: 3 mg Percentage calories from fat: 13%

251   SCALLOPED POTATOES
Prep: 15 minutes   Cook: 1 hour   Serves: 6

This comfy potato dish is one of my favorites. I had to stop myself from eating the whole thing! Substituting a low-fat milk for the whole milk reduces the fat content considerably.

Vegetable cooking spray
3 tablespoons flour
½ to ¾ teaspoon salt
⅛ to ¼ teaspoon pepper
3 cups peeled and thinly
    sliced all-purpose
    potatoes (2 to 3 medium,
    about 1¼ pounds)

½ cup diced onion
1½ teaspoons butter
1½ cups 1% low-fat milk,
    heated to scalding

1. Preheat oven to 350°F. Coat a 1-quart baking dish with cooking spray.

2. In a small cup, combine flour, salt, and pepper. Layer one-third of potatoes on bottom of baking dish. Sprinkle with half of flour mixture. Sprinkle half of onion on top. Top with another third of potatoes, then remaining flour mixture and onion. Top with remaining potatoes. Dot with butter. Pour scalded milk over all.

3. Bake, uncovered, 1 hour, or until sauce is bubbly and thick and potatoes are tender. Let stand 10 minutes before serving.

Per Serving: Calories: 114   Total fat: 2 g   Saturated fat: 1 g
Cholesterol: 5 mg   Percentage calories from fat: 15%

252   WHIPPED RUTABAGA
Prep: 10 minutes   Cook: 40 minutes   Serves: 6

Rutabagas are plentiful during the fall and winter months. When purchasing, buy small to medium-sized rutabagas, as the larger ones tend to get woody.

2 pounds rutabaga, peeled
    and cut into 1-inch cubes
1½ teaspoons salt
1 teaspoon sugar

1 tablespoon butter
3 to 4 tablespoons buttermilk
¼ teaspoon ground nutmeg

1. In a medium saucepan, combine rutabaga with enough cold water to cover. Bring to a boil over high heat. Add salt and sugar. Reduce heat to medium-low and cook at a low boil, with lid slightly ajar, until fork-tender, about 40 minutes; drain well.

2. Whip rutabaga with an electric mixer or puree rutabaga in a food processor with the butter, buttermilk, and nutmeg until fluffy and smooth.

Per Serving: Calories: 69   Total fat: 2 g   Saturated fat: 1 g
Cholesterol: 6 mg   Percentage calories from fat: 28%

253 SPINACH WITH RAISINS AND PINE NUTS
Prep: 20 minutes   Cook: 6 to 7 minutes   Serves: 6

Anchovy paste gives this savory side dish extra zest, but if you don't tell, no one will realize it's there.

2 **pounds fresh spinach**	1 **teaspoon olive oil**
2 **tablespoons pine nuts**	¼ **teaspoon anchovy paste**
1 **garlic clove, minced**	⅓ **cup golden raisins**

1. Trim tough stems from spinach. Rinse leaves thoroughly; do not shake off water. Place spinach in a large nonreactive saucepan. Cover and cook over medium heat just until spinach begins to wilt but is still bright green, about 3 minutes.

2. In a small skillet, toast pine nuts over medium-high heat, shaking pan often, until golden, 1 to 2 minutes; place in a small cup. In same skillet, cook garlic in olive oil over medium heat until golden, about 2 minutes. Immediately remove from heat and stir in anchovy paste, raisins, and pine nuts.

3. Place spinach in a large bowl. Pour pine nut mixture on top and toss gently to combine. Serve warm or at room temperature.

Per Serving: Calories: 71 Total fat: 3 g Saturated fat: 0 g
Cholesterol: 0 mg Percentage calories from fat: 29%

254 GARLIC ROASTED POTATOES
Prep: 10 minutes   Cook: 1 hour   Serves: 8

Vegetable cooking spray	½ **teaspoon salt**
3 **pounds medium baking**	¼ **teaspoon freshly ground**
potatoes, scrubbed and	**cracked black pepper**
cut into ½-inch slices	1 **tablespoon chopped fresh**
1 **tablespoon extra-virgin**	**parsley**
olive oil	
1 **head garlic, cloves lightly**	
crushed and peeled	

1. Preheat oven to 375°F. Coat a 10 x 15-inch jelly roll pan with cooking spray.

2. In a large bowl, combine potatoes, olive oil, garlic, salt, and pepper. Toss to coat potatoes with oil. Place on baking sheet. Coat potatoes with cooking spray.

3. Bake 1 hour, or until potatoes are golden and tender, turning a few times. Coat potatoes with cooking spray halfway through baking. Place in a serving dish. Sprinkle on parsley and toss lightly to combine. Season with additional salt and pepper to taste.

Per Serving: Calories: 172 Total fat: 3 g Saturated fat: 0 g
Cholesterol: 0 mg Percentage calories from fat: 15%

255 ORANGE-BAKED ACORN SQUASH
Prep: 10 minutes   Cook: 1 hour   Serves: 4

2 small acorn squash (about ¾
    pound each)
1 teaspoon butter, melted
1 cup orange juice

2 teaspoons sugar
⅛ teaspoon cinnamon
¼ teaspoon salt

1. Preheat oven to 400°F. Cut squash lengthwise in half. Scoop out and discard seeds and stringy fibers. Lightly brush cut sides of squash with melted butter. Arrange cut side down in a shallow baking dish just large enough to hold squash. Pour ¾ cup orange juice into baking dish.

2. Bake 30 minutes, basting top of squash with pan juices occasionally.

3. In a small bowl, combine remaining ¼ cup orange juice with sugar and cinnamon. Turn squash over and season lightly with salt. Spoon 1 tablespoon spiced orange juice into each half. If orange juice in baking dish has evaporated, pour ½ cup water into pan.

4. Bake 30 minutes longer, or until squash is tender, basting occasionally.

*Per Serving: Calories: 96   Total fat: 1 g   Saturated fat: 1 g
      Cholesterol: 3 mg   Percentage calories from fat: 9%*

256 HONEY-GLAZED SHALLOTS
Prep: 15 minutes   Cook: 25 to 30 minutes   Serves: 4

Try to get shallots all the same size for even cooking, and use a large enough skillet to hold them in a single layer.

1 pound shallots
2 teaspoons butter
1 tablespoon honey
⅛ teaspoon salt
  Pinch of pepper

1 cup homemade or canned
    reduced-sodium chicken
    broth
1 tablespoon chopped parsley
1 tablespoon chopped fresh
    mint

1. Trim root ends and tips from shallots. Remove papery brown skins.

2. In a large nonstick skillet, melt butter over medium heat. Stir in honey. Add shallots, salt, and pepper. Pour in chicken broth and bring to a simmer. Cook, uncovered, shaking pan several times, until shallots are tender and almost all of liquid has evaporated to glaze, 25 to 30 minutes. Stir in parsley and mint.

*Per Serving: Calories: 112   Total fat: 3 g   Saturated fat: 1 g
      Cholesterol: 5 mg   Percentage calories from fat: 18%*

257   SPAGHETTI SQUASH WITH HONEYED ONIONS
Prep: 8 minutes   Cook: 36 to 41 minutes   Serves: 6

Spaghetti squash is sometimes called vegetable spaghetti, because the strands, when cooked, resemble spaghetti. Here caramelized onions and honey are tossed with the strands.

1 **(2-pound) spaghetti squash**
1 **cup thinly sliced onion**
1 **tablespoon butter**

2 **tablespoons honey**
¼ **teaspoon salt**

1. In a large saucepan, cook squash, covered, in boiling water until tender, 25 to 30 minutes. Remove from water and let cool slightly. Cut in half lengthwise. With a spoon, scoop out and discard seeds and loose fibers. With a fork, comb out the spaghetti-like strings of flesh from each half until only shell remains. Place strands in a large bowl; cover to keep warm.

2. In a large skillet, cook onions in butter over medium-low heat, stirring occasionally, until golden, about 10 minutes. Stir in honey and salt. Cook 1 minute longer, or until bubbly. Pour over squash. Toss with forks to combine. Serve at once.

Per Serving: Calories: 84   Total fat: 3 g   Saturated fat: 1 g
Cholesterol: 5 mg   Percentage calories from fat: 26%

258   POTATO KNISHES
Prep: 30 minutes   Cook: 15 minutes   Bake: 1 hour   Serves: 6

Potato knishes usually have a dough wrapped around them. I've eliminated this coating, but the taste is the same. Serve them with deli mustard.

1½ **pounds all-purpose potatoes, peeled and cut into 1-inch cubes**
  Vegetable cooking spray
2 **teaspoons vegetable oil**

¾ **cup finely chopped onion**
¼ **cup frozen egg substitute, thawed**
1 **teaspoon salt**
¼ **teaspoon pepper**

1. Place potatoes in a large saucepan with enough cold water to cover. Bring to a boil over high heat. Reduce heat to medium and cook 15 minutes, or until potatoes are tender.

2. While potatoes are cooking, preheat oven to 350°F. Coat a large baking sheet with cooking spray. Heat oil in a nonstick skillet. Add onion and cook, stirring frequently, until onion is lightly browned, about 10 minutes.

3. Drain potatoes. Return to saucepan and mash with a fork until smooth. Add browned onion, egg substitute, salt, and pepper. Stir until well mixed. Shape potato mixture into 6 rounds about 2½ inches in diameter and 1 inch thick. Place on baking sheet. Lightly coat rounds with cooking spray.

4. Bake 30 minutes. Turn knishes over and lightly coat tops with cooking spray. Bake 30 minutes longer, or until lightly browned. Serve hot.

*Per Serving: Calories: 101 Total fat: 3 g Saturated fat: 0 g
Cholesterol: 0 mg Percentage calories from fat: 22%*

---

259   GINGERED SWEET POTATO GALETTE
Prep: 22 minutes   Cook: 1 hour   Serves: 8

Vegetable cooking spray
2 pounds sweet potatoes
1 tablespoon canola oil
1 tablespoon butter, melted

¾ teaspoon salt
⅛ teaspoon pepper
1 tablespoon finely chopped candied ginger

1. Preheat oven to 400°F. Generously coat a 9-inch pie plate with cooking spray.

2. Peel potatoes and thinly slice with a food processor fitted with a slicer blade, a mandoline, or cut potatoes paper-thin with a sharp knife. Place potatoes in a large bowl. Add oil, melted butter, salt, and pepper; toss to coat well.

3. Arrange one-third of sweet potato slices in prepared pie plate in a slightly overlapping concentric circle, starting from center. Sprinkle half of candied ginger over sweet potatoes. Repeat with half of remaining sweet potatoes and remaining ginger. Top with remaining potato slices. With palm of hand, press down on potatoes to fit them firmly into pan. Coat a piece of foil large enough to cover dish with cooking spray. Cover potatoes with foil, sprayed side down, and secure tightly. Weight down with another pie plate or flat, heavy lid.

4. Bake 30 minutes. Remove weight and foil. Bake 30 minutes longer, or until sweet potatoes are tender and brown on bottom and top. Using mitts, carefully place a large, flat serving platter over top of pie plate; flip over and shake slightly. If some potatoes should stick to bottom of pie plate, use a wide spatula to remove them and replace over top of galette.

*Per Serving: Calories: 123 Total fat: 4 g Saturated fat: 1 g
Cholesterol: 4 mg Percentage calories from fat: 27%*

260   INDIAN-SPICED SWEET POTATO CAKES

Prep: 10 minutes   Stand: 30 minutes   Cook: 12 minutes
Makes: 8

Minted yogurt provides a lovely contrast to these sweet potato cakes. You can also serve them as an hors d'oeuvre, snack, or first course. Allow one per serving.

Vegetable cooking spray
½ cup chopped onion
½ cup chopped green bell
   pepper
1 teaspoon salt
1 teaspoon curry powder
½ teaspoon ground coriander
½ teaspoon ground cumin
½ teaspoon turmeric
¼ teaspoon cayenne

2 (15- to 16-ounce) cans sweet
   potatoes, drained and
   mashed
3 to 4 tablespoons yellow
   cornmeal
1 cup nonfat plain yogurt
2 tablespoons chopped mint
   leaves or 1½ teaspoons
   dried

1. Coat a large nonstick skillet with cooking spray and heat pan over medium heat. Add onion and pepper and cook until soft but not brown, about 5 minutes. Stir in salt, curry powder, coriander, cumin, turmeric, and cayenne. Cook, stirring, 1 minute. Blend in sweet potatoes. Remove from heat and let stand 30 minutes.

2. Place cornmeal on a sheet of wax paper. Shape sweet potato mixture into 8 patties about 2½ inches in diameter and ½ inch thick (⅓ cup). Coat well with cornmeal.

3. Coat a large nonstick skillet with cooking spray and heat pan over medium heat. Add patties to skillet and cook over medium-low heat, turning, until golden on both sides, about 3 minutes per side.

4. In a small bowl, stir together yogurt and mint. Serve with sweet potato cakes.

Per Serving: Calories: 141   Total fat: 1 g   Saturated fat: 0 g
Cholesterol: 1 mg   Percentage calories from fat: 6%

261   SAUTÉ OF PEAR TOMATOES
Prep: 5 minutes   Cook: 3½ to 5½ minutes   Serves: 6

During the summer, tiny pear-shaped tomatoes are in plentiful supply at farmers' markets, roadside stands, and in specialty food stores. You can also use red or yellow cherry tomatoes in this recipe.

1½ teaspoons extra-virgin olive oil	2 tablespoons minced cilantro, basil, or parsley
2 garlic cloves, minced	⅛ teaspoon salt
3 cups tiny red and yellow pear tomatoes, cherry tomatoes, or a combination	⅛ teaspoon pepper Herbed Sourdough Croutons (recipe follows)

1. In a large nonstick skillet, heat olive oil over medium-low heat. Add garlic and cook 30 seconds.

2. Add tomatoes to skillet. Increase heat to medium and cook, shaking pan frequently, just until skins begin to burst, 3 to 5 minutes. Sprinkle with cilantro, salt, and pepper. Add croutons, toss, and serve at once.

*Per Serving: Calories: 37   Total fat: 1 g   Saturated fat: 0 g
Cholesterol: 0 mg   Percentage calories from fat: 29%*

---

262   HERBED SOURDOUGH CROUTONS
Prep: 5 minutes   Cook: 12 minutes   Makes: 1 cup

These croutons can also be served over a salad or sprinkled into a bowl of soup.

1 cup diced (½-inch) sourdough bread (1¼ ounces)	½ teaspoon dried marjoram, basil, and/or oregano
1 garlic clove, crushed through a press	

1. Preheat oven to 350°F. In a heavy-duty plastic bag, combine bread cubes, garlic, and marjoram. Close bag and shake vigorously to coat bread cubes.

2. Place bread cubes in a 9-inch pie plate in a single layer. Bake 12 minutes, or until light golden and crisp.

*Per ¼-Cup Serving: Calories: 26   Total fat: < 1 g   Saturated fat: 0 g
Cholesterol: 0 mg   Percentage calories from fat: 10%*

263   OVEN-ROASTED VEGETABLES
Prep: 25 minutes   Cook: 30 minutes   Serves: 6

I like to serve these vegetables with game hens or over rice with a sprinkling of Parmesan cheese.

2 medium red bell peppers, quartered and seeded
2 medium green bell peppers, quartered and seeded
½ pound small button or cremini mushrooms, wiped clean and trimmed
½ pound small white boiling onions, papery skins removed and onions halved

½ teaspoon salt
¼ teaspoon pepper
2 teaspoons extra-virgin olive oil
1 garlic clove, minced
1 tablespoon fresh lemon juice
1 tablespoon minced parsley

1. Preheat oven to 450°F. In a large bowl, place red and green bell peppers, mushrooms, and onions. Add salt, pepper, olive oil, and garlic; toss to coat. Spread out vegetables in a single layer on a 10 x 15-inch jelly roll pan.

2. Roast 20 minutes. Sir vegetables to turn over. Reduce oven temperature to 400°. Sprinkle lemon and parsley over vegetables. Roast 10 minutes longer, stirring once, until vegetables are tender and lightly browned.

Per Serving: Calories: 51   Total fat: 2 g   Saturated fat: 0 g
Cholesterol: 0 mg   Percentage calories from fat: 28%

264   SAUTÉED SPRING VEGETABLES
Prep: 20 minutes   Cook: 8 minutes   Serves: 6 to 8

These delicate spring vegetables are lightly sautéed and tossed with a lime-parsley gremolata. I like to serve this with grilled chicken.

2 teaspoons grated lime zest
1 teaspoon minced garlic
2 tablespoons minced parsley
1 tablespoon olive oil
½ cup red onion slivers
½ pound thin asparagus spears, trimmed and cut into 2-inch lengths
2 or 3 medium carrots, peeled and cut into thin strips

1 small red bell pepper (6 ounces), cut into thick strips
2 small zucchini (½ pound), cut into thick strips
2 small yellow squash (½ pound), cut into thick strips
4 ounces cremini mushrooms, halved
2 teaspoons fresh lime juice

1. In a small bowl, combine lime zest with garlic and parsley. Set gremolata aside.

2. In a large deep nonstick skillet or flameproof casserole, heat olive oil over medium-high heat. Add red onion, asparagus, carrots, and bell pepper. Cook, stirring frequently, 3 minutes.

3. Add zucchini, yellow squash, and mushrooms. Cook, stirring frequently, until vegetables are crisp-tender and mushrooms are softened, about 5 minutes. Sprinkle with lime juice. Top with lime gremolata, toss gently, and serve.

Per Serving: Calories: 59   Total fat: 2 g   Saturated fat: 0 g
Cholesterol: 0 mg   Percentage calories from fat: 30%

---

265   DOMATES DOLMASI
Prep: 30 minutes   Cook: 52 to 65 minutes   Serves: 4

Stuffed tomatoes in the Turkish style make a wonderful first course, side dish, or colorful addition to a buffet. These are good hot or at room temperature.

¾ cup long-grain white rice	¼ teaspoon cinnamon
4 large, firm, ripe tomatoes	⅛ teaspoon pepper
(about 8 ounces each)	2 tablespoons toasted
Vegetable cooking spray	pine nuts
1 tablespoon olive oil	2 tablespoons chopped
½ cup chopped scallions	parsley
1 garlic clove, minced	2 tablespoons chopped fresh
¼ cup currants or raisins	mint
½ teaspoon salt	

1. In a medium saucepan, bring 1½ cups water to a boil. Add rice, cover, and cook over low heat until rice is tender and liquid has been absorbed, 15 to 18 minutes.

2. Meanwhile, cut a thin slice from top of each tomato; reserve slices. Scoop out pulp from tomatoes into a sieve set over a bowl to catch juices. Set tomato shells upside down on paper towels to drain. Discard seeds from tomato pulp; chop pulp and reserve.

3. Preheat oven to 375°F. Coat an 8-inch square pan with cooking spray. Heat olive oil over medium heat while rice is cooking. Add scallions and garlic; sauté until soft, about 2 minutes. Stir in currants, salt, cinnamon, pepper, and 2 tablespoons of reserved tomato juice. Remove from heat. Stir in tomato pulp, cooked rice, pine nuts, parsley, and mint.

4. Arrange tomato shells upright in prepared pan. Spoon equal amounts of rice filling into shells, mounding slightly; top each with a reserved tomato slice. Bake 35 to 45 minutes, or until filling is hot and tomatoes have softened.

Per Serving: Calories: 389   Total fat: 7 g   Saturated fat: 1 g
Cholesterol: 0 mg   Percentage calories from fat: 16%

266 TOMATO FANS
Prep: 5 minutes   Cook: 13 minutes   Serves: 4

Vegetable cooking spray
2 large firm, ripe tomatoes
   (8 ounces each)
¼ cup plain fine dry bread
   crumbs

2 tablespoons chopped
   cilantro or parsley
1 teaspoon olive oil
   Pinch of cayenne

1. Preheat oven to 400°F. Coat a 9-inch pie plate or other shallow baking dish with cooking spray.

2. Place uncored tomatoes upside down on work surface. With a small sharp knife, cut tomatoes in half, then cut each half into 3 to 4 slices to within ⅛ inch of core. Press cut side of tomatoes with palm of hand to fan out slightly. Place tomato fans, cut side up, in prepared pie plate.

3. In a small cup, combine bread crumbs, cilantro, olive oil, cayenne, and 1 teaspoon water. Stir to moisten. Sprinkle over top of tomatoes.

4. Bake 12 minutes, or until tomatoes are hot and have softened slightly. Place dish under broiler and broil about 1 minute, or until crumbs brown; watch carefully to prevent burning.

Per Serving: Calories: 62   Total fat: 2 g   Saturated fat: 0 g
Cholesterol: 0 mg   Percentage calories from fat: 28%

267 MINTED ZUCCHINI WITH GOLDEN RAISINS
Prep: 10 minutes   Cook: 6 to 7 minutes   Serves: 4

This recipe can also be made with yellow summer squash, or try teaming the two squashes together for an attractive color combination.

1½ teaspoons olive oil
1 pound zucchini, trimmed
   and thinly sliced
¼ cup golden raisins

2 tablespoons chopped fresh
   mint
¼ teaspoon salt
   Pinch of freshly ground
   pepper

1. In a large dry nonstick skillet, toast walnuts over medium-low heat, shaking pan frequently, until lightly browned and fragrant, about 1 to 2 minutes. Remove to a small bowl.

2. In the same skillet, heat walnut oil over medium-high heat. Add zucchini and cook, stirring often, until crisp-tender, about 5 minutes. Add walnuts, raisins, mint, salt, and pepper, toss, and serve.

Per Serving: Calories: 52   Total fat: 2 g   Saturated fat: 0 g
Cholesterol: 0 mg   Percentage calories from fat: 29%

Chapter 11

Healthful Beans, Grains, and Rice

Most of us want to eat less fat. As a result we are rediscovering more unusual, versatile, and convenient ways to use beans, grains, and rice in a healthy, low-fat diet. Since ancient times, these foods have been an economical staple for most of the world. Now they are achieving the recognition and appreciation they deserve.

Beans, grains, and rice are exceptional sources of complex carbohydrates. All three are rich in dietary fiber for bulk and water-soluble fiber, which helps the body lower cholesterol levels, an important aid in a low-fat diet.

Beans are high in protein; when eaten with rice or a grain, 30 percent more protein is released. Beans, rice, and grains each lack one of the eight essential amino acids; combining beans with rice or a grain makes them a complete protein. You can also substitute beans for meat, but, again, they must be combined with a grain or corn, or a small amount of meat, fish, poultry, or eggs to be "complete." The trio is also rich in the B vitamins—thiamine, riboflavin, B6, and niacin, iron, zinc, and calcium. All are low in sodium and except for soy beans, virtually fat-free.

Dried beans need to be rehydrated by soaking in water before being cooked. For convenience and to save time, in this chapter I've used canned beans, which simply need to be rinsed and drained before using. Recipes such as Garbanzo Beans with Escarole and Fennel, White Beans Italian Style, and Cowboy Beans use some of the more popular beans: garbanzos, also called chickpeas; cannellini beans, which are white kidney beans; and pinto beans. The high-protein Japanese adzuki bean is used to flavor Adzuki Beans with Small Shells, a complete meal in itself, and the flat fava bean creates substantial Fava Beans with Broccoli and Red Pepper.

A low-fat, healthier diet has also spurred an interest in rice. We all know of white rice, converted (parboiled) rice, instant rice, and wild rice, which is really a wild grass. Now we are using more brown rice and including aromatic rices (such as basmati, Texmati, and jasmine rice) in our diet. Short-grain rice, such as Italian Arborio, used in making risottos, is also gaining in popularity. In this collection, these specialty rices are featured in Brown Rice Pilaf with Wild Mushrooms, Basmati and Wild Rice with Almonds and Raisins, and Risotto Milanese.

You'll also find recipes using quinoa (KEEN-wah), the ancient Incan grain; grits, the Southern favorite that is a coarsely ground cornmeal; and an old-world grain and one of my favorites, kasha, or buckwheat groats.

268   ADZUKI BEANS WITH SMALL SHELLS

Prep: 8 minutes   Cook: 28 to 30 minutes
Serves: 4 as a main dish; 8 as a side dish.

Adzuki, sometimes spelled azuki, are very small, oval-shaped, russet-colored beans with a thin white line down the side. They have been a staple in Japan and China for thousands of years and have been called the "King of Beans." They are a very high source of protein. You can usually find them in health food stores or in Asian markets.

1⅓ cups small shells or ditalini
2 teaspoons olive oil
½ cup coarsely chopped green bell pepper
1 tablespoon finely chopped garlic
1 (16-ounce) can whole tomatoes, drained, ½ cup juice reserved
¼ teaspoon crushed hot red pepper

1 (16-ounce) can adzuki beans, rinsed and drained
2 tablespoons slivered fresh basil leaves
2 tablespoons chopped parsley
¼ cup finely shredded Asiago cheese

1. In a medium saucepan filled with boiling water, cook pasta, without adding salt or oil, until tender but still firm, about 12 minutes; drain.

2. Meanwhile, in a medium saucepan, heat olive oil over medium heat. Add bell pepper and garlic. Cook, stirring occasionally, until vegetables are soft, 3 to 5 minutes.

3. Add tomatoes, reserved ½ cup tomato juice, and hot pepper. Breaking up tomatoes with a wooden spoon, bring to a boil over high heat. Reduce heat and simmer, uncovered, 10 minutes, stirring occasionally.

4. Stir in adzuki beans, basil, and parsley. Cook until beans are heated through, about 2 minutes, stirring occasionally. Stir in hot cooked pasta. Spoon into shallow serving bowls and sprinkle with Asiago cheese.

Per Serving: Calories: 304 Total fat: 5 g Saturated fat: 2 g
Cholesterol: 5 mg Percentage calories from fat: 15%

269 BLACK BEANS WITH FETA CHEESE

Prep: 20 minutes   Cook: none   Chill: 1 hour   Serves: 6

2 (16-ounce) cans black beans,
    rinsed and drained
½ cup diced red onion
2 tablespoons finely chopped
    fresh mint
2 tablespoons finely chopped
    parsley

¼ cup fresh lemon juice
2 teaspoons extra-virgin olive
    oil
1 garlic clove, minced
2 ounces crumbled feta cheese
    (¼ cup)

In a large bowl, combine black beans, red onion, mint, and parsley. In a small bowl, whisk together lemon juice, olive oil, 1 tablespoon water, and garlic. Pour over beans and mix to combine. Fold in feta. Cover and refrigerate at least 1 hour for flavors to mellow. Serve cold or at room temperature.

Per Serving: Calories: 131 Total fat: 4 g Saturated fat: 2 g
Cholesterol: 2 mg Percentage calories from fat: 29%

270 COWBOY BEANS

Prep: 15 minutes   Cook: 2 hours 9 minutes   Serves: 12

This bean dish reminds me of the baked beans that were served at "Aggie" Day during my college years at the University of Arizona.

2 slices of lean hickory-
    smoked bacon, cut into
    ¼-inch dice
2 cups chopped onions
½ cup chopped green bell
    pepper
1 tablespoon minced garlic
2 teaspoons ground cumin

3 (16-ounce) cans pinto
    beans, drained
1 (15-ounce) can tomato puree
1 (16-ounce) jar medium-hot
    enchilada sauce
½ cup firmly packed dark
    brown sugar

1. Preheat oven to 325°F. In a large heavy saucepan, cook bacon over medium heat until crisp, about 4 minutes. With a slotted spoon, remove to paper towels. Pour off all but 1 teaspoon drippings.

2. Add onions, bell pepper, garlic, and cumin to saucepan. Cook over medium heat, stirring occasionally, until vegetables are soft, about 5 minutes. Add pinto beans, tomato puree, enchilada sauce, brown sugar, and cooked bacon; stir to combine.

3. Spoon beans into a 3-quart casserole. Bake, uncovered, 2 hours. Stir before serving.

Per Serving: Calories: 148 Total fat: 1 g Saturated fat: 0 g
Cholesterol: 1 mg Percentage calories from fat: 8%

271   WHITE BEANS ITALIAN STYLE
Prep: 5 minutes   Cook: 10 minutes   Serves: 4

Try serving these savory white beans with a grilled garlic- and rosemary-scented lamb chop.

2 teaspoons extra-virgin olive oil	1 (19-ounce) can cannellini beans, rinsed and drained
2 garlic cloves, minced	¼ teaspoon salt
½ teaspoon crumbled dried sage leaves	⅛ teaspoon pepper
1 (16-ounce) can whole peeled tomatoes, coarsely chopped, juices reserved	1 teaspoon fresh lemon juice or red wine vinegar
	1 tablespoon finely chopped parsley

1. In a medium saucepan, heat olive oil over medium heat. Add garlic and sage and cook until garlic softens, about 30 seconds. Add drained chopped tomatoes and reserved tomato juice. Cook over medium heat 5 minutes, stirring occasionally.

2. Add beans to saucepan. Season with salt and pepper. Simmer, uncovered, over low heat, stirring occasionally, until beans are hot, about 5 minutes. Stir in lemon juice and parsley and serve.

*Per Serving: Calories: 141   Total fat: 3 g   Saturated fat: 0 g
Cholesterol: 0 mg   Percentage calories from fat: 21%*

---

272   POLENTA PUMPKIN CASSEROLE
Prep: 5 minutes   Cook: 40 to 45 minutes   Serves: 4

This side dish would be a perfect addition to a Thanksgiving table. Try it with a little honey spooned over each serving.

⅓ cup yellow cornmeal	1 (12-ounce) can evaporated skim milk
½ cup canned solid-pack pumpkin	1 cup skim milk
½ teaspoon salt	1 tablespoon butter
¼ teaspoon ground nutmeg	

1. Preheat oven to 350°F. In a medium saucepan, combine cornmeal, pumpkin, salt, and nutmeg. Gradually stir in evaporated skim milk and skim milk until mixture is smooth. Cook and stir over medium heat until mixture thickens, about 10 minutes. Stir in butter.

2. Spoon mixture into a 1-quart casserole. Bake 30 to 35 minutes, or until casserole is firm on top and lightly golden.

*Per Serving: Calories: 174   Total fat: 3 g   Saturated fat: 2 g
Cholesterol: 13 mg   Percentage calories from fat: 18%*

273 HERBED YELLOW HOMINY
Prep: 5 minutes   Cook: 4 to 5 minutes   Serves: 4 to 5

Hominy is dried corn that has been processed and cooked until soft. Double-grinding the dried corn kernels results in grits, and further grinding produces cornmeal. Hominy is considered a Southern staple, and to some is an acquired taste.

2 (15½-ounce) cans yellow hominy, drained
2 teaspoons canola oil
1 tablespoon finely chopped fresh oregano or 1 teaspoon dried

1 tablespoon finely chopped cilantro
¼ teaspoon salt
¼ teaspoon pepper

In a large nonstick skillet, combine hominy, oil, 1 tablespoon water, and oregano. Cook over medium-high heat, stirring, until hominy is heated through and water has evaporated, 4 to 5 minutes. Add cilantro, salt, and pepper; toss gently to combine.

Per Serving: Calories: 144 Total fat: 3 g Saturated fat: 0 g Cholesterol: 0 mg Percentage calories from fat: 21%

274 KASHA WITH APRICOTS
Prep: 15 minutes   Cook: 16 to 20 minutes   Serves: 6

Kasha is cracked buckwheat, which is also called buckwheat groats. I prefer to use the whole-granulation kasha for this recipe as it keeps its shape when cooked. The apricots add a burst of tart sweetness to this dish. To cut the apricots easily, snip them with kitchen shears.

2 cups homemade or canned reduced-sodium chicken broth
1 cup whole-granulation kasha (buckwheat groats)

1 egg white
2 teaspoons butter
½ cup sliced scallions
½ cup slivered dried apricots (3 ounces)

1. In a small saucepan, bring chicken broth to a boil over medium heat. Meanwhile, in a small bowl, combine kasha with egg white and mix until thoroughly moistened. Heat a large nonstick skillet over medium heat. Add kasha. Cook, stirring, until grains are hot and separated, 2 to 4 minutes. Carefully pour in boiling broth (watch, as it spatters). Cover and simmer over low heat until liquid is absorbed, 12 to 14 minutes.

2. In a small skillet, melt butter over medium heat, Add scallions and cook, stirring often, until soft, about 2 minutes. Add scallions and apricots to kasha. Toss with a fork to combine and fluff up kasha.

Per Serving: Calories: 154 Total fat: 3 g Saturated fat: 1 g Cholesterol: 3 mg Percentage calories from fat: 15%

275   BUTTERMILK SPOON BREAD

Prep: 14 minutes   Cook: 40 to 45 minutes   Serves: 6

This Southern specialty, similar to a soufflé, is a very soft side dish that is literally spooned out of the dish; hence its name. Spoon bread puffs up upon baking, then deflates, so serve it right from the oven.

Vegetable cooking spray	**1 cup buttermilk**
1½ cups boiling water	**1 teaspoon sugar**
1 cup yellow cornmeal	**1 teaspoon baking powder**
2 teaspoons butter	**1 teaspoon salt**
2 whole eggs, separated, plus	**1 teaspoon baking soda**
1 additional egg white	

1. Preheat oven to 375°F. Coat a 1½-quart casserole with cooking spray.

2. In a large bowl, stir boiling water into cornmeal, mixing constantly to prevent lumps. Blend in butter and egg yolks. Stir in buttermilk, sugar, baking powder, salt, and baking soda.

3. In small bowl of an electric mixer, beat egg whites at high speed until soft peaks form. Fold beaten egg whites into cornmeal mixture until no streaks of white remain. Pour batter into casserole.

4. Bake 40 to 45 minutes, or until puffed and golden brown. Serve at once.

Per Serving: Calories: 144   Total fat: 4 g   Saturated fat: 2 g
Cholesterol: 76 mg   Percentage calories from fat: 24%

---

276   FAVA BEANS WITH BROCCOLI AND RED PEPPER

Prep: 15 minutes   Cook: 14 to 18 minutes   Serves: 6

This savory bean and vegetable dish can quickly be turned into a vegetarian main dish for four. To do so, spoon over couscous or rice and dollop with a nonfat plain yogurt.

1¼ pounds broccoli spears	**1 (19-ounce) can fava beans,**
1 tablespoon olive oil	**drained and rinsed**
1 medium red bell pepper	**2 tablespoons finely chopped**
(6 ounces), seeded and cut	**fresh mint leaves**
into thin strips	**2 tablespoons fresh lemon**
2 teaspoons finely chopped	**juice**
garlic	**¼ teaspoon salt**
⅛ teaspoon crushed hot red	
pepper	

1. Remove leaves and tough ends of broccoli spears. Cut broccoli into florets to equal 3 cups and cut stems into ¼-inch diagonal slices to equal 1 cup. Place florets and stems in a steamer basket and steam, covered, over 1 inch boiling water until crisp-tender, 5 to 8 minutes.

2. In a large skillet, heat olive oil over medium-high heat. Add bell pepper and cook, stirring occasionally, until it begins to brown, 4 to 5 minutes. Add garlic and hot pepper; cook, stirring, 30 seconds.

3. Add fava beans and steamed broccoli to skillet and toss gently to combine. Reduce heat to low, cover, and cook until beans are heated through, about 4 minutes, stirring occasionally. Add mint, lemon juice, and salt; toss gently to combine.

Per Serving: Calories: 109 Total fat: 3 g Saturated fat: 0 g Cholesterol: 0 mg Percentage calories from fat: 20%

277 GARBANZO BEANS WITH ESCAROLE AND FENNEL

Prep: 15 minutes   Cook: 11 to 13 minutes   Serves: 6

Escarole is a slightly bitter salad green that adds just the right flavor bite to the garbanzo beans. I like this side dish with a squeeze of lemon. To make this into a main dish, toss with 12 ounces cooked pasta.

2 **teaspoons extra-virgin olive oil**	6 **cups rinsed and drained chopped escarole (14 ounces)**
½ **cup diced red onion**	
½ **cup coarsely chopped fennel bulb, cored**	1 **(19-ounce) can garbanzo beans (chickpeas), rinsed and drained**
2 **garlic cloves, minced**	
¼ **teaspoon crushed hot red pepper**	¼ **teaspoon salt**
	1 **lemon, cut into 6 wedges**

1. In a large nonstick skillet, heat olive oil over medium heat. Add red onion, fennel, garlic, and hot pepper. Cook and stir until vegetables are soft, 3 to 4 minutes.

2. Add escarole, cover, and cook over medium-low heat until escarole is wilted, 5 to 6 minutes. Add garbanzo beans and salt; stir to combine. Cook, covered, until garbanzos are heated through, about 2 minutes. Serve with lemon wedges.

Per Serving: Calories: 98 Total fat: 3 g Saturated fat: 0 g Cholesterol: 0 mg Percentage calories from fat: 27%

278   RED BEANS AND RICE
Prep: 8 minutes   Cook: 28 to 30 minutes   Serves: 4 to 6

This is a superquick version of a Southern favorite. It's usually made with a ham hock; I eliminated that and substituted lean smoked ham to add flavor.

1 teaspoon canola oil	1½ teaspoons dried thyme
¾ cup chopped onion	leaves
¾ cup chopped green bell	¼ teaspoon cayenne
pepper	1 bay leaf
1 teaspoon minced garlic	1 cup long-grain white rice
4 ounces lean smoked ham	1 (16-ounce) can small red
(95% fat-free), cut into	beans, rinsed and
3 x ¼-inch strips	drained
(1 cup)	¼ teaspoon salt

1. In a medium nonstick saucepan, heat oil over medium heat. Add onion, bell pepper, garlic, ham, thyme, and cayenne. Cook, stirring occasionally, until vegetables are softened, 3 to 5 minutes. Add 3 cups water and bay leaf. Bring to a boil over high heat. Add rice; stir once. Quickly bring to a boil. Reduce heat to low, cover, and simmer 10 minutes.

2. Add beans to rice (do not stir); cover and simmer until rice is tender and water is absorbed, about 10 minutes. Remove from heat; let stand 3 minutes. Remove bay leaf. Add salt. Stir with a fork to combine and fluff up rice.

*Per Serving: Calories: 319 Total fat: 3 g Saturated fat: 1 g
Cholesterol: 13 mg Percentage calories from fat: 9%*

279   GARLIC CHEESE GRITS
Prep: 10 minutes   Cook: 37 to 39 minutes   Serves: 6 to 8

The first time I had grits was in the Deep South, and they were made with lots of garlic and butter. Alas, the butter had to go in this recipe, but the addition of jalapeño pepper and parsley gives this great taste.

Vegetable cooking spray	5 ounces shredded reduced-
1 cup homemade or canned	fat Cheddar cheese
reduced-sodium chicken	2 tablespoons finely chopped
broth	parsley
2 large garlic cloves, minced	1 tablespoon minced seeded
¾ cup quick-cooking grits	jalapeño pepper

1. Preheat oven to 350°F. Coat a 7 x 11-inch baking pan with cooking spray.

2. In a medium saucepan, bring chicken broth, 1 cup water, and garlic to a boil over high heat. Stir in grits, reduce heat to low, cover, and simmer 5 to 7 minutes, or until grits are thick, stirring occasionally. Stir in cheese, parsley, and jalapeño pepper; stir until cheese melts.

3. Spoon mixture into prepared pan, spreading evenly. Bake 30 minutes, or until slightly firm and lightly browned around edges.

Per Serving: Calories: 120 Total fat: 4 g Saturated fat: 3 g
Cholesterol: 14 mg Percentage calories from fat: 30%

---

280 KASHA WITH BOW TIES
Prep: 10 minutes   Cook: 23 to 29 minutes   Serves: 6 to 8

½ cup small egg bows
1 tablespoon canola oil
1½ cups chopped onions
2 cups homemade or canned reduced-sodium chicken broth

1 cup whole-granulation kasha (buckwheat groats)
1 egg white
¼ teaspoon pepper

1. In a medium saucepan filled with boiling water, cook egg bows until tender, 9 to 11 minutes. Drain and transfer to a bowl.

2. Meanwhile, in a medium nonstick saucepan, heat oil over medium-low heat. Add onions and cook, stirring occasionally, until golden brown, about 10 minutes. Add onions to egg bows. Pour broth into skillet and bring to a boil. Remove from heat.

3. In a medium bowl, combine kasha with egg white and mix until thoroughly moistened. Heat a large nonstick skillet over medium heat. Add kasha. Cook, stirring, until grains are hot and separated, 2 to 4 minutes. Carefully pour hot broth into kasha (watch, as it spatters). Cover and simmer over low heat, until liquid is absorbed, 12 to 14 minutes. Add cooked egg bows, onions, and pepper. Stir with a fork to combine and fluff up kasha.

Per Serving: Calories: 147 Total fat: 4 g Saturated fat: 1 g
Cholesterol: 6 mg Percentage calories from fat: 20%

281   ORANGE-FLAVORED QUINOA
Prep: 8 minutes   Cook: 20 to 25 minutes . Serves: 6

This refreshing quinoa can be served either hot or cold. I like it with fish or chicken.

2 teaspoons extra-virgin olive oil	¼ cup minced fresh parsley
½ cup chopped onion	¼ cup minced fresh mint
1 cup orange juice	2 tablespoons currants or raisins
½ teaspoon salt	2 teaspoons grated orange zest
1 cup quinoa	

1. In a medium nonstick saucepan, heat olive oil over medium heat. Add onion and cook, stirring occasionally, until soft, about 3 minutes.

2. Add orange juice, 1 cup water, and salt. Bring to a boil. Add quinoa and stir once. Quickly return to a boil. Reduce heat to low, cover, and simmer 15 to 20 minutes, until water is absorbed and quinoa is tender. Remove from heat; let stand 3 minutes.

3. Add parsley, mint, currants, and orange zest to quinoa. Stir with a fork to combine and fluff up grain.

Per Serving: Calories: 154 Total fat: 3 g Saturated fat: 0 g
Cholesterol: 0 mg Percentage calories from fat: 18%

---

282   CURRIED RICE WITH CURRANTS AND PUMPKIN SEEDS
Prep: 8 minutes   Cook: 21 minutes   Serves: 6 to 7

Hulled pumpkin seeds, sometimes called pepitas, can be found in health food stores, specialty food shops, and Mexican markets.

2 teaspoons olive oil	1 (2-inch) cinnamon stick
1 cup converted long-grain white rice	2 tablespoons currants or raisins
1 teaspoon curry powder	2 tablespoons hulled pumpkin seeds (pepitas)
½ teaspoon ground turmeric	
½ teaspoon salt	

1. In a medium nonstick saucepan, heat olive oil over medium heat. Stir in rice and cook, stirring, until rice is coated with oil, about 1 minute. Add 2¼ cups water, curry powder, turmeric, salt, and cinnamon stick. Quickly bring to a boil, stirring once. Reduce heat to low, cover, and simmer 20 minutes, or until water is absorbed and rice is tender. Discard cinnamon stick.

2. Add currants and pumpkin seeds to rice. Stir with a fork to combine and fluff up rice.

Per Serving: Calories: 124 Total fat: 2 g Saturated fat: 0 g
Cholesterol: 0 mg Percentage calories from fat: 12%

283   ITALIAN RICE BALLS

Prep: 30 minutes   Cook: 35 to 45 minutes   Serves: 6

I used to have as landlords a lovely, elderly Italian couple who would invite me to Sunday dinner. It was in their home where I first tasted this dish, which is usually deep-fried. When you pulled the balls apart, the cheese in the center would string; hence the name "Suppli al Telefono," or telephone wires. I've adapted the recipe to include spinach, used a low-fat mozzarella cheese, and baked them. This dish is a perfect way to use up leftover rice. I like them with a squeeze of lemon, but I've given the option of serving them with a light marinara sauce if you prefer.

¾ cup raw long-grain white
    rice or 2 cups cold cooked
    rice
1 (10-ounce) package frozen
    chopped spinach
    Olive oil cooking spray
½ cup fine dry seasoned bread
    crumbs
¼ cup finely shredded Asiago
    or Parmesan cheese
¼ cup finely chopped scallions
2 teaspoons finely chopped
    fresh oregano or
    ½ teaspoon dried

½ teaspoon salt
¼ teaspoon pepper
⅛ teaspoon grated nutmeg
2 egg whites, slightly beaten
1½ ounces reduced-fat
    mozzarella cheese, cut
    into 12 (½-inch) cubes
1 lemon, cut into 6 wedges
2 cups marinara sauce, heated
    (optional)

1. In a medium saucepan, bring 2 cups water to a boil. Add rice; stir once. Cover and simmer 15 to 20 minutes, or until water is absorbed and rice is tender. (Eliminate this step if you use cold cooked rice.) Meanwhile, cook spinach following package directions, 11 to 13 minutes; drain and squeeze dry.

2. Preheat oven to 375°F. Coat an 11 x 15-inch jelly roll pan with cooking spray. In a large bowl, combine rice, spinach, ¼ cup bread crumbs, cheese, scallions, oregano, salt, pepper, and nutmeg. Mix with a fork to blend well. Add egg whites and stir until mixture is thoroughly moistened.

3. Divide rice mixture into 12 equal mounds (a scant ¼ cup each). Place a mozzarella cube in center of each and shape into a ball with moistened hands, thoroughly enclosing cheese.

4. Place remaining ¼ cup bread crumbs on a sheet of wax paper. Roll rice balls in crumbs to coat thoroughly. Place on prepared baking sheet. Bake 20 to 25 minutes, or until heated through and light brown on bottom. Serve with lemon wedges or marinara sauce.

Per Serving: Calories: 181   Total fat: 3 g   Saturated fat: 2 g
Cholesterol: 6 mg   Percentage calories from fat: 15%

284   BASMATI AND WILD RICE WITH ALMONDS AND RAISINS
Prep: 10 minutes   Cook: 20 to 25 minutes   Serves: 6 to 7

Packaged rice blends, without seasoning packets, are becoming more available on supermarket shelves. This rice blend uses a combination of aromatic basmati and wild rice, which is technically a wild grass. You can use homemade or canned reduced-sodium chicken broth when cooking the rice instead of the water; just eliminate the salt from the recipe.

2 teaspoons olive oil
¼ cup chopped onion
1 cup basmati and wild rice blend
2 cups homemade or canned reduced-sodium chicken broth or water
½ teaspoon salt (optional)

¼ cup golden raisins
2 tablespoons slivered almonds, preferably toasted
1 teaspoon grated lemon zest
2 tablespoons chopped parsley

1. In a medium nonstick saucepan, heat olive oil over medium heat. Add onions and cook, stirring occasionally, until softened, 2 to 3 minutes. Add chicken broth or 2 cups water and salt and bring to a boil. Add rice and stir once. Quickly return to a boil. Reduce heat to low, cover, and simmer 15 to 20 minutes, until water is absorbed and rice is tender. Remove from heat; let stand 3 minutes.

2. Add raisins, almonds, and lemon zest to rice. Stir with a fork to combine and fluff up rice. Serve garnished with parsley.

Per Serving: Calories: 149   Total fat: 4 g   Saturated fat: 1 g
Cholesterol: 0 mg   Percentage calories from fat: 20%

---

285   YELLOW RICE
Prep: 5 minutes   Cook: 10 to 12 minutes   Serves: 8

Turmeric colors this rice yellow; cumin and cinnamon add to the flavor. I occasionally like to add currants and sliced scallions to this dish.

½ teaspoon ground turmeric
¼ teaspoon ground cumin
1 cup basmati rice

1 (2-inch) cinnamon stick
½ teaspoon salt

Place turmeric and cumin in a medium saucepan and toast over low heat until fragrant, about 30 seconds. Add rice, 2 cups water, cinnamon stick, and salt; stir once. Bring to a boil; reduce heat. Cover and simmer 10 to 12 minutes, or until water is absorbed and rice is tender. Remove from heat; let stand 3 minutes. Remove cinnamon stick. Stir with a fork to fluff up rice.

Per Serving: Calories: 79   Total fat: < 1 g   Saturated fat: 0 g
Cholesterol: 0 mg   Percentage calories from fat: 4%

286 BASIL BROWN RICE AND PEAS

Prep: 8 minutes   Cook: 43 to 48 minutes   Serves: 6 to 7

½ teaspoon salt
1 cup brown rice
1 (10-ounce) package frozen
   peas

2 tablespoons chopped fresh
   basil
2 teaspoons fresh lemon juice

1. In a medium saucepan, bring 2½ cups water and salt to a boil. Add brown rice and stir once. Quickly return to a boil. Reduce heat to low, cover, and simmer 35 to 40 minutes, until water is almost absorbed.

2. Add peas (do not stir in). Continue to cook 5 minutes longer, or until water is absorbed and rice is tender. Remove from heat; let stand 3 minutes.

3. Add basil and lemon juice to rice. Stir with a fork to combine and fluff up rice.

Per Serving: Calories: 130 Total fat: 1 g Saturated fat: 0 g
            Cholesterol: 0 mg Percentage calories from fat: 6%

287 BROWN RICE PILAF WITH WILD MUSHROOMS

Prep: 5 minutes   Cook: 48 minutes   Serves: 6

2 teaspoons butter
1 cup brown rice
2½ cups homemade or canned
   reduced-sodium chicken
   broth
   Vegetable cooking spray

1½ cups sliced wild
   mushrooms, such as
   shiitake or cremini
   (about 5 ounces)
½ cup chopped onion

1. In a medium saucepan, melt 1 teaspoon butter over medium heat. Add brown rice and quickly toss to coat. Cook over medium-low heat, stirring, until rice is lightly toasted, about 3 minutes. Add chicken broth and quickly bring to a boil. Reduce heat to low, cover, and simmer 45 minutes, or until broth is absorbed and rice is tender. Remove from heat; let stand 3 minutes.

2. Just before rice is done, coat a large nonstick skillet with cooking spray. Add remaining 1 teaspoon butter and melt over medium heat. Add mushrooms and onion. Cook, stirring often, until mushrooms begin to brown at edges and liquid they exude evaporates, 6 to 8 minutes.

3. Add mushrooms and onion to rice. Stir with a fork to combine and fluff up rice. Serve at once.

Per Serving: Calories: 149 Total fat: 3 g Saturated fat: 1 g
            Cholesterol: 3 mg Percentage calories from fat: 19%

288 GREEN RICE
Prep: 10 minutes   Cook: 25 minutes   Serves: 6

Spinach, parsley, and Parmesan cheese accent this classic rice dish. It is important that the spinach be dry before chopping. Either spin it dry in a salad spinner or pat dry between paper towels.

2 teaspoons olive oil	1½ cups finely chopped fresh
½ cup chopped onion	spinach
1 teaspoon finely chopped	½ cup finely chopped parsley
garlic	¼ cup grated fresh Parmesan
1 cup long-grain white rice	or Asiago cheese

1. In a medium saucepan, heat olive oil over medium heat. Add onion and garlic and cook, stirring occasionally, until soft, about 3 minutes. Add rice and quickly toss to coat with oil. Cook, stirring, 2 minutes. Add 2 cups water. Quickly bring to a boil. Reduce heat to low, cover, and simmer 15 minutes.

2. Add spinach and parsley to rice; stir once or twice with a fork to combine. Cover and simmer until spinach is wilted, water has evaporated, and rice is tender, about 5 minutes. Remove from heat; let stand 3 minutes. Add Parmesan cheese. Stir with a fork to combine and fluff up rice.

Per Serving: Calories: 155 Total fat: 3 g Saturated fat: 1 g
Cholesterol: 3 mg Percentage calories from fat: 18%

---

289 RISOTTO MILANESE
Prep: 7 minutes   Cook: 25 to 30 minutes   Serves: 6

Risotto is made with short-grain Italian Arborio rice. It differs from a pilaf in that it must be continuously stirred to develop its distinctive creamy texture. Ladling in the broth gives a consistent measure.

4 to 5 cups homemade or	1½ cups Arborio rice
canned reduced-sodium	¼ cup grated Parmesan cheese
chicken broth	2 tablespoons chopped fresh
¼ teaspoon crushed saffron	parsley
threads	2 teaspoons butter, cut into
Olive oil cooking spray	small pieces
1 teaspoon olive oil	¼ teaspoon freshly ground
¼ cup minced onion	pepper

1. In a medium saucepan, bring chicken broth to a boil. Remove ¼ cup of the broth and place in a small bowl with the saffron. Keep remaining broth at a simmer.

2. Coat a large deep skillet with cooking spray. Add olive oil and heat pan over medium-low heat. Add onion and cook, stirring often, until soft, about 3 minutes. Add rice and stir to coat with oil. Cook, stirring, 2 minutes.

3. Add a ladleful (about ⅓ cup) of hot broth to rice. Cook over medium-low heat, stirring, until almost all of broth has been absorbed, about 3 minutes. Add saffron broth mixture. Cook, stirring constantly, until all broth has been absorbed. Continue adding remaining broth, a ladleful at a time, and cooking and stirring, until rice is creamy and firm but not chalky in center, about 15 to 20 minutes longer.

4. Add cheese, parsley, butter, and pepper. Stir to mix. Spoon into shallow bowls and serve at once with additional cracked pepper.

*Per Serving: Calories: 237   Total fat: 5 g   Saturated fat: 2 g
          Cholesterol: 6 mg   Percentage calories from fat: 19%*

---

290 WILD RICE PILAF WITH RED GRAPES AND PECANS

Prep: 10 minutes   Cook: 45 to 50 minutes   Serves: 6

The nutty flavor of wild rice is accented with the sweetness of grapes and herbs. I've noticed that the amount of water will vary with the type of wild rice purchased. Use the amount of water called for on the package to cook 1 cup rice.

1 **cup wild rice**	½ **cup minced fresh parsley**
⅔ **cup halved seedless red grapes**	2 **tablespoons coarsely chopped toasted pecans**
½ **cup coarsely chopped scallions**	¼ **teaspoon salt**
	¼ **teaspoon pepper**

1. In a large saucepan, bring 6 cups water to a boil. Rinse wild rice under cold water and add to saucepan; stir once. Quickly bring to a boil. Reduce heat to low, cover, and simmer 40 to 45 minutes, until water is absorbed and rice is tender. Remove from heat; let stand 3 minutes.

2. Add grapes, scallions, parsley, pecans, salt, and pepper to wild rice. Stir with a fork to combine and fluff up rice.

*Per Serving: Calories: 121   Total fat: 2 g   Saturated fat: 0 g
          Cholesterol: 0 mg   Percentage calories from fat: 13%*

Chapter 12

Eye-Opening Ideas for Breakfast and Brunch

Breakfast is still considered the most important meal of the day, yet over one-third of the population skips this necessary meal. If they do, it's to grab a cup of coffee with a fat-laden doughnut, a cheese Danish, or a candy bar. If they sit down, it's to a plate of scrambled eggs, greasy bacon, hash browns sautéed in bacon fat, and toast slathered with butter and jam. Does this sound like someone in your family?

It is still possible to have a healthy breakfast and keep to a low-fat style of eating. In this chapter, I've tried to tempt everyone to the morning table. Set the pace of the day with a nutritious breakfast, even breakfast in a glass, such as Banana Pineapple Shake or Chocolate Malted Milkshake. If the kids need to grab and go, have them tote a hearty Blueberry Muffin or Currant Walnut Scone with low-fat cheese or yogurt, and a banana. If everyone in your family has time to sit down to breakfast, a bowl of Raisin Date Granola with skim milk or a hot bowl of Apricot Couscous will surely satisfy.

Still want your bacon and eggs? Bacon and Egg Strata is made healthier with low-fat smoked turkey bacon, skim milk, and egg substitute. Hash browns a favorite? Then the Hash Brown Omelet will surely be a hit for breakfast or brunch. I've also included lower-fat versions of French toast, waffles, and pancakes. Cheese Blintzes, usually butter-fried, are not fried at all! To reduce the fat, I substituted 2 egg whites for one of the eggs, used skim milk, fat-free cottage cheese, and a low-fat ricotta and baked them. Top them with a sprinkling of powdered sugar, mixed fresh berries, a nonfat sour cream, or a low-sugar cherry pie filling. Dutch Baby with Fresh Fruits will draw raves, too.

291   DUTCH BABY WITH FRESH FRUITS
Prep: 10 to 15 minutes   Cook: 16 to 21 minutes   Serves: 4

This big, puffy, German classic, also called a Bismarck, never bakes up exactly the same way twice. It must be served immediately after leaving the oven, as it will collapse within minutes. The usual topping is a generous squeeze of lemon juice and a dusting of powdered sugar.

½ cup flour
2 tablespoons granulated sugar
¼ teaspoon salt
½ cup 1% low-fat milk
2 eggs
1 teaspoon vanilla extract
1 tablespoon reduced-fat margarine

4 cups mixed fresh fruit (blueberries, strawberry halves, blackberries, raspberries; fresh pineapple pieces; nectarine, peach, banana, or kiwi slices)
2 teaspoons powdered sugar

1. Preheat oven to 425°F. In a medium bowl, place flour, sugar, salt, milk, eggs, and vanilla. Beat with a wire whisk until smooth, about 1 minute.

2. In a 9-inch pie plate, melt margarine in oven until sizzling, 2 to 3 minutes. Remove pan from oven and tilt to coat bottom of pan with margarine. Immediately pour batter into pan.

3. Bake 14 to 18 minutes, or until omelet is puffed and golden brown. Immediately fill center with fresh fruit and dust with powdered sugar. Serve at once.

Per Serving: Calories: 229   Total fat: 5 g   Saturated fat: 1 g
Cholesterol: 107 mg   Percentage calories from fat: 19%

292   BACON AND EGG STRATA
Prep: 10 minutes   Stand: 15 minutes   Cook: 50 minutes
Serves: 4 to 6

Still want your bacon and eggs for breakfast? Here's an interesting variation of the two. There is no need to cook the turkey bacon before using.

Vegetable cooking spray
16 slices of French, Italian or semolina bread, cut ½ inch thick (about 6 ounces)
1 (8-ounce) container frozen egg substitute, thawed
2 cups skim milk
2 tablespoons grated Parmesan cheese

1 tablespoon Dijon mustard
¼ teaspoon pepper
8 slices of 95% fat-free smoked turkey bacon, cut into ½-inch pieces (4 ounces)
⅓ cup sliced scallions
1 large tomato (8 ounces), seeded and coarsely chopped

1. Coat a 1½-quart shallow baking dish with cooking spray. Overlap bread slices in bottom of dish.

2. In a medium bowl, whisk together egg substitute, milk, Parmesan cheese, mustard, and pepper. Pour egg mixture over bread and press bread down into mixture. Let stand at least 15 minutes, or cover and refrigerate overnight.

3. Preheat oven to 350°F. In a small bowl, combine bacon, scallions, and tomato; toss to mix. Sprinkle evenly over bread.

4. Bake uncovered 50 minutes, or until strata is lightly golden on top and a knife inserted near center comes out clean. Let stand 5 minutes before serving.

Per Serving: Calories: 223 Total fat: 6 g Saturated fat: 2 g
Cholesterol: 20 mg Percentage calories from fat: 25%

---

293 HASH BROWN OMELET
Prep: 15 minutes   Cook: 9 to 13 minutes   Serves: 4

I love potatoes and eggs, so I teamed their flavor for this delightful dish. It is easier to make the dish in two batches rather than one huge omelet. If you prefer to make one omelet, use a 12-inch nonstick skillet. For brunch, I like to serve this omelet with salsa and hot flour tortillas.

Vegetable cooking spray
2 cups cubed (½-inch) cooked potatoes (about 2 medium)
½ cup thinly sliced onion
½ cup diced (½-inch) red bell pepper
1 tablespoon seeded and chopped fresh jalapeño pepper

2 tablespoons chopped cilantro or parsley
½ teaspoon salt
⅛ teaspoon cayenne
1 teaspoon reduced-fat margarine
2 (8-ounce) containers frozen egg substitute, thawed

1. Coat a large nonstick skillet with cooking spray. Add potatoes, onion, bell pepper, and jalapeño pepper. Coat vegetables with cooking spray and toss to coat. Cook over medium heat, stirring occasionally, until vegetables begin to soften and potatoes begin to brown slightly, 6 to 8 minutes. Stir in cilantro, salt, and cayenne. Transfer vegetables to a large bowl; cover to keep warm. Wipe out skillet.

2. Melt ½ teaspoon margarine in skillet over medium heat. Add 1 cup of egg substitute. Cook, lifting edges to allow uncooked portion to flow underneath, until almost set, 2 to 3 minutes. Spoon half of hash brown mixture over half of omelet. Fold other half over filling.

3. Cover skillet and let cook 1 to 2 minutes longer to heat filling. Slide onto serving platter and keep warm. Repeat with remaining margarine, egg substitute, and hash brown mixture. Serve at once.

Per Serving: Calories: 145 Total fat: 1 g Saturated fat: 0 g
Cholesterol: 0 mg Percentage calories from fat: 5%

294 CHEESE BLINTZES

Prep: 1 hour 40 minutes (includes chilling time)
Cook: 17 to 19 minutes   Serves: 8

Who can resist cheese blintzes? I like to prepare the blintzes and freeze them on a baking sheet. When frozen, transfer to a shallow freezer container with wax paper between. They can be baked from the frozen state in about 12 minutes. Serve with cinnamon sugar, sweetened berries, nonfat sour cream, or a canned pie filling.

2 whole eggs	¼ teaspoon salt
2 egg whites	No-Fat Cheese Filling
1 cup skim milk	(recipe follows)
1 cup flour	Vegetable cooking spray

1. In a food processor or blender, place eggs, egg whites, milk, flour, and salt. Process until smooth, scraping sides of container (with motor off), if necessary. Pour batter into a 4-cup glass measure. Cover and refrigerate 1 hour.

2. Prepare cheese filling. Cover and refrigerate while preparing crepes.

3. Heat a 7-inch crepe pan or skillet over medium heat. Coat with cooking spray. Pour in 2 tablespoons batter, rotating pan quickly to spread batter evenly. Cook until lightly browned on underside and dry on top, about 30 seconds. Turn over and cook 5 seconds longer. Remove crepe from pan to a large baking sheet. Repeat with remaining batter to make 16 crepes. Coat pan when necessary and stir batter occasionally. Place wax paper between crepes to prevent them from sticking.

4. Preheat oven to 350°F. Coat a large baking sheet with cooking spray. To assemble, place 2 tablespoons cheese filling on whiter side of each crepe. Fold opposite sides over filling, then overlap ends envelope-style to cover filling completely. Place blintzes on baking sheet and bake until filling is hot, about 8 to 10 minutes.

Per Serving: Calories: 178 Total fat: 3 g Saturated fat: 0 g
Cholesterol: 57 mg Percentage calories from fat: 13%

295   NO-FAT CHEESE FILLING
Prep: 5 minutes   Cook: none   Makes: about 2½ cups, 8 servings

This rich-tasting but fat-free filling can also be used to fill crepes or can be layered with fresh fruit to make a stylish parfait.

1 cup nonfat cottage cheese
1 cup nonfat ricotta cheese
⅓ cup nonfat cream cheese

¼ cup sugar
1 teaspoon grated lemon zest

In a food processor, combine cottage cheese, ricotta, cream cheese, sugar, and lemon zest. Puree until smooth. Spoon into a bowl. Cover and refrigerate while making crepes.

Per Serving: Calories: 80 Total fat: 0 g Saturated fat: 0 g Cholesterol: 3 mg Percentage calories from fat: 0%

296   ORANGE FRENCH TOAST
Prep: 10 minutes   Cook: 4 to 6 minutes   Serves: 4

1 large orange
1 whole egg
2 egg whites
⅓ cup skim milk
⅛ teaspoon grated nutmeg
8 slices of French, Italian, or white bread, cut ½ inch thick

1 teaspoon reduced-fat margarine
2 teaspoons powdered sugar

1. Grate 1 teaspoon zest from orange into a large bowl. Squeeze in enough juice from orange to yield ⅓ cup. Add whole egg, egg whites, milk, and nutmeg. Whisk until well blended.

2. Dip bread into egg mixture to coat both sides. Place bread slices on a 10 x 15-inch jelly roll pan. Pour remaining egg mixture over bread. Let stand 10 minutes, or until egg mixture is absorbed, turning once.

3. Heat a nonstick griddle over medium heat until a few drops of water dance about. Spread ½ teaspoon margarine over griddle until melted. Add half of bread slices and cook, turning once, until golden brown on both sides, about 2 to 3 minutes. Remove to a serving platter; cover to keep warm. Repeat with remaining margarine and bread. Dust French toast with powdered sugar and serve at once.

Per Serving: Calories: 190 Total fat: 3 g Saturated fat: 1 g Cholesterol: 54 mg Percentage calories from fat: 16%

297 PLUM COOLER
Prep: 5 minutes   Cook: none   Serves: 6

This plum beverage is a perfect thirst-quencher. For variation, try it with equal amounts of a flavored seltzer or white wine.

1 (16-ounce) can whole plums
    in heavy syrup
1 cup orange juice
2 tablespoons fresh lemon
    juice

¼ teaspoon ground cinnamon
Ice cubes

1. Drain juice from plums into a 4-cup glass measure; reserve. Pit plums and place plums in a blender or food processor. Puree until smooth, about 1 minute. Add to reserved plum juice.

2. Add orange juice, lemon juice, and cinnamon. Stir to dissolve cinnamon. Pour over ice cubes in tall glasses.

*Per Serving: Calories: 87   Total fat: 0 g   Saturated fat: 0 g
Cholesterol: 0 mg   Percentage calories from fat: 0%*

298 ZUCCHINI, RED PEPPER, AND MUSHROOM FRITTATA
Prep: 25 minutes   Cook: 8 to 9 minutes   Serves: 4

This colorful frittata tastes like a pizza without the crust. If you don't have an ovenproof skillet, be sure to cover the handle snugly with aluminum foil before placing the pan in the oven.

1 whole egg
2 egg whites
¼ teaspoon salt
¼ teaspoon crushed hot red
    pepper
¼ cup nonfat ricotta cheese
1 tablespoon chopped fresh
    basil or 1 teaspoon dried
1 teaspoon olive oil
1 cup sliced fresh mushrooms
    (3 ounces)
1 medium scallion, cut into
    1-inch pieces

1 garlic clove, minced
2 medium zucchini (about
    8 ounces total), trimmed
    and cut into thin rounds
1 small red bell pepper,
    seeded and cut into thin
    strips
2 tablespoons grated
    Parmesan cheese
¼ cup shredded nonfat
    mozzarella cheese

1. Preheat broiler. In a medium bowl, whisk together whole egg, egg whites, salt, and hot pepper. Stir in ricotta and basil.

2. In a 10-inch ovenproof nonstick skillet, heat olive oil over medium-high heat. Add mushrooms, scallions, and garlic. Cook, stirring often, until mushrooms begin to give up their liquid, about 2 minutes. Add zucchini and bell pepper. Cook, stirring, until vegetables are crisp-tender and liquid has evaporated, about 4 minutes. Remove from heat. Stir in Parmesan cheese.

3. Press vegetables down into skillet to form an even layer. Gradually pour on egg mixture, tilting pan to coat bottom evenly. Return to heat and cook over medium heat until eggs are set, about 1 minute. Sprinkle mozzarella cheese on top.

4. Transfer frittata to broiler and broil about 4 inches from heat until cheese begins to brown, 1 to 2 minutes. Serve directly from skillet or slide onto a large plate. Cut into wedges to serve.

Per Serving: Calories: 84 Total fat: 3 g Saturated fat: 1 g
Cholesterol: 56 mg Percentage calories from fat: 30%

---

299 CORNMEAL GRIDDLE CAKES
Prep: 10 minutes   Cook: 15 to 20 minutes   Makes: 18

Sour cream and yogurt, the nonfat varieties, are used to make these corn-meal-based pancakes. You can serve them laced with warmed maple syrup or topped with Cranberry-Orange Sauce (page 224).

1 cup yellow cornmeal, preferably stone-ground	1 cup nonfat plain yogurt
½ cup flour	1 cup nonfat sour cream
1 teaspoon baking soda	1 whole egg
1 teaspoon sugar	2 egg whites
½ teaspoon salt	6 tablespoons skim milk
	Vegetable cooking spray

1. In a large bowl, combine cornmeal, flour, baking soda, sugar, and salt; mix with a fork to combine. In a small bowl, whisk together yogurt, sour cream, whole egg, and egg whites. Stir in milk. Pour into cornmeal mixture. Mix gently just until moistened.

2. Coat a nonstick griddle with cooking spray. Heat griddle over medium heat until a few drops of water dance about. Drop batter, 2 tablespoons at a time, onto griddle. Cook griddle cakes, turning once, until golden brown on both sides, 3 to 4 minutes. Transfer to a serving platter and cover to keep warm while preparing remaining griddle cakes.

Per Pancake: Calories: 67 Total fat: 1 g Saturated fat: 0 g
Cholesterol: 12 mg Percentage calories from fat: 9%

300   RICOTTA PANCAKES WITH CRANBERRY-ORANGE SAUCE

Prep: 12 minutes   Cook: 6 to 8 minutes   Serves: 4 to 6

1 cup all-purpose flour
1 teaspoon baking powder
½ teaspoon baking soda
¼ teaspoon salt
1 cup reduced-fat ricotta
   cheese
¾ cup buttermilk

1 whole egg
1 egg white
2 teaspoons sugar
1 teaspoon grated orange zest
   Vegetable cooking spray
   Cranberry-Orange Sauce
   (recipe follows)

1. Sift flour, baking powder, baking soda, and salt onto a sheet of wax paper.

2. In a food processor or blender, place ricotta, buttermilk, whole egg, egg white, sugar, and orange zest. Puree until smooth. Pour into a large bowl. Add flour mixture and whisk just until combined. Batter will be stiff.

3. Coat a nonstick griddle with cooking spray and heat over medium heat until a few drops of water dance about. Ladle a scant ¼ cup batter (about 3 tablespoons) per pancake onto griddle. Cook, turning once, until golden brown, about 1½ to 2 minutes for each side. Serve warm with Cranberry-Orange Sauce.

Per Serving: Calories: 332 Total fat: 6 g Saturated fat: 2 g
Cholesterol: 52 mg Percentage calories from fat: 15%

301   CRANBERRY-ORANGE SAUCE

Prep: 5 minutes   Cook: 15 minutes   Makes: 2 cups

You can also serve this sauce over a nonfat frozen yogurt or a piece of plain cake.

½ cup sugar
1 tablespoons cornstarch
1½ cups orange juice

2 cups fresh or frozen
   cranberries

In a medium nonreactive saucepan, combine sugar and cornstarch. Stir in orange juice until mixture is smooth. Add cranberries. Bring to a boil over high heat. Reduce heat to medium-low and simmer, stirring occasionally, 15 minutes, or until mixture thickens slightly and cranberries pop. Sauce will thicken more upon standing. Serve warm.

Per Serving: Calories: 87 Total fat: < 1 g Saturated fat: 0 g
Cholesterol: 0 mg Percentage calories from fat: 1%

302 RAISIN FRENCH TOAST WITH CARAMELIZED PEARS

Prep: 1 hour 10 minutes (includes chilling time)   Cook: 35 minutes
Serves: 4

For convenience, make this up the night before and bake it the next day.

8 slices of raisin bread or
   raisin-cinnamon bread
1½ cups skim milk
2 whole eggs
2 egg whites
1 tablespoon granulated sugar

1 teaspoon vanilla extract
1 teaspoon grated lemon zest
   Vegetable cooking spray
1 teaspoon powdered sugar
   Carmelized Pears (recipe
   follows)

1. Place bread in a single layer in a 10 x 15-inch jelly roll pan.

2. In a medium bowl, whisk together milk, whole eggs, egg whites, sugar, vanilla, and lemon zest. Pour evenly over bread slices. Cover and refrigerate until milk mixture is absorbed, at least 1 hour or overnight.

3. Preheat oven to 400°F. Coat a large baking sheet with cooking spray. With a wide spatula, carefully transfer bread slices to baking sheet.

4. Bake 20 minutes. Turn bread slices over and continue to bake 15 minutes longer, or until French toast is browned and lightly puffed. Dust with powdered sugar and serve with Caramelized Pears.

Per Serving: Calories: 354 Total fat: 6 g Saturated fat: 1 g
Cholesterol: 108 mg Percentage calories from fat: 14%

---

303 CARAMELIZED PEARS

Prep: 5 minutes   Cook: 7 to 8 minutes   Serves: 4

The pears do not need to be peeled, and should be cooked just until they soften but still keep their shape. You can also serve them as a compote or over low-fat yogurt or a piece of plain cake.

¼ cup sugar
2 large firm-ripe pears (1 pound)

2 tablespoons fresh lemon
   juice

1. In a large skillet, combine sugar and 4 teaspoons water. Cook over low heat until sugar melts and syrup turns a light amber color, about 5 minutes.

2. Meanwhile, cut pears lengthwise in half and scoop out cores. Cut each half into 6 thick slices. Place in a medium bowl and toss gently with 1 tablespoon lemon juice.

3. Remove skillet from heat. Add remaining 1 tablespoon lemon juice to caramelized sugar and quickly stir until mixture is smooth. Add pears and juices in bowl to skillet. Return to medium heat. Cook, stirring gently, until pears are softened and lightly glazed, 2 to 3 minutes. Serve warm.

Per Serving: Calories: 112 Total fat: 1 g Saturated fat: 0 g
Cholesterol: 0 mg Percentage calories from fat: 3%

304   BREAKFAST POLENTA WITH ORANGE-MAPLE SYRUP

Prep: 5 minutes   Cook: 16 to 18 minutes   Chill: 3 hours
Serves: 6

Polenta is a favorite Italian dish. I've added orange juice and made it into individual rounds to be topped with a delicate orange-maple syrup.

1 tablespoon reduced-fat
    margarine
¾ teaspoon salt
1 cup yellow cornmeal,
    preferably stone-ground

Vegetable cooking spray
Orange-Maple Syrup
    (recipe follows)

1. In a large saucepan, bring 3 cups of water to a boil over medium heat. Add margarine and salt. In a small bowl, combine cornmeal with 1 cup cold water. Slowly add cornmeal mixture to boiling water, stirring constantly. Return to a boil, reduce heat to low, and cook, uncovered, stirring frequently, until mixture begins to mound onto itself when dropped from a spoon, about 10 minutes.

2. Spoon mixture into 6 (4 x ½-inch) tart pans with removable bottoms. Cover and chill until very firm, at least 3 hours or overnight. (If you don't have individual tart pans, place cornmeal mixture in a foil-lined 9-inch square pan.)

3. Preheat broiler. Unmold polenta rounds from tart pans (or remove polenta from square pan and cut into 4 large squares, then cut each square diagonally into 4 triangles). Place polenta on unheated broiler pan lightly coated with cooking spray. Coat tops of polenta pieces with spray.

4. Broil 4 inches from heat 2 to 3 minutes, or until browned. Turn polenta over and coat lightly with cooking spray. Broil 2 to 3 minutes longer, or until browned. Serve with Orange-Maple Syrup.

Per Serving: Calories: 204 Total fat: 2 g Saturated fat: 0 g
Cholesterol: 0 mg Percentage calories from fat: 8%

305   ORANGE-MAPLE SYRUP

Prep: 2 minutes   Cook: 3 minutes   Makes: 1 cup

Make up a double batch of this syrup and store in the refrigerator for whenever you need a topping for French toast, waffles, or pancakes.

¾ cup pure maple syrup

¼ cup orange juice

In a small saucepan, bring maple syrup and orange juice to a boil over high heat, stirring frequently. Serve warm.

Per Tablespoon: Calories: 40 Total fat: 0 g Saturated fat: 0 g
Cholesterol: 0 mg Percentage calories from fat: 0%

306 CHOCOLATE MALTED MILKSHAKE
Prep: 3 minutes   Cook: none   Serves: 2

Kids, big and small, will enjoy this quick-fix beverage. Look for other flavors of nonfat frozen yogurts and design your own milkshakes.

2 **large scoops (⅓ cup each) nonfat frozen chocolate mousse yogurt**

2 **tablespoons chocolate malted milk powder**
1½ **cups skim milk**

In a blender, combine frozen yogurt, chocolate malted milk powder, and skim milk. Process until smooth. Pour into tall glasses.

*Per Serving: Calories: 160   Total fat: 1 g   Saturated fat: 0 g
Cholesterol: 4 mg   Percentage calories from fat: 4%*

307 LEMON HONEY BELGIAN WAFFLES
Prep: 10 minutes   Cook: 16 to 20 minutes   Serves: 4

This hearty, fiber-rich waffle includes the addition of cereal nuggets to give it a slightly nutty crunch. You can substitute orange zest for the lemon and maple syrup for the honey. If you do not have a Belgian waffle iron maker, the batter can be cooked in a traditional waffle iron.

Vegetable cooking spray
1 **egg, separated**
¾ **cup all-purpose flour**
¾ **cup whole wheat flour**
1 **teaspoon baking powder**
½ **teaspoon baking soda**
½ **teaspoon salt**
¼ **cup natural wheat and barley cereal nuggets (such as Grape-Nuts)**

1½ **cups buttermilk**
2 **tablespoons canola or vegetable oil**
1 **tablespoon honey or maple syrup**
2 **teaspoons grated lemon or orange zest**
Warmed honey or Orange-Maple Syrup (page 226)

1. Lightly coat a waffle iron with cooking spray; wipe off excess. Heat waffle iron.

2. In small bowl of an electric mixer, beat egg white until stiff but not dry. In a large bowl, stir together all-purpose flour, whole wheat flour, baking powder, baking soda, salt, and cereal. In another bowl, whisk together buttermilk, oil, egg, honey, and lemon zest; add to dry ingredients. Stir just until moistened. Fold in beaten egg white.

3. Pour ⅓ cup batter per waffle onto hot waffle iron, spreading batter to cover grids. Cook until steaming stops and waffle is crisp and brown, about 4 to 5 minutes. Repeat with remaining batter. Serve with warmed honey or Orange-Maple Syrup.

*Per Serving: Calories: 329   Total fat: 11 g   Saturated fat: 1 g
Cholesterol: 57 mg   Percentage calories from fat: 28%*

308 LEMON PEPPER POPOVERS
Prep: 10 minutes   Cook: 30 to 35 minutes   Makes: 6

Lemon and pepper accent these puffy popovers. Make sure you preheat the popover pans when preheating the oven.

Vegetable cooking spray	1 teaspoon grated lemon zest
1 cup skim milk	¼ teaspoon salt
1 whole egg	⅛ teaspoon coarsely cracked
2 egg whites	black pepper
1 tablespoon canola oil	1 cup flour

1. Preheat oven to 425°F. Lightly coat 6 popover pans or 6-ounce custard cups with cooking spray. If using custard cups, place on a baking sheet. Place popover pans or custard cups in oven to warm while preheating.

2. In a blender or food processor, combine milk, egg, egg whites, oil, lemon zest, salt, pepper, and flour. Whirl until smooth, stirring down sides of container occasionally (with machine off). Divide batter evenly among preheated popover pans or custard cups.

3. Bake 30 to 35 minutes, or until popovers are puffy and golden. Serve at once.

Per Serving: Calories: 132 Total fat: 4 g Saturated fat: 0 g
Cholesterol: 36 mg Percentage calories from fat: 27%

309 BANANA PINEAPPLE SHAKE
Prep: 3 hours (including freezing time)   Cook: none   Serves: 2

Somehow, bananas overripen in my house before they can be eaten. I just plop the overripe bananas in the freezer and use them when I need them. If you don't have frozen bananas in the freezer, use the method below. Freezing the bananas also helps to chill the drink and make it thick.

2 small slightly overripe
   bananas, peeled and cut
   into 2-inch chunks
	1 cup buttermilk or nonfat
	   plain yogurt

1 (8-ounce) can crushed
   pineapple in pineapple
   juice, chilled
	¼ cup pineapple-orange juice
	2 teaspoons honey (optional)
	2 ice cubes

1. Arrange bananas on a small baking sheet and place in freezer until hard, about 3 hours.

2. In a blender, place frozen banana chunks, crushed pineapple with juice, buttermilk, pineapple-orange juice, honey, and ice cubes. Process, using pulses, until mixture is smooth. Pour into tall glasses.

Per Serving: Calories: 237 Total fat: 2 g Saturated fat: 1 g
Cholesterol: 5 mg Percentage calories from fat: 6%

310 MANGO YOGURT SMOOTHIE
Prep: 5 minutes   Cook: none   Serves: 2

1 large ripe mango
1 cup nonfat plain yogurt
1 cup skim milk

1 tablespoon honey
2 ice cubes
Pinch of grated nutmeg

Peel mango with a swivel-bladed vegetable peeler. Cut fruit into large chunks. Place in a blender or food processor. Include any fruit remaining on pit, which can be scraped off with a small paring knife. Add yogurt, milk, honey, and ice cubes. Whirl until smooth. Pour into tall glasses. Dust with nutmeg. Serve at once.

Per Serving: Calories: 223 Total fat: 1 g Saturated fat: 0 g
Cholesterol: 5 mg Percentage calories from fat: 3%

311 BLUEBERRY MUFFINS
Prep: 15 minutes   Cook: 20 minutes   Makes: 12

For the greatest enjoyment, serve these hearty, coarse-grained muffins warm, as soon as they come out of the oven. If you are using frozen blueberries, be sure to add them right out of the freezer without thawing first, to preserve their texture.

Vegetable cooking spray
¾ cup all-purpose flour
¾ cup whole wheat flour
1 cup quick-cooking
    multigrain cereal (rye,
    barley, oats, wheat, etc.)
¼ cup firmly packed light
    brown sugar
2 teaspoons baking powder
½ teaspoon baking soda

½ teaspoon salt
¾ cup buttermilk
4 tablespoons (½ stick)
    reduced-fat margarine,
    melted
1 egg
1 teaspoon vanilla extract
1 cup fresh or frozen
    blueberries

1. Preheat oven to 400°F. Coat 12 medium-size muffin pan cups with cooking spray.

2. In a large bowl, combine all-purpose flour, whole wheat flour, cereal, brown sugar, baking powder, baking soda, and salt. Make a well in the center. In another bowl, whisk together buttermilk, margarine, egg, and vanilla. Add to dry ingredients; stir with a fork just until moistened. Gently stir in blueberries. Batter will be stiff.

3. Spoon batter evenly into muffin cups, filling almost to tops; then spread batter out to fill muffin cups. Bake 20 minutes, or until muffins are browned. Remove from pans and serve warm.

Per Serving: Calories: 132 Total fat: 3 g Saturated fat: 1 g
Cholesterol: 18 mg Percentage calories from fat: 21%

312   CURRANT WALNUT SCONES

Prep: 15 minutes   Cook: 20 minutes   Makes: 8

Serve these not-too-sweet scones warm with honey or an orange marmalade fruit spread.

1½ cups all-purpose flour
½ cup whole wheat flour
¼ cup plus 1 tablespoon sugar
1 tablespoon baking powder
¼ teaspoon salt
4 tablespoons (½ stick) reduced-fat margarine

½ cup currants
2 tablespoons toasted chopped walnuts
⅔ cup evaporated skimmed milk
2 egg whites

1. Preheat oven to 400°F. In a large bowl, combine all-purpose flour, whole wheat flour, ¼ cup sugar, baking powder, and salt. With a pastry blender or 2 knives, cut in margarine until mixture is size of small peas. Stir in currants and walnuts.

2. In a small bowl, blend together milk and egg whites. Add to dry ingredients and stir with a fork just until evenly moistened. Dough will be sticky.

3. Turn out dough onto a well-floured surface and knead gently 5 to 6 times with floured hands. Place dough on a large baking sheet. Shape into an 8-inch circle about 1 inch thick. Cut into 8 wedges, but do not separate (a hot knife helps). Sprinkle remaining 1 tablespoon sugar evenly over top.

4. Bake 20 minutes, or until scones are golden. Serve warm.

*Per Serving: Calories: 232 Total fat: 4 g Saturated fat: 1 g
Cholesterol: 1 mg Percentage calories from fat: 16%*

313   STRAWBERRY BANANA NOG

Prep: 5 minutes   Cook: none   Serves: 2 to 3

This creamy rich drink is thickened with a low-fat silken tofu, which you won't even taste. If you have time, freeze bananas chunks and strawberry slices before pureeing to make an even thicker nog.

2 small ripe bananas, cut into chunks
1 cup fresh strawberries, sliced, plus 2 or 3 whole berries
1 cup skim milk

⅔ cup 1% fat silken tofu
1 to 2 teaspoons sugar, depending upon sweetness of fruit
½ teaspoon vanilla extract
2 ice cubes

In a blender or food processor, combine bananas, strawberries, milk, tofu, sugar, vanilla, and ice cubes. Whirl until creamy smooth. Pour into tall glasses. Garnish each with a fresh strawberry.

*Per Serving: Calories: 131 Total fat: 1 g Saturated fat: 0 g
Cholesterol: 2 mg Percentage calories from fat: 8%*

314   APRICOT COUSCOUS
Prep: 5 minutes   Cook: 2 minutes   Serves: 4

Couscous for breakfast? Why not! This can also be a side dish to poultry, pork, or fish.

1 cup orange juice	1 cup whole wheat couscous
8 dried apricots, snipped	4 teaspoons sliced almonds
¼ teaspoon salt	

In a medium saucepan, place orange juice, 1 cup water, apricots, and salt; bring to a boil over high heat, about 2 minutes. Remove pan from heat; stir in couscous. Let stand 5 minutes, or until liquid is absorbed. Top each serving with 1 teaspoon almonds. Serve warm.

Per Serving: Calories: 246 Total fat: 1 g Saturated fat: 0 g
Cholesterol: 0 mg Percentage calories from fat: 5%

---

315   RAISIN DATE GRANOLA
Prep: 10 minutes   Cook: 31 to 36 minutes   Serves: 6

Most granolas are loaded with fat-laden ingredients, especially coconut, seeds, and butter. I eliminated these, increased the amount of fiber-rich dried fruits, and substituted oil. The molasses gives the granola an old-fashioned taste that I like. Have it with yogurt or skim milk, or over fresh fruit with a dollop of yogurt.

2 cups rolled oats (not instant)	¼ cup unsulfured molasses
¼ cup unblanched sliced almonds or coarsely chopped pecans or walnuts	1 tablespoon canola oil
	¼ teaspoon cinnamon
	½ teaspoon vanilla extract
	⅓ cup golden raisins
¼ cup maple syrup or honey	⅓ cup chopped pitted dates

1. Preheat oven to 325°F. In a large bowl, combine oats with almonds. Stir to combine.

2. In a small saucepan, combine maple syrup, molasses, 2 tablespoons water, oil, and cinnamon. Cook over medium heat, stirring, until heated through, about 1 minute. Stir in vanilla. Pour over oats and stir to coat. Spread evenly into a 10 x 15-inch jelly roll pan.

3. Bake 30 to 35 minutes, or until granola is toasted, stirring every 10 minutes. Remove from oven. Stir in raisins and dates. Let cool. Granola will crisp up upon cooling. Stir in an airtight container.

Per Serving: Calories: 270 Total fat: 6 g Saturated fat: 1 g
Cholesterol: 0 mg Percentage calories from fat: 20%

316   CURRANT CARAWAY BISCUITS

Prep: 15 minutes   Cook: 15 minutes   Makes: 24

These mini biscuits taste just like a hearty Irish soda bread.

2 cups all-purpose flour	3 tablespoons reduced-fat
1 cup whole wheat flour	margarine
2 tablespoons light brown	⅓ cup currants
sugar	2 teaspoons caraway seeds
2 teaspoons baking powder	1 egg or ¼ cup frozen egg
1 teaspoon baking soda	substitute, thawed
¼ teaspoon salt	1 cup buttermilk

1. Preheat oven to 350°F. In a large bowl, combine all-purpose flour, whole wheat flour, brown sugar, baking powder, baking soda, and salt. Whisk gently or stir to blend. Cut in margarine until mixture resembles small peas. Stir in currants and caraway seeds. In a small bowl, blend together egg and buttermilk. Add to dry ingredients and stir just until moistened.

2. Turn out dough onto a lightly floured surface and gently knead together 8 to 10 times. Shape into a ball. Roll out dough to a round about ½ inch thick. With a floured 2-inch biscuit cutter, cut dough into biscuits. Place on an ungreased baking sheet. Reroll dough to make additional biscuits.

3. Bake 15 minutes, or until biscuits are golden brown. Serve warm.

*Per Serving: Calories: 79   Total fat: 1 g   Saturated fat: 0 g
Cholesterol: 9 mg   Percentage calories from fat: 13%*

Chapter 13

Low-Fat Cakes, Cookies, and Puddings

How sweet it is! While Jackie Gleason was talking about life, these sumptuous desserts will fulfill your greatest expectations. What makes these desserts so exceptionally pleasing is that all are low in fat, low in calories, and surprisingly easy to prepare.

If you like chocolate the way I like chocolate, you won't be disappointed here. Hot Fudge Brownie Pudding uses unsweetened cocoa instead of chocolate baking squares, which reduces the fat by half; vegetable oil replaces the butter and 1% skim milk instead of the full-fat whole milk. Chocolate Cinnamon Angel Food Cake, made with no-cholesterol egg whites and unsweetened cocoa, and accented with cinnamon, is a cloud of low-fat lightness.

Apples, a high-fiber fruit, raisins, and loads of spices are wrapped in flaky filo pastry for Easy Apple Strudel, made with only tablespoons of fat! Individual Cherry-Topped Cheesecakes include crunchy, nutlike cereal nuggets in the crust and light Neufchâtel in place of high-fat cream cheese. Carrot Cake with Pineapple Drizzle is a favorite of mine. Substituting 2 egg whites for one of the eggs and using canola oil and buttermilk are some of my tricks. Since reducing the fat in cakes and cookies increases toughness, I have found that using cake flour and sometimes cornstarch instead of all-purpose flour replaces part of the tenderness.

Another favorite of mine is tapioca pudding. In this, an egg substitute and skim milk replace eggs and whole milk, and a spiced fruit sauce, for added fiber, combine for Tapioca with Spiced Plum Sauce. Orzo Pudding with Raspberry Coulis is a takeoff on rice pudding made with only 1 egg, skim milk, and lemon zest for added flavor.

Cookie monsters won't be able to keep their hands out of the cookie jar. Chocolate Chip Cookies and Ginger, Almond, and Raisin Biscotti use low-fat ingredients. Prune puree replaces the fat in Oatmeal Cookies to make them more nutritious. Who says you can't have your cake—or cookie or pudding—and eat it, too!

317   CHOCOLATE CINNAMON ANGEL FOOD CAKE

Prep: 27 minutes   Bake: 30 to 35 minutes   Serves: 12 to 16

Tender, airy, and fluffy as a cloud! Very stiff beating of the egg whites is necessary to achieve a high-volume cake. If you want to make the traditional angel food cake, eliminate the cocoa and increase the cake flour to 1 cup.

¾ cup unsifted cake flour	12 egg whites (1½ cups), at
1¼ cups sugar	room temperature
¼ cup unsweetened cocoa	1½ teaspoons cream of tartar
powder	¼ teaspoon salt
½ teaspoon cinnamon	1½ teaspoons vanilla extract

1. Place oven rack at lowest position in oven. Preheat oven to 375°F. In a small bowl, sift together flour, ½ cup sugar, cocoa, and cinnamon. Mix lightly with a fork until well mixed.

2. In large bowl of an electric mixer, beat egg whites with cream of tartar, salt, and vanilla on medium speed until mixture forms soft peaks. Gradually add remaining ¾ cup sugar, beating at highest speed, until stiff but not dry peaks form. Spoon flour mixture, part at a time, over beaten egg whites, folding in gently until blended. Spoon batter into an ungreased 10 x 4-inch tube pan with removable bottom. Gently cut through batter with a knife to remove any air pockets.

3. Bake 30 to 35 minutes, or until cake springs back when tapped with a small metal spatula. Immediately invert cake onto funnel or soft drink bottle; let stand until completely cool.

Per Serving: Calories: 111 Total fat: < 1 g Saturated fat: 0 g
Cholesterol: 0 mg Percentage calories from fat: 2%

318   CHOCOLATE ORANGE MINI-CUPCAKES

Prep: 15 minutes   Bake: 12 minutes   Makes: 24

These bite-size cupcakes are sumptuous.

Vegetable cooking spray	½ cup unsweetened orange
1½ cups flour	juice
½ cup granulated sugar	3 tablespoons canola oil
¼ cup European-style	1 tablespoon distilled white
unsweetened cocoa	vinegar
powder	2 teaspoons grated orange zest
1 teaspoon baking soda	1 teaspoon vanilla extract
¼ teaspoon salt	1 teaspoon powdered sugar

1. Preheat oven to 375°F. Coat two mini-muffin pans (12 cups each) with cooking spray.

2. In a large bowl, combine flour, sugar, cocoa, baking soda, and salt. Stir with a fork until mixed. In another bowl, whisk together orange juice, 1/3 cup water, oil, vinegar, orange zest, and vanilla. Add to dry ingredients, stirring just until blended. Batter will be stiff. Spoon into prepared muffin cups, filling almost to top.

3. Bake 12 minutes, or until a wooden pick inserted near center comes out clean. Carefully remove cupcakes from pans. Let cool completely on a wire rack. Dust cupcakes with powdered sugar just before serving.

*Per Serving: Calories: 67   Total fat: 2 g   Saturated fat: 0 g
Cholesterol: 0 mg   Percentage calories from fat: 28%*

---

319   CHERRY-TOPPED CHEESECAKES
Prep: 19 minutes   Bake: 10 minutes   Makes: 24

These creamy two-bite cheesecakes are a snap to prepare. The crust is a crunchy nutlike cereal, and the topping is prepared cherry pie filling. You will have some of the thickened pie filling juices left over. Simply discard or thin out with some orange juice and use as a sauce for plain cake or over frozen yogurt.

1/3 cup crunchy nutlike cereal nuggets, such as Grape-Nuts	2 teaspoons orange juice Cheese Filling (recipe follows)
1/4 cup plus 2 tablespoons sugar	1 (21-ounce) can light cherry pie filling

1. Preheat oven to 375°F. Line 24 mini-muffin pan cups with paper liners.

2. In a small bowl, combine cereal, 2 tablespoons sugar, and orange juice. Stir just until moistened. Press 1 teaspoon of crumbs into bottom of each paper-lined muffin cup. Place 1 level measuring tablespoon of cheese filling into each cup.

3. Bake cheesecakes 10 minutes, or until firm. Let cool in pans 10 minutes. Remove from pans and let cool completely. Top cheesecakes with cherry pie filling, including 3 to 4 cherries in each. Refrigerate until ready to serve.

CHEESE FILLING
Makes: 1 1/2 cups

1 (8-ounce) package Neufchâtel cheese, at room temperature	1/4 cup sugar 1 egg 1/8 teaspoon almond extract

In small bowl of an electric mixer, beat cream cheese, sugar, egg, and almond extract on high speed, until light and fluffy, about 5 minutes.

*Per Serving: Calories: 73   Total fat: 2 g   Saturated fat: 1 g
Cholesterol: 16 mg   Percentage calories from fat: 30%*

320 BROWN SUGAR SHORTCAKES WITH MIXED SUMMER FRUITS

Prep: 20 minutes   Bake: 12 minutes   Serves: 10

A big bowl of mixed summer fruits is surrounded with shortcake biscuits and a honey-yogurt sauce to top. If fruits are too tart, you can add 1 to 2 tablespoons sugar, but I find the sauce is adequate. Let the guests make their own shortcakes.

Vegetable cooking spray
2 cups flour
2 tablespoons light brown sugar
2 teaspoons baking powder
¾ teaspoon baking soda
½ teaspoon salt
¾ cup buttermilk
¼ cup vegetable oil

1 pint strawberries, halved
1 pint blueberries
2 large peaches or nectarines, pitted and sliced
1 cup raspberries
1 tablespoon fresh lemon juice
Honey-Yogurt Sauce (recipe follows)

1. Preheat oven to 425°F. Coat a large baking sheet with cooking spray. In a large bowl, combine flour, brown sugar, baking powder, baking soda, and salt. Mix with fork to blend well. Add buttermilk and oil; stir just until ingredients are moistened. Turn dough out onto a lightly floured surface and knead 5 to 6 times.

2. With a floured rolling pin, roll dough out to ½ inch thick. Cut out shortcakes with a 2½-inch cutter and place 1 inch apart on prepared baking sheet. Gather trimmings to make more shortcakes. Bake shortcakes 12 minutes, or until lightly golden.

3. Meanwhile in a large bowl, combine strawberries, blueberries, peaches, raspberries, and lemon juice. Toss lightly to combine.

4. To serve, place fruit bowl on large serving platter. Surround with warm shortcakes and serve honey-yogurt sauce in a separate bowl.

*Per Serving: Calories:275   Total fat: 6 g   Saturated fat: 1 g
Cholesterol: 1 mg   Percentage calories from fat: 21%*

321 HONEY-YOGURT SAUCE

Prep: 3 minutes   Cook: none   Makes: 2½ cups

1¼ cups nonfat plain yogurt
1¼ cups nonfat sour cream

⅓ cup honey

In a medium bowl, combine yogurt, sour cream, and honey. Stir to blend well. Cover and refrigerate until ready to use.

*Per ¼-Cup Serving: Calories: 70   Total fat: 0 g   Saturated fat: 0 g
Cholesterol: 1 mg   Percentage calories from fat: 0%*

322 PALACSINTA

Prep: 1 hour 20 minutes (includes chilling time)
Cook: 12 to 14 minutes   Serves: 6

This Hungarian crepe dessert, pronounced *pah-lah-chin-tahk,* is simple and sumptuous. For ease of preparation when making crepes, scoop up 2 tablespoons crepe batter into a ¼-cup dry measure to fill it halfway.

2 **egg whites**	**Vegetable cooking spray**
1 **cup skim milk**	¼ **cup apricot fruit spread**
1 **cup flour**	1 **tablespoon ground toasted**
3 **tablespoons sugar**	**walnuts**
¼ **teaspoon salt**	

1. In a blender container, place egg whites, milk, flour, 2 tablespoons of sugar, and salt. Blend until smooth; scrape down sides of container. Pour into a 2-cup measure. Cover and refrigerate at least 1 hour.

2. Heat a 7-inch crepe pan or skillet over medium heat until hot. Coat pan with cooking spray. Pour in 2 tablespoons batter, rotating pan quickly to spread batter evenly. Cook until crepe is lightly browned on underside and dry on top, about 30 seconds. Turn it over and cook 5 seconds on other side. Remove crepe from pan to a large baking sheet. Repeat with remaining batter to make a total of 12 crepes. Coat pan when necessary and stir batter occasionally. Place wax paper between crepes to prevent them from sticking.

3. Preheat oven to 350°F. Spread 2 level teaspoonfuls of apricot fruit spread over whiter side of each crepe. Fold in half, then in half again, to form a triangle, or roll up loosely to form a cylinder. Place on a baking sheet. Heat palacsinta 5 to 7 minutes, or until warm.

4. In a small cup, combine remaining 1 tablespoon sugar with walnuts. Place 2 palacsinta on each dessert place. Sprinkle each serving with 1 teaspoon of sugar-walnut mixture.

Per Serving: Calories: 163 Total fat: 2 g Saturated fat: 0 g
Cholesterol: 1 mg Percentage calories from fat: 11%

323   EASY APPLE STRUDEL
Prep: 30 minutes   Bake: 35 minutes   Serves: 8

As a child I used sit at my Grandma Lena's feet as she pared the apples for strudel, the peel coming off in one spiral piece and falling in mounds in front of me on the newspaper-lined kitchen floor. Then I watched in awe as she stretched and pulled the dough to paper-thinness and filled it with the spiced apple mixture. This short-cut version of strudel still fills my house with the same aromas, and brings back those happy memories.

Vegetable cooking spray
1 slice of firm-textured white
   bread
3 large apples, such as
   Granny Smith, red
   or Golden Delicious,
   peeled and chopped
   (about 4 cups)
½ cup golden raisins

1 tablespoon fresh lemon
   juice
1 teaspoon grated lemon zest
⅓ cup sugar
¾ teaspoon cinnamon
1½ teaspoons butter, melted
1½ teaspoons canola oil
6 sheets of filo pastry, thawed
   if frozen

1. Preheat oven to 375°F. Line a 10 x 15-inch jelly roll pan with aluminum foil. Coat foil with cooking spray. In a food processor, grind bread into fine crumbs. Place crumbs in a pie plate and toast in oven until golden, about 5 minutes. Watch carefully to prevent burning.

2. In a large bowl, combine apples, raisins, lemon juice, and lemon zest; toss to mix. In a small bowl, stir together sugar and cinnamon. In another small bowl, combine melted butter and oil.

3. Unroll filo and place on a large baking sheet; cover with plastic wrap and top with a slightly dampened kitchen towel to prevent filo from drying out. Place 1 filo sheet on a sheet of plastic wrap. Using a pastry brush, dab with part of butter-oil mixture; coat with cooking spray. Sprinkle with part of bread crumbs. Repeat layering with remaining filo, butter-oil mixture, cooking spray, and crumbs. Top sheet should just be brushed with the butter-oil mixture and coated with cooking spray.

4. Spread apple filling along one long edge of dough, leaving a 2-inch border along edge and at sides. Sprinkle cinnamon sugar over apples. Fold bottom edge up over apple filling; fold in at sides. Starting at longer side and using plastic wrap, lift filo and carefully roll up like a jelly roll. Place strudel, seam side down, on prepared baking sheet. Brush with remaining butter-oil mixture. Coat with cooking spray.

5. Bake 15 minutes. Reduce oven temperature to 350° and bake 15 minutes longer, or until golden. Serve warm.

Per Serving: Calories: 165 Total fat: 4 g Saturated fat: 1 g
Cholesterol: 2 mg Percentage calories from fat: 19%

324   TAPIOCA WITH SPICED PLUM SAUCE
Prep: 15 minutes (includes standing time)   Cook: 8 minutes
Chill: 2 hours   Serves: 6

Quick-cooking tapioca topped with a delicious plum sauce. Try the sauce over rice pudding, too.

¼ cup sugar
¼ cup quick-cooking tapioca
⅛ teaspoon salt
¼ cup frozen egg substitute,
    thawed, or 1 egg

2 cups skim milk
¼ teaspoon almond extract
    Spiced Plum Sauce (recipe
    follows)

1. In a medium saucepan, combine sugar, tapioca, salt, and egg substitute. Stir in milk. Let stand 5 minutes to soften tapioca. Cook tapioca mixture over medium heat, stirring constantly, until mixture comes to a full rolling boil, about 8 minutes.

2. Remove from heat and stir in almond extract. Cover surface with plastic wrap. Let stand 20 minutes and stir again. Refrigerate at least 2 hours, or until very cold. To serve, stir chilled tapioca. Spoon into compote dishes or wine goblets. Top with sauce.

Per Serving: Calories: 224 Total fat: 1 g Saturated fat: 0 g
Cholesterol: 2 mg Percentage calories from fat: 2%

325   SPICED PLUM SAUCE
Prep: 10 minutes   Cook: 10 to 12 minutes   Chill: 2 hours
Makes: 2 cups

1 pound fresh purple plums,
    halved, pitted, and sliced
½ cup sugar

½ teaspoon ground cinnamon
½ cup ruby port

In a medium saucepan, combine plums, sugar, cinnamon, and port. Bring to a boil, reduce heat, cover, and simmer, stirring occasionally, until plums are soft, 10 to 12 minutes. Remove from heat and let cool slightly. Cover and refrigerate at least 2 hours, or until cold.

Per ⅓-Cup Serving: Calories: 135 Total fat: 1 g Saturated fat: 0 g
Cholesterol: 0 mg Percentage calories from fat: 3%

326   CHOCOLATE CHIP COOKIES
Prep: 13 minutes   Cook: 8 to 10 minutes   Makes: 32

Here's a low-fat version of America's favorite cookie. Make sure you use the mini-chocolate chips, as their smaller size is more evenly distributed in the cookies.

1 cup flour	4 tablespoons (½ stick) butter,
½ teaspoon baking soda	at room temperature
¼ teaspoon salt	1 egg white
¼ teaspoon cinnamon	1½ teaspoons vanilla extract
½ cup firmly packed light	½ cup semisweet chocolate
brown sugar	mini-morsels
⅓ cup granulated sugar	

1. Preheat oven to 375°F. On a sheet of wax paper, combine flour, baking soda, salt, and cinnamon; stir well to mix.

2. In small bowl of an electric mixer, beat together brown sugar, granulated sugar, butter, egg white, and vanilla on medium speed until smooth and creamy. Blend in flour mixture just until combined. Stir in chocolate mini-morsels.

3. Drop batter by teaspoonfuls 2 inches apart on large ungreased baking sheets. Bake 8 to 10 minutes, or until golden. Transfer cookies to a wire rack, let cool completely. Cookies will puff during baking, flatten upon cooling.

*Per Serving: Calories: 57   Total fat: 2 g   Saturated fat: 1 g
Cholesterol: 4 mg   Percentage calories from fat: 30%*

---

327   LEMON ROLL
Prep: 15 minutes   Bake: 12 to 13 minutes   Serves: 8 to 10

Prepare the filling a few hours before making the cake so it has time to set up and chill. For an even easier dessert, omit the lemon filling and spread the cake with a no-sugar fruit spread or refrigerated whipped topping and sliced strawberries.

Vegetable cooking spray	⅔ cup granulated sugar
1 cup sifted cake flour	1 teaspoon vanilla extract
1 teaspoon baking powder	3 tablespoons powdered
¼ teaspoon salt	sugar
2 egg whites	Light Lemon Filling (recipe
⅛ teaspoon cream of tartar	follows)
½ cup frozen egg substitute,	
thawed	

1. Preheat oven to 375°F. Coat a 10 x 15-inch jelly roll pan with cooking spray. Line bottom of pan with wax paper; trim off excess paper from edges and coat again with cooking spray. On a sheet of wax paper, combine flour, baking powder, and salt.

2. In small bowl of an electric mixer, beat egg whites with cream of tartar on high speed until firm peaks form; set aside. In large bowl of electric mixer, beat egg substitute until thick and creamy, about 1 minute; lower speed. Gradually add sugar, beating constantly, until mixture is very thick, about 2 minutes. Stir in ⅓ cup water and vanilla. Add flour mixture, stirring until combined. Fold in beaten egg whites. Spread batter evenly in prepared pan.

3. Bake 12 to 13 minutes, or just until cake begins to pull away from the sides of the pan and springs back when lightly pressed with a small metal spatula.

4. Loosen cake around edges with a knife. Invert pan onto a clean kitchen towel dusted with 2 tablespoons powdered sugar; peel off wax paper. Gently roll up cake and towel together from short end. Place roll, seam side down, on a wire rack; let cool completely. When cool, unroll cake carefully. Spread with lemon filling. To start rerolling, lift end of cake with towel. Place roll, seam side down, on serving platter. Dust with remaining 1 tablespoon powdered sugar.

Per Serving: Calories: 195   Total fat: 1 g   Saturated fat: 0 g
Cholesterol: 24 mg   Percentage calories from fat: 3%

---

328   LIGHT LEMON FILLING
Prep: 5 minutes   Cook: 8 to 10 minutes   Chill: 3 hours
Makes: 1 cup plus 2 tablespoons

The egg yolk is added to the filling to give it richness. Make sure the filling is well chilled before filling cake roll. You can also use this filling in meringue cups or the little sponge cake shells usually found in the produce section of the supermarket near the strawberries.

⅔ **cup sugar**
3 **tablespoons cornstarch**
1 **egg yolk**

¼ **cup fresh lemon juice**
2 **teaspoons grated lemon zest**

1. In a small saucepan, combine sugar and cornstarch. Stir in ⅔ cup water. Cook over medium-low heat, stirring constantly, until mixture becomes translucent, thickens, and bubbles, 6 to 8 minutes. Cook 1 minute longer. Remove from heat.

2. In a small bowl, beat half of hot mixture into egg yolk, then stir back into saucepan. Cook, stirring, 1 minute longer. Stir in lemon juice and lemon zest. Pour into a small bowl. Press plastic wrap directly on surface. Refrigerate at least 3 hours, or until very cold.

Per Tablespoon: Calories: 38   Total fat: 1 g   Saturated fat: 0 g
Cholesterol: 12 mg   Percentage calories from fat: 6%

329 CARROT CAKE WITH PINEAPPLE DRIZZLE

Prep: 30 minutes   Cook: 30 to 35 minutes   Serves: 24

Vegetable cooking spray
2¼ cups sifted cake flour
1 teaspoon baking powder
1 teaspoon baking soda
½ teaspoon salt
1½ teaspoons cinnamon
½ teaspoon ground nutmeg
1 whole egg
2 egg whites
¾ cup firmly packed light
  brown sugar

¾ cup buttermilk
¼ cup canola or vegetable oil
2 teaspoons vanilla extract
2 cups coarsely shredded
  carrots (about 4 large)
1 (8-ounce) can crushed
  pineapple in pineapple
  juice, drained, with juice
  reserved
½ cup golden raisins
¾ cup sifted powdered sugar

1. Preheat oven to 350°F. Coat a 9 x 13-inch baking pan with cooking spray. In a small bowl, place cake flour, baking powder, baking soda, salt, cinnamon, and nutmeg. Stir with a fork to mix well.

2. In large bowl of an electric mixer, beat egg and egg whites on high speed until light, fluffy, and thick, about 2 minutes. Beat in brown sugar, buttermilk, oil, and vanilla until smooth. Reduce speed to low; blend in dry ingredients. Stir in carrots, drained crushed pineapple, and raisins until thoroughly combined. Pour mixture into prepared pan.

3. Bake 30 to 35 minutes, or until a wooden pick inserted near center comes out clean. Let cake cool completely in pan on a wire rack.

4. In a small bowl, blend together powdered sugar and 3 to 4 teaspoons of reserved pineapple juice to make a thick but runny glaze. Drizzle over cooled cake in pan in both directions to make an uneven crisscross pattern. Let stand until set. Cut cake into 24 squares to serve.

Per Serving: Calories: 119 Total fat: 3 g Saturated fat: 0 g
Cholesterol: 9 mg Percentage calories from fat: 20%

330 CARAMELIZED APPLES IN FILO NESTS
Prep: 20 minutes   Cook: 21 minutes   Serves: 6

Believe it or not, this tastes like pie à la mode. The filo nests can be made ahead of time and stored in an airtight container.

Butter-flavored cooking
   spray
4 teaspoons butter
6 frozen filo pastry sheets,
   thawed and stacked
½ cup sugar
½ teaspoon cinnamon
⅛ teaspoon ground nutmeg

3 medium baking apples
   (about 6 ounces each),
   such as Rome Beauty or
   Golden Delicious
1½ teaspoons fresh lemon juice
Nonfat vanilla ice cream or
   vanilla frozen yogurt

1. Preheat oven to 350°F. Coat 6 medium-size muffin cups with cooking spray. In a small skillet over low heat or in a small cup in a microwave, melt 2 teaspoons butter.

2. Fold filo sheets in half, then fold in half again; trim to 5-inch squares. For each filo nest, place one filo square on work surface. Using a pastry brush, lightly dab with melted butter; coat with cooking spray. Set a second square on top; dab with butter and coat with cooking spray. Set a third square at a 45-degree angle, forming an 8-pointed star; dab with butter and coat with cooking spray. Cover with a fourth square in same way; dab with butter and coat with cooking spray.

3. Gently press each stacked filo into a muffin cup, making sure edges of filo come up sides of cup. Bake 8 minutes, or until lightly browned and crisp. Let cool 5 minutes. Carefully remove filo nests from muffin cups to a wire rack.

4. In a heavy, medium saucepan, stir together sugar, cinnamon, nutmeg, and 1 tablespoon water. Bring to a boil, stirring to dissolve sugar. Cook without stirring until syrup is light amber in color, about 5 minutes. Remove pan from heat. Add remaining 2 teaspoons butter; swirl pan to melt butter. Add apples and sprinkle with lemon juice. *Do not stir.* Return pan to heat, cover, and cook 5 minutes. Uncover and cook, stirring occasionally, until apples are tender and slightly glazed, about 3 minutes.

5. To serve, place each filo nest on a flat dessert plate. Place a scoop of ice cream (⅓ cup) into nest and top with ⅓ cup of warmed apples.

Per Serving: Calories: 267   Total fat: 5 g   Saturated fat: 2 g
Cholesterol: 7 mg   Percentage calories from fat: 17%

331   HOT FUDGE BROWNIE PUDDING

Prep: 15 minutes   Bake: 40 minutes   Serves: 10 to 12

This decadent dessert is a combination of a brownie and a soft chocolate pudding, which you spoon over the top. Make sure your oil is fresh.

1 cup sifted flour
¾ cup granulated sugar
¼ cup plus 2 tablespoons unsweetened cocoa powder
2 teaspoons baking powder
¼ teaspoon salt

½ cup 1% low-fat milk
2 tablespoons vegetable oil
1½ teaspoons vanilla extract
¼ cup coarsely chopped toasted walnuts
½ cup firmly packed light brown sugar

1. Preheat oven to 350°F. In an ungreased 9-inch square baking pan, combine flour, sugar, 2 tablespoons of cocoa, baking powder, and salt. Mix well until smooth. Stir in milk, oil, and vanilla. Stir in walnuts. Spread batter evenly in pan. Sprinkle with brown sugar and remaining ¼ cup cocoa. Pour 1¾ cups hot water over batter. *Do not stir.*

2. Bake 40 minutes, or until top is set. Serve warm, spooning out cake with soft pudding that forms on the bottom. If desired, serve with a nonfat frozen vanilla yogurt.

Per Serving: Calories: 167   Total fat: 4 g   Saturated fat: 1 g
Cholesterol: 0 mg   Percentage calories from fat: 23%

332   PEACHY ORANGE COBBLER

Prep: 8 minutes   Cook: 6 to 8 minutes
Bake: 26 to 33 minutes   Serves: 6

An old-fashioned favorite. You can substitute nectarines or combine plums with the peaches or nectarines.

1 pound (3 to 4 medium) firm-ripe peaches
1 tablespoon fresh lemon juice
⅓ cup plus 1 tablespoon sugar
1 tablespoon cornstarch

¾ cup unsweetened orange juice
1 teaspoon grated orange zest
Buttermilk Biscuit Topping (recipe follows)

1. Preheat oven to 375°F. Halve, pit, and slice peaches into a large bowl. Add lemon juice and toss to coat; set aside. You should have about 4 cups.

2. In a medium saucepan, combine ⅓ cup sugar with cornstarch. Gradually stir in orange juice. Cook and stir over medium heat until mixture comes to a boil, has thickened slightly, and is clear, about 4 to 5 minutes. Add peaches; stir to combine with sauce. Cook until fruit is hot, about 2 to 3 minutes, stirring occasionally. Stir in orange zest.

3. Spoon mixture into a 9-inch square pan. Drop biscuit topping by table-spoons over hot fruit. Sprinkle with remaining 1 tablespoon sugar. Bake 20 to 25 minutes, or until biscuits are golden and juices bubble up around the fruit. Serve warm.

BUTTERMILK BISCUIT TOPPING

1 **cup all-purpose flour**	¼ **teaspoon grated nutmeg**
2 **tablespoons sugar**	½ **cup buttermilk**
1 **teaspoon baking powder**	3 **tablespoons canola oil**
¼ **teaspoon baking soda**	

In a medium bowl, combine flour, sugar, baking powder, baking soda, and nutmeg; mix well. Stir in buttermilk and oil just until mixture is moistened. Dough is now ready to spoon on fruit.

*Per Serving: Calories: 257   Total fat: 7 g   Saturated fat: 1 g
Cholesterol: 1 mg   Percentage calories from fat: 25%*

---

333 LEMON SQUARES
Prep: 8 minutes   Bake: 30 minutes   Makes: 28

Very few people can resist buttery rich lemon squares. After several attempts, I was able to produce a cookie almost as rich as the original. If the top cracks slightly, don't be alarmed. Once dusted with powdered sugar and cut into tiny squares, no one will notice.

1¼ **cups sifted cake flour**	¼ **cup fresh lemon juice**
¾ **cup granulated sugar**	2 **tablespoons grated lemon**
¼ **cup reduced-fat margarine**	**zest**
¼ **cup Neufchâtel cheese,**	1 **tablespoon powdered sugar**
softened	
½ **cup frozen egg substitute,**	
thawed	

1. Preheat oven to 350°F. In a medium bowl, stir together 1 cup of flour and ¼ cup of granulated sugar. Cut in margarine and Neufchâtel with a pastry blender or fingertips until mixture is crumbly. Press mixture evenly into bottom of an 8-inch square baking pan. Bake crust 15 minutes, or until lightly browned.

2. Meanwhile, in a medium bowl, combine egg substitute, lemon juice, lemon zest, and remaining ¼ cup flour and ½ cup granulated sugar.

3. Remove crust from oven. Pour lemon mixture over hot prebaked crust. Return to oven and bake 15 minutes, or until top is set. Cool cookies in pan on a wire rack. Just before serving, dust with powdered sugar. Cut into approximately 2 x 1-inch bars with a sharp knife sprayed with cooking spray.

*Per Serving: Calories: 53   Total fat: 1 g   Saturated fat: 0 g
Cholesterol: 2 mg   Percentage calories from fat: 22%*

334   ORZO PUDDING WITH RASPBERRY COULIS

Prep: 3 minutes   Bake: 11 to 13 minutes
Chill: 3 to 4 hours   Serves: 4

A change of pace from rice pudding, orzo, the rice-shaped pasta, is used to make this lemon-flavored pudding. Place individual servings of the orzo pudding into custard cups, then unmold onto coulis, or use an ice-cream scoop.

⅓ cup uncooked orzo (rice-shaped pasta)	Pinch of salt
2 cups skim milk	1 teaspoon grated lemon zest
1 egg	Raspberry Coulis (recipe
1 tablespoon sugar	follows)
½ teaspoon vanilla extract	Mint sprigs (optional)

1. In a large saucepan over medium heat, bring orzo and milk just to a boil, stirring occasionally. Reduce heat and simmer, partially covered, until orzo is soft, 10 to 12 minutes. Watch carefully at end of cooking time that milk does not bubble over.

2. In a medium bowl, beat egg lightly with sugar, vanilla, salt, and lemon zest. Stir in half of warm milk from orzo mixture, then stir back into saucepan. Return to heat and cook 1 minute longer. Pour into a bowl, cover surface with plastic wrap, and let cool. Cover and refrigerate 3 to 4 hours, or until very cold. Pudding will thicken upon chilling. If too thick when ready to serve, stir in 1 to 2 tablespoons additional skim milk until creamy.

3. To serve, spread ¼ cup raspberry coulis onto each of 4 dessert plates. Mound ½ cup pudding in center of each. Garnish each serving with a mint sprig.

Per Serving: Calories: 235   Total fat: 2 g   Saturated fat: 1 g
Cholesterol: 56 mg   Percentage calories from fat: 7%

---

335   RASPBERRY COULIS

Prep: 5 minutes   Cook: none   Makes: 1 cup

This is the perfect low-fat (actually nonfat) dessert sauce; instant, tart-sweet, and ruby-colored.

1 (10-ounce) package frozen red raspberries in light syrup	2 tablespoons sugar

In a food processor or blender, place berries and sugar. Puree until smooth. Pour into a sieve set over a bowl and press puree with a wooden spoon to remove seeds.

Per Tablespoon: Calories: 24   Total fat: 0 g   Saturated fat: 0 g
Cholesterol: 0 mg   Percentage calories from fat: 0%

336   CRANBERRY CRUNCH BARS
Prep: 20 minutes   Bake: 43 to 48 minutes   Makes: 32

Two kinds of cranberries, fresh and dried, make up the tangy filling sandwiched between a cookie crust and a crumb topping.

Vegetable cooking spray
4 ounces Neufchâtel cheese, at room temperature
⅓ cup canola oil
½ cup firmly packed light brown sugar
¼ teaspoon grated nutmeg

¼ teaspoon salt
1½ cups sifted cake flour
¼ cup cornstarch
Double Cranberry Filling (recipe follows)
¼ cup granulated sugar

1. Preheat oven to 375°F. Coat a 9-inch square baking pan with cooking spray.

2. In small bowl of an electric mixer, beat cheese, oil, brown sugar, nutmeg, and salt on medium speed until smooth, about 30 seconds. On low speed, blend in flour and cornstarch just until combined. Remove ½ cup of cookie base and reserve. Spread remainder in prepared pan, using a metal spatula; press down to make an even layer.

3. Bake 15 minutes. Spoon double cranberry filling over cookie base, spreading evenly. In a small bowl, combine granulated sugar with reserved cookie crust using fingertips or a fork. Crumble evenly over filling.

4. Bake 20 to 25 minutes, or until crumb topping is golden. Let cool in pan on wire rack, then cut into bars.

DOUBLE CRANBERRY FILLING
Makes: 2 cups

2 cups fresh or partially thawed frozen cranberries
½ cup dried cranberries
¼ cup honey
¼ cup sugar

¾ teaspoon cinnamon
½ teaspoon nutmeg
¼ cup orange juice
2 teaspoons grated orange zest

In a medium nonreactive saucepan, bring fresh cranberries, dried cranberries, honey, sugar, cinnamon, nutmeg, orange juice, and orange zest to a boil over medium heat, about 5 minutes. Cook, stirring occasionally, until mixture thickens, about 8 minutes.

*Per Serving: Calories: 93   Total fat: 3 g   Saturated fat: 1 g
Cholesterol: 3 mg   Percentage calories from fat: 30%*

337   LEMON BUTTERMILK POUND CAKE

Prep: 20 minutes   Cook: 1 hour 10 minutes   Serves: 16

Pound cakes were so called because they were made with a pound each of butter, sugar, and flour, and loads of eggs, and had a dense texture. This pound cake has a less dense texture, no whole eggs, a minimum of fat, and lots of flavor. After baking, allow the cake to mellow for 24 hours before serving.

Vegetable cooking spray
4 tablespoons (½ stick) butter, softened to room temperature
3 tablespoons solid vegetable shortening
1⅓ cups sugar
3 egg whites

1 cup buttermilk
½ teaspoon baking soda
2¼ cups sifted cake flour
⅛ teaspoon salt
2 tablespoons grated lemon zest
1 teaspoon vanilla extract

1. Preheat oven to 325°F. Coat a 9 x 5 x 3-inch loaf pan with cooking spray. In large bowl of an electric mixer, beat butter, shortening, and sugar at high speed for 5 minutes, scraping down sides of bowl frequently. Beat in egg whites, one at a time, just until combined.

2. In a 1-cup glass measure, stir together buttermilk and baking soda. Combine flour and salt on wax paper. Add dry ingredients to creamed ingredients alternately with buttermilk, beginning and ending with dry ingredients. Stir in lemon zest and vanilla. Spoon batter into prepared pan.

3. Bake 1 hour 10 minutes, or until a wooden pick inserted near center comes out clean. Let cake cool in pan on a wire rack 5 minutes. Remove cake from pan and let cool completely. Wrap in aluminum foil; let stand overnight before slicing.

Per Serving: Calories: 171   Total fat: 6 g   Saturated fat: 2 g
Cholesterol: 8 mg   Percentage calories from fat: 29%

338 OATMEAL COOKIES

Prep: 10 minutes   Bake: 8 to 10 minutes   Makes: 36

Prune puree can be used to reduce the fat in baked products. You won't even notice it's gone in these fiber-rich, chewy cookies.

Vegetable cooking spray	1 teaspoon vanilla extract
½ cup granulated sugar	1 cup flour
½ cup firmly packed light brown sugar	½ teaspoon baking powder
	½ teaspoon baking soda
¼ cup Prune Puree (recipe follows)	¼ teaspoon salt
	1 cup rolled oats
¼ cup orange juice	½ cup raisins

1. Preheat oven to 350°F. Lightly coat 2 baking sheets with cooking spray.

2. In a small bowl, beat together granulated sugar, brown sugar, prune puree, orange juice, and vanilla until combined. In a large bowl, mix together flour, baking powder, baking soda, and salt. Stir in prune mixture. Fold in oats and raisins. Drop by heaping teaspoonfuls (2 level teaspoon measures) about 2 inches apart on prepared baking sheets. Spread each to a 1¼-inch round.

3. Bake 8 to 10 minutes, or until lightly brown. Transfer cookies to wire racks and let cool completely. Cookies will be soft after baking and will crisp up upon standing.

Per Serving: Calories: 55 Total fat: 1 g Saturated fat: 0 g
Cholesterol: 0 mg Percentage calories from fat: 4%

---

339 PRUNE PUREE

Prep: 2 minutes   Cook: none   Makes: 1 cup

To cut fat from baked goods, use a one-to-one substitution. For example, for 1 cup butter or shortening use 1 cup of this prune puree. The puree can be kept up to two weeks stored in an airtight container in the refrigerator.

1⅓ cups (8 ounces) pitted prunes

1. If prunes are not soft and moist, soak in a bowl of hot water just to cover 5 minutes. Drain, reserving soaking water. Use 6 tablespoons reserved liquid in place of water in Step 2.

2. Place prunes in a food processor with 6 tablespoons water. Process, using pulses, until puree is smooth, about 1 minute.

Per ¼ Cup: Calories: 136 Total fat: < 1 g Saturated fat: 0 g
Cholesterol: 0 mg Percentage calories from fat: 2%

340 GINGER, ALMOND, AND RAISIN BISCOTTI

Prep: 1 hour 10 minutes   Chill: 30 minutes
Bake: 40 to 45 minutes   Cool: 10 minutes   Makes: 36

With the ever-growing popularity of specialty coffee shops, biscotti, crisp Italian twice-baked biscuits, are the latest rage to hit the cookie scene. Crystallized ginger adds to the flavor of this version.

Vegetable cooking spray
1⅔ cups flour
1 teaspoon baking powder
½ teaspoon salt
1 whole egg
2 egg whites
⅔ cup sugar

1 teaspoon vanilla extract
½ cup unblanched sliced almonds
½ cup golden raisins
3 tablespoons finely chopped crystallized ginger

1. Preheat oven to 350°F. Coat a large baking sheet with cooking spray. Dust lightly with flour. On a sheet of wax paper, combine flour, baking powder, and salt.

2. In small bowl of electric mixer, beat egg, egg whites, sugar, and vanilla on high speed until very pale and double in volume, about 3 minutes. Blend in dry ingredients on low speed. Stir in almonds, raisins, and ginger. Place in refrigerator 30 minutes, or until dough is easy to handle.

3. Divide dough in half. Place on prepared baking sheet about 4 inches apart. With moistened hands, shape each half into a 10-inch-long log. Bake 25 to 30 minutes, or until firm and golden. Let cool on baking sheet 10 minutes.

4. Slide logs onto a cutting board. Cut crosswise on a diagonal into ½-inch slices. Place slices back on baking sheet and bake 15 minutes, or until dry and lightly toasted. Transfer to a wire rack and let cookies cool completely. Biscotti keep well in an airtight container at room temperature.

Per Serving: Calories: 58 Total fat: 1 g Saturated fat: 0 g
Cholesterol: 6 mg Percentage calories from fat: 14%

Chapter 14

Light Fruits and Frozen Desserts

Improving on Mother Nature's bounty is hard to do, yet fresh fruit desserts are ripe for the picking. Arranged in elegant still-life perfection, fresh fruit desserts are fiber-rich, fat-free, and bursting with vitamins and minerals. If you add a splash of citrus juice or liqueur, or spices, fresh herbs, or citrus zest to flavor, and garnish with fresh citrus strips or mint, these desserts are fast, easy, refreshing—and naturally light.

Venetian Strawberries sprinkled with brown sugar and a splash of red wine vinegar, and Watermelon with White Zinfandel, or Papaya and Blackberries, take minutes to prepare. A mélange of summer fruits—peaches, nectarines, plums, pears, and cherries—are lightly cooked for the Summer Fruit Compote. And all are virtually nonfat.

The "cream" in Nectarines and Plums with Amaretto Cream is actually a combination of nonfat sour cream, amaretto liqueur, and crushed amaretti cookies. Crisp, sugar-coated baked wonton triangles top a mélange of summer berries, and nonfat vanilla yogurt replaces the whipped heavy cream for Warm Berries with Wonton Crisps. Peaches with Raspberry Sauce is a takeoff on peaches Melba, with low-fat frozen yogurt sitting in for the higher-fat vanilla ice cream, and a crunchy brown sugar praline is blended into a low-fat vanilla yogurt and a nonfat cream cheese for Blueberries with Praline Cream.

Frozen nonfat desserts are gaining in popularity. Espresso Granita, Cranberry Wine Sorbet, and Pineapple Ice, made with a frozen juice concentrate, are all superquick to prepare. Serve them between courses in a meal to refresh the palate, or as icy-cool endings.

Don't want to bother with making a fresh fruit dessert? Biting into a crisp apple, eating a juicy peach or pear, or popping fresh berries in the mouth are just as satisfying. Remember to eat two to four servings of fruit a day to meet the minimum daily requirement for a healthy diet.

341   APRICOTS WITH ORANGE CREAM
Prep: 5 minutes   Cook: none   Serves: 4

½ cup nonfat sour cream
1 tablespoon sugar
½ teaspoon grated orange
  zest
2 tablespoons orange juice

4 large ripe fresh apricots
  or 8 large canned apricot
  halves
1 tablespoon sliced almonds
  Fresh mint sprigs (optional)

1. In a small bowl, blend together sour cream, sugar, and orange zest. Stir in orange juice until combined. Cover and refrigerate orange cream, if desired.

2. Cut apricots around natural separation. Twist and separate into halves; remove pits. Fill centers with orange cream. Place 2 filled apricot halves on each of 4 small chilled dessert plates. Sprinkle almonds on top. Garnish each with a mint sprig.

*Per Serving: Calories: 66 Total fat: 1 g Saturated fat: 0 g
              Cholesterol: 0 mg Percentage calories from fat: 13%*

342   FRUIT COMPOTE ORIENTALE
Prep: 10 minutes   Cook: none   Chill: 2 hours   Serves: 6

Litchi, also spelled lichee, is the fruit of a Chinese evergreen, the litchi tree. The fruit consists of a single seed surrounded by a sweet raisinlike white pulp enclosed in a rough, brown, papery shell. You can buy them fresh in oriental marketplaces or canned. The crystallized ginger adds a sharp bite to this easy fruit compote.

1 (20-ounce) can pineapple
  chunks in unsweetened
  pineapple juice, drained
1 (20-ounce) can litchi nuts,
  drained
¼ cup white rum
3 tablespoons fresh lime juice

2 tablespoons honey
2 tablespoons chopped
  crystallized ginger
2 kiwis, peeled, halved
  lengthwise, and cut into
  ¼-inch slices

1. In a large bowl, combine pineapple chunks, litchi nuts, rum, lime juice, honey, and crystallized ginger. Cover and refrigerate at least 2 hours for flavors to mellow, stirring occasionally.

2. When ready to serve, fold in kiwi slices. Spoon fruits evenly among chilled compote dishes with some of the ginger syrup.

*Per Serving: Calories: 202 Total fat: < 1 g Saturated fat: 0 g
              Cholesterol: 0 mg Percentage calories from fat: 2%*

343 ORANGE-HONEY BAKED APPLES
Prep: 7 minutes   Cook: 45 to 50 minutes   Serves: 4

4 large baking apples (9
   ounces each), such as
   Cortland
½ cup orange juice

2 tablespoons honey
1 teaspoon grated orange zest
⅛ teaspoon grated nutmeg

1. Preheat oven to 375°F. Rinse and core apples. Using a vegetable peeler, remove about a 1-inch strip of apple skin around center of each apple. Stand apples up in an 8-inch square baking pan.

2. In a 1-cup glass measure, combine orange juice, honey, orange zest, and nutmeg. Stir to dissolve honey. Pour mixture over apples. Cover tightly with aluminum foil.

3. Bake apples 25 minutes. Uncover and bake, basting frequently with the sauce, 20 to 25 minutes longer, or until apples are tender. Remove from oven. Let cool slightly, spooning sauce over apples occasionally. Serve warm or cold.

Per Serving: Calories: 186   Total fat: 1 g   Saturated fat: 0 g
Cholesterol: 0 mg   Percentage calories from fat: 4%

344 DRIED FRUIT COMPOTE WITH PORT
Prep: 5 minutes   Cook: 10 minutes   Serves: 6

Dried fruit compote has always been a favorite of mine. It was always one of the desserts my family served after a festive meal.

1 cup dried apricot halves
   (½ pound)
1¼ cups dried pitted prunes
   with orange flavor
   (½ pound)
½ cup golden raisins

½ cup orange juice
4 thin lemon slices
3 tablespoons sugar
1 (2-inch) cinnamon stick
½ cup port

1. In a medium nonreactive saucepan, combine apricots, prunes, raisins, orange juice, lemon slices, sugar, cinnamon stick, and 2½ cups water. Bring to a boil over medium heat. Reduce heat to low, cover, and simmer 10 minutes, or until fruits are plump and tender.

2. Remove from heat and stir in port. Serve warm or chilled. If serving cold, refrigerate with lemon slices and cinnamon stick; remove them before serving.

Per Serving: Calories: 286   Total fat: 0 g   Saturated fat: 0 g
Cholesterol: 0 mg   Percentage calories from fat: 0%

345 SUMMER FRUIT COMPOTE

Prep: 15 minutes   Cook: 15 minutes   Chill: 3 hours   Serves: 6

I have to thank my friend and neighbor, Carol, for this compote. She varies it with whatever fruit is in season, sometimes adding apples or fresh apricots. The plums provide the compote with a rosy color; leaving the stems on the cherries gives an interesting appearance to the compote when it is served.

½ **pound fresh peaches**
½ **pound fresh nectarines**
½ **pound fresh prune plums**
2 **firm-ripe pears, such as
   Bartlett or Comice**
½ **pound dark Bing cherries,
   with stems**

2 **lemon slices**
1 **(2-inch) cinnamon stick**
¼ **to ½ cup sugar, depending
   upon sweetness of fruit**

1. Halve and pit peaches, nectarines, and plums. Cut fruits into thick slices directly into a large nonreactive saucepan. Halve pears, core, and cut into thick slices; add to saucepan. Add cherries with their stems, lemon slices, cinnamon stick, sugar, and 1 cup water.

2. Bring to a boil. Reduce heat to low, cover, and simmer 15 minutes, or until fruit softens but still holds its shape. Let compote cool, uncovered; then cover and refrigerate until very cold, at least 3 hours.

3. When ready to serve, mix fruits lightly to combine. Spoon evenly among chilled compote dishes with some of fruit juices.

*Per Serving: Calories: 164 Total fat: 1 g Saturated fat: 0 g
   Cholesterol: 0 mg Percentage calories from fat: 4%*

346 HONEYDEW MELON WITH CILANTRO-HONEY TOPPING

Prep: 5 minutes   Cook: none   Serves: 4

2 **tablespoons fresh lime juice**
1½ **teaspoons honey**
1 **tablespoon minced cilantro**
4 **(3-inch-wide) honeydew
   wedges**

Cracked black pepper
(optional)

In a small cup, combine lime juice, honey, and cilantro. Place honeydew on shallow chilled dessert plates. Drizzle with honey mixture. Top with a few grindings of pepper over each serving.

*Per Serving: Calories: 65 Total fat: < 1 g Saturated fat: 0 g
   Cholesterol: 0 mg Percentage calories from fat: 2%*

347   WARM BERRIES WITH WONTON CRISPS
Prep: 20 minutes   Cook: 9 minutes   Serves: 6

A mélange of berries is served warm topped with a vanilla yogurt cream and a sugar-coated crisp wonton. You can find wonton wrappers in the produce or frozen food sections of some supermarkets or in Asian food markets.

3 tablespoons granulated sugar	1 cup blueberries
1 tablespoon butter	1 cup red or yellow raspberries
6 wonton wrappers (3-inch squares)	1 cup blackberries
¼ cup firmly packed light brown sugar	1 cup small strawberries, halved
1 tablespoon orange juice	2 cups nonfat vanilla yogurt

1. Preheat oven to 425°F. Spread granulated sugar on a sheet of wax paper. In a small skillet over low heat, melt 2 teaspoons of butter. Using a pastry brush, brush wonton wrappers lightly on both sides with butter. Press wonton wrappers into sugar to coat evenly on both sides. Cut diagonally in half to form triangles. Place on a large nonstick baking sheet.

2. Bake 4 minutes, or until wonton wrappers begin to turn golden. Turn and bake 1 minute longer, or until evenly browned (watch carefully). Transfer wrappers to a wire rack and let cool.

3. In a large nonstick skillet, melt remaining 1 teaspoon butter over medium heat. Add brown sugar and orange juice. Cook, stirring until sugar dissolves, about 2 minutes. Add blueberries and cook just until berries start to release juice, about 1 minute. Add raspberries, blackberries, and strawberries. Cook, shaking pan frequently or turning berries with a heatproof rubber spatula, until fruit has softened but still holds its shape, about 1 minute.

4. To serve, spoon warm berries evenly among 6 shallow dessert plates. Top each with ⅓ cup vanilla yogurt and 2 wonton crisps.

Per Serving: Calories: 210   Total fat: 2 g   Saturated fat: 1 g
Cholesterol: 8 mg   Percentage calories from fat: 10%

348 NECTARINES AND PLUMS WITH AMARETTO CREAM

Prep: 10 minutes   Cook: none   Chill: 1 hour   Serves: 4

½ cup nonfat or low-fat sour
   cream
3 tablespoons amaretto
   liqueur
4 firm-ripe fresh nectarines or
   peaches
4 ripe purple plums

2 tablespoons light brown
   sugar
1 tablespoon fresh lemon
   juice
  Pinch of cinnamon
4 amaretti cookies, coarsely
   crushed

1. In a small bowl, whisk together sour cream with liqueur until blended. Cover and refrigerate until very cold, at least 1 hour.

2. Meanwhile, halve and pit nectarines and slice into a medium bowl. Quarter and pit plums into same bowl. Toss fruit with brown sugar, lemon juice, and cinnamon. Cover and refrigerate until very cold, at least 1 hour.

3. When ready to serve, divide fruit evenly among chilled compote dishes. Dollop with amaretto cream and sprinkle crushed cookies on top.

Per Serving: Calories: 204   Total fat: 2 g   Saturated fat: 0 g
Cholesterol: 0 mg   Percentage calories from fat: 7%

349 BLUEBERRIES WITH PRALINE CREAM

Prep: 15 minutes   Cook: 1 minute   Chill: 1 hour 15 minutes
Serves: 4

You won't miss whipped cream with this fresh summer berry dessert. In its place I've blended brown sugar praline into low-fat vanilla yogurt and nonfat cream cheese. Fold the praline into the cream just before serving so it keeps its crunch.

  Butter-flavored cooking
   spray
¼ cup firmly packed light
   brown sugar
½ cup low-fat vanilla yogurt
½ cup nonfat cream cheese,
   softened

1 pint strawberries, halved
1 cup fresh blueberries
1 cup fresh red or yellow
   raspberries

1. Preheat broiler. Place a large baking sheet in freezer to chill, about 15 minutes. Coat the *chilled* baking sheet with cooking spray. Rub brown sugar with fingertips through a wire strainer onto baking sheet. Sugar should be ⅛ to ¼ inch thick; it will not cover sheet. Broil sugar 6 inches from heat just until it is bubbly, about 1 minute. Watch carefully to prevent sugar from burning. Place baking sheet on a wire rack; let cool completely. Remove praline with a wide spatula and break into small pieces.

2. In a small bowl, whisk together yogurt with cream cheese until smooth. In a medium bowl, combine strawberries, blueberries, and raspberries. Cover and refrigerate yogurt mixture and berries separately until cold, at least 1 hour.

3. When ready to serve, spoon berries evenly among 4 dessert dishes or wine goblets. Combine praline with yogurt mixture and dollop over berries. Serve at once.

*Per Serving: Calories: 164   Total fat: 1 g   Saturated fat: 0 g
Cholesterol: 4 mg   Percentage calories from fat: 7%*

---

350   PEACHES WITH RASPBERRY SAUCE
Prep: 15 minutes   Cook: 5 minutes   Chill: 2 hours   Serves: 4

My variation on the classic peach Melba, attributed to Chef Georges Auguste Escoffier for the Australian opera singer Nellie Melba, substitutes low-fat frozen yogurt for vanilla ice cream and uses frozen raspberries for convenience. Otherwise, it is quite true to the original.

1 tablespoon sugar
2 teaspoons cornstarch
1 (10-ounce) package frozen
   raspberries in light syrup,
   thawed
1 tablespoon orange liqueur,
   such as Cointreau or
   Triple Sec, or orange juice

4 medium firm-ripe peaches
1 pint low-fat frozen vanilla
   bean yogurt
Mint sprigs (optional)

1. In a small saucepan, stir together sugar and cornstarch. Stir in raspberries with syrup until mixture is smooth. Cook over medium heat, stirring constantly, until sauce thickens and clears, about 5 minutes. Strain through a sieve set over a bowl to remove seeds, if desired. Add liqueur or orange juice to bowl. Cover and refrigerate raspberry sauce until very cold, at least 2 hours.

2. When ready to serve, halve peaches and remove pits. Cut into thin even slices, keeping slices from halves together. Spoon about ¼ cup raspberry sauce onto 4 large chilled dessert plates. Fan out peach slices on sauce. Place a ½-cup scoop of frozen yogurt alongside peach slices. Garnish each serving with a mint sprig.

*Per Serving: Calories: 257   Total fat: 1 g   Saturated fat: 0 g
Cholesterol: 5 mg   Percentage calories from fat: 4%*

351   PAPAYA AND BLACKBERRIES
Prep: 10 minutes   Cook: none   Chill: 2 hours   Serves: 4

Pretty and quick, this fruit dessert is laced with Moscato, a sweet Italian dessert wine made from the muscat grape. You can substitute mango for the papaya and raspberries for the blackberries.

1 ripe medium papaya	1 cup sweet white wine, such
2 teaspoons crushed fresh	as Italian Moscato or
mint plus some leaves for	French Sauternes
garnish	1 cup blackberries or
1½ teaspoons fresh lime or	raspberries
lemon juice	

1. Peel, halve, and seed papaya. Cut each half crosswise into slices. Place fruit in a shallow bowl. Crush mint leaves with fingertips and add to fruit. Sprinkle with lime juice and pour wine over fruit. Cover and refrigerate until very cold, at least 2 hours.

2. When ready to serve, divide papaya slices evenly among chilled shallow dessert plates. Drizzle juices in bowl over fruit. Sprinkle berries on top, garnish with mint leaves, and serve cold.

Per Serving: Calories: 141   Total fat: < 1 g   Saturated fat: 0 g
Cholesterol: 0 mg   Percentage calories from fat: 3%

352   GRAPEFRUIT WITH GINGERED CREAM
Prep: 10 minutes   Cook: none   Chill: 1 hour   Serves: 4

This ginger-flavored cream with citrus sections would be a perfect addition to breakfast or brunch.

1 cup nonfat or low-fat sour	1 tablespoon finely chopped
cream	crystallized ginger
¼ cup skim milk	2 large pink grapefruits

1. In a small bowl, stir together sour cream, milk, and crystallized ginger. Cover and refrigerate gingered cream, at least 1 hour for flavors to mellow.

2. With a small sharp knife, peel grapefruits, removing white pith. Section grapefruits over a bowl to catch juices. Spoon grapefruit sections evenly among chilled compote dishes along with some of the grapefruit juice in bowl. Top with gingered cream.

Per Serving: Calories: 105   Total fat: < 1 g   Saturated fat: 0 g
Cholesterol: 0 mg   Percentage calories from fat: 1%

353   ORANGES IN ORANGE-FLOWER WATER
Prep: 10 minutes   Cook: none   Chill: 2 hours   Serves: 4

Orange-flower water can usually be found in the spice and herb section of some supermarkets or at Middle Eastern food stores. When pomegranates are in season, I love their bright color as a garnish.

¼ cup orange juice
¼ teaspoon orange-flower
   water
4 large navel oranges
8 dried pitted dates, quartered
   lengthwise

1 tablespoon pomegranate
   seeds or chopped
   pistachio nuts

1. In a medium bowl, combine orange juice and orange-flower water.

2. With a sharp knife, peel oranges, removing colored skin and white pith. Cut oranges into ¼-inch-thick slices. Add orange slices and dates to orange juice mixture; toss gently to combine. Cover and refrigerate until very cold, at least 2 hours.

3. When ready to serve, spoon oranges and dates evenly among chilled compote dishes. Drizzle juice over each serving. Garnish with pomegranate seeds. Serve cold.

Per Serving: Calories: 133   Total fat: < 1 g   Saturated fat: 0 g
Cholesterol: 0 mg   Percentage calories from fat: 1%

---

354   CARAMELIZED PINEAPPLE AND BANANAS
Prep: 5 minutes   Cook: 3 minutes   Serves: 2

This hot fruit dessert is an easy version of bananas Foster, with the addition of pineapple.

1 tablespoon butter
1 tablespoon brown sugar
2 tablespoons golden rum
½ teaspoon vanilla extract
1 (8-ounce) can pineapple
   chunks in unsweetened
   pineapple juice, drained

1 large banana, peeled and cut
   into ½-inch diagonal
   slices
2 scoops (½ cup each) nonfat
   frozen vanilla yogurt or
   ice cream

1. In a medium nonstick skillet, melt butter over low heat. Add brown sugar and stir until mixture is bubbly. Stir in rum and vanilla. Immediately add pineapple chunks and banana slices. Cook, stirring, until fruit is glazed and heated through but not mushy, about 2 minutes.

2. To serve, place a scoop of frozen yogurt into each of 2 chilled compote dishes. Top with hot fruit and any sauce left in pan.

Per Serving: Calories: 340   Total fat: 6 g   Saturated fat: 4 g
Cholesterol: 15 mg   Percentage calories from fat: 17%

355   RED PEARS IN RED WINE SYRUP
Prep: 5 minutes   Cook: 20 minutes   Chill: 3 hours   Serves: 4

There's no need to peel the skin off these pears, as they maintain some of their red color during poaching. Quick trick: Use a melon-baller to core the pears.

1½ **cups dry red wine, such as Burgundy**
⅓ **cup sugar**
1 **(2-inch) cinnamon stick**
¾ **teaspoon ground cardamom**

4 **medium firm-ripe red pears with stems (about 6 ounces each)**
1 **tablespoon fresh lemon juice**

1. In a large nonreactive skillet, combine wine, sugar, cinnamon stick, and cardamom. Bring to a boil over medium heat. Reduce heat and simmer, uncovered, 10 minutes. Cut pears in half, leaving stem intact on one half; scoop out cores. Brush cut sides of pear halves with lemon juice.

2. Place pears, cut sides down, in spiced wine syrup. Cover skillet and simmer 10 minutes, or until pears are firm-tender. Remove pears with a slotted spoon and place, cut sides down, in a 9-inch glass pie plate or a nonreactive shallow dish large enough to hold them in a single layer. Let syrup cool slightly, then pour over pears.

3. Cover and refrigerate until very cold, at least 3 hours, spooning sauce over pears occasionally. To serve, place 2 pear halves, one with a stem, into chilled compote dishes. Spoon some of wine syrup over each dessert.

Per Serving: Calories: 223   Total fat: 1 g   Saturated fat: 0 g
Cholesterol: 0 mg   Percentage calories from fat: 3%

356   WATERMELON WITH WHITE ZINFANDEL
Prep: 5 minutes   Cook: none   Chill: 2 hours   Serves: 4

12 **triangular wedges of seedless red or yellow watermelon, cut ½ inch thick, with rind left on**
1 **cup white zinfandel**

1 **tablespoon fresh lime juice**
1 **cup yellow or red raspberries**
Lime wedges (optional)

1. In a large shallow dish, place watermelon. Pour zinfandel over fruit and sprinkle with lime juice. Cover and refrigerate until well chilled, at least 2 hours.

2. When ready to serve, arrange 3 watermelon triangles on each dessert plate. Spoon juices over and sprinkle with raspberries. Garnish each serving with a lime wedge.

Per Serving: Calories: 95   Total fat: 1 g   Saturated fat: 0 g
Cholesterol: 0 mg   Percentage calories from fat: 10%

357 VENETIAN STRAWBERRIES
Prep: 5 minutes   Cook: none   Serves: 4

Nobody will figure out the unusual combination of ingredients unless you tell them. I first tasted berries with vinegar and brown sugar at an Italian friend's home. It's really good! The tartness of the vinegar enhances the sweet fruit flavor of the strawberries.

1 pint strawberries	3 tablespoons red wine
3 tablespoons brown sugar	vinegar

1. Just before serving, rinse strawberries; pat dry. Hull and halve strawberries lengthwise; quarter large strawberries.

2. Place strawberries in a medium bowl. Add sugar; toss to coat. Let stand, mixing occasionally, until moisture of berries melts sugar, about 2 minutes.

3. Stir in vinegar; toss lightly to coat. Spoon evenly among 4 compote dishes. Serve at once.

Per Serving: Calories: 64 Total fat: < 1 g Saturated fat: 0 g
Cholesterol: 0 mg Percentage calories from fat: 4%

---

358 PINEAPPLE PIÑA COLADA
Prep: 15 minutes   Cook: 8 minutes   Chill: 1 hour   Serves: 4

The choice of nonfat frozen yogurts available in the market is exciting. It's hard to pick a favorite. Here is one flavor atop fresh pineapple. Or make one of the sorbets or ices in this chapter and use it instead of the yogurt. Garnish with fresh mint leaves if you have them.

4 slices of fresh pineapple, cut ½ inch thick, rind and eyes removed	1 pint low-fat piña colada frozen yogurt or your favorite flavor
1 tablespoon sugar	12 strawberries, halved if large
1 tablespoon fresh lime juice	1 teaspoon finely shredded lime zest (optional)

1. Cut each slice of pineapple into 4 wedges. Place in a bowl and sprinkle with sugar and lime juice. Cover and refrigerate until cold, at least 1 hour.

2. When ready to serve, arrange 4 pineapple wedges, slightly overlapping, on 4 shallow chilled dessert plates with points toward center. Place a scoop of frozen yogurt in center.

3. Divide strawberries among plates. Sprinkle lime zest on top.

Per Serving: Calories: 164 Total fat: 3 g Saturated fat: 0 g
Cholesterol: 6 mg Percentage calories from fat: 16%

359   LEMON HONEY GRANITA

Prep: 5 minutes   Cook: 3 minutes   Stand: 30 minutes
Freeze: 2½ hours   Serves: 4

Refreshing Italian-style granitas have a coarser texture than sorbets. They are easy to make without any kind of specialized equipment.

¼ cup sugar
2 tablespoons honey

½ cup fresh lemon juice
2 teaspoons grated lemon zest

1. In a medium saucepan, combine 2 cups water, sugar, and honey. Simmer over medium heat, stirring until sugar and honey are dissolved, about 3 minutes. Stir in lemon juice and lemon zest. Let cool to room temperature, about 30 minutes.

2. Pour mixture into a chilled 9-inch square metal pan. Freeze until ice crystals form around edges, about 30 minutes. Stir ice crystals into center of mixture. Return pan to freezer and stir in same fashion every 30 minutes until mixture is firm but not frozen hard, 2 to 4 hours.

3. To serve, scrape granita with a fork to lighten texture. Spoon into chilled parfait glasses or wine goblets.

Per Serving: Calories: 89   Total fat: 0 g   Saturated fat: 0 g
        Cholesterol: 0 mg   Percentage calories from fat: 0%

360   CHOCOLATE ICE

Prep: 3 minutes   Stand: 30 minutes   Cook: 8 minutes
Freeze: 2½ hours   Serves: 6

⅔ cup sugar
¼ cup unsweetened cocoa
    powder

¼ teaspoon ground cinnamon
    (optional)

1. In a medium saucepan, stir together sugar, cocoa powder, and cinnamon. Gradually add 2 cups water, stirring constantly, until mixture is smooth. Cook over medium heat, stirring occasionally, until syrup boils, about 5 minutes. Reduce heat and simmer, uncovered, 3 minutes. Remove from heat and let cool to room temperature, about 30 minutes.

2. Pour mixture into a chilled 9-inch square metal pan. Freeze until ice crystals form around edges, about 30 minutes. Stir ice crystals into center of mixture. Return pan to freezer and stir every 30 minutes until mixture is firm, 2 to 4 hours.

3. Break up chocolate ice with a wooden spoon. Place in a food processor and process, using pulses, just until smooth. Scoop into chilled parfait glasses or wine goblets. Serve at once.

Per Serving: Calories: 95   Total fat: < 1 g   Saturated fat: 0 g
        Cholesterol: 0 mg   Percentage calories from fat: 4%

361 KIWI MINT SORBET
Prep: 10 minutes   Cook: none   Freeze: 2½ hours   Serves: 6

8 firm-ripe kiwi
½ cup sugar
3 tablespoons finely chopped
   fresh mint leaves

1 tablespoon fresh lime or
   lemon juice
1 teaspoon grated lime or
   lemon zest

1. Peel and quarter kiwis. Place in a food processor with sugar, mint, lime juice, and lime zest. Process, using pulses, just until the mixture is smooth and liquid, about 1 minute.

2. Pour fruit mixture into a chilled 9-inch square metal pan. Freeze until ice crystals form around edges, about 30 minutes. Stir ice crystals into center of mixture. Return pan to freezer and stir every 30 minutes until firm, 2 to 4 hours.

3. Break up frozen mixture with a wooden spoon. Place in a food processor and process, using pulses, just until sorbet is smooth. Scoop into chilled parfait glasses or wine goblets.

Per Serving: Calories: 128   Total fat: > 1 g   Saturated fat: 0 g
Cholesterol: 0 mg   Percentage calories from fat: 3%

362 ESPRESSO GRANITA
Prep: 5 minutes   Stand: 30 minutes   Freeze: 2½ hours   Serves: 4

Whether you brew your espresso in an espresso machine or through a drip coffee maker, this light Italian ice is a refreshing treat. Since everyone's taste buds differ as to espresso strength, I left the choice of preparation up to you. You can eliminate the liqueur if you wish and add ½ teaspoon ground cinnamon to the hot espresso.

2 cups hot strong espresso
   coffee
⅓ cup sugar

1 tablespoon sambuca or
   amaretto liqueur

1. In a 4-cup glass measure, stir together hot espresso coffee and sugar until sugar is dissolved. Let cool to room temperature, about 30 minutes. Stir in liqueur.

2. Pour mixture into a chilled 9-inch square metal pan. Freeze until ice crystals form around edges, about 30 minutes. Stir ice crystals into center of mixture. Return pan to freezer and stir every 30 minutes until mixture is firm but not frozen hard, 2 to 4 hours.

3. To serve, scrape granita with a fork to lighten texture. Spoon into chilled parfait glasses or wine goblets. Serve at once.

Per Serving: Calories: 78   Total fat: 0 g   Saturated fat: 0 g
Cholesterol: 0 mg   Percentage calories from fat: 0%

363   CRANBERRY WINE SORBET
Prep: 3 minutes   Stand: 30 minutes   Cook: 7 minutes
Freeze: 3 hours   Serves: 4

1½ cups fresh or frozen
       cranberries (½ of a
       12-ounce package)

¼ cup dry red wine, such as
      Burgundy
¾ cup sugar
1 teaspoon fresh lemon juice

1. In a medium nonreactive saucepan, place cranberries, red wine, and 1 cup water. Bring to a simmer over medium heat. Cook just until cranberries soften and begin to pop, about 3 minutes.

2. Pour mixture into a sieve set over a bowl. Press with a wooden spoon against sieve to remove seeds. Stir sugar and lemon juice into cranberry juice in bowl.

3. Pour fruit mixture into a chilled 9-inch square metal pan. Freeze until ice crystals form around edges, about 1 hour. Stir ice crystals into center of mixture. Return pan to freezer and stir every 30 minutes until sorbet is firm, 2 to 4 hours.

4. Break up frozen mixture with a wooden spoon. Place in a food processor and process, using pulses, just until sorbet is smooth. Scoop into chilled parfait glasses or wine goblets. Serve at once.

Per Serving: Calories: 177   Total fat: 0 g   Saturated fat: 0 g
Cholesterol: 0 mg   Percentage calories from fat: 0%

364   SPICED RHUBARB
Prep: 10 minutes   Cook: 25 minutes   Chill: 3 hours   Serves: 6

Tart-sweet rhubarb is wonderful so many ways. This spiced version can be enjoyed by itself or over angel food slices or frozen yogurt. You can vary the rhubarb by stirring in a cup of halved strawberries at the very end. The heat of the sauce just softens the strawberries and doesn't make them mushy. If you are using frozen rhubarb, increase the baking time by 5 to 10 minutes, or until the rhubarb is cooked through.

1 pound fresh rhubarb,
      trimmed and cut into
      ½-inch pieces, or
      1 (1-pound) package
      frozen cut rhubarb,
      thawed

1 cup sugar
1 (2-inch) cinnamon stick
4 whole cloves
4 whole allspice
1 (4-inch) strip of lemon zest

1. Preheat oven to 400°F. Toss rhubarb with sugar in a shallow 2-quart baking dish. Add cinnamon, cloves, allspice, and lemon zest. Cover with lid or foil.

2. Bake rhubarb 10 minutes. Stir gently to dissolve sugar. Bake, covered, until rhubarb is tender but not mushy, about 15 minutes longer. Let cool, covered, in dish set on a wire rack.

3. Refrigerate until well chilled, at least 3 hours. Remove cinnamon stick, cloves, and allspice before serving. Divide fruit evenly among chilled compote dishes. Serve cold.

Per Serving: Calories: 142   Total fat: < 1 g   Saturated fat: 0 g
Cholesterol: 0 mg   Percentage calories from fat: 1%

---

365   PINEAPPLE ICE
Prep: 3 minutes   Cook: 5 minutes   Freeze: 2½ hours   Serves: 6

A frozen juice concentrate is the base for this creamy smooth dessert. As a variation, try frozen pineapple-orange juice concentrate.

¾ **cup sugar**
1 **(6-ounce) can frozen pineapple juice concentrate**

1 **tablespoon fresh lemon juice**
1 **teaspoon grated lemon zest**

1. In a medium saucepan, combine 2 cups water with sugar. Bring to a boil, stirring to dissolve sugar. Reduce heat and simmer 5 minutes. Remove from heat and stir in pineapple juice concentrate, lemon juice, and lemon zest. Stir until pineapple juice is melted.

2. Pour mixture into a chilled 9-inch square metal pan. Freeze until ice crystals form around edges, about 30 minutes. Stir ice crystals into center of pan. Return pan to freezer and stir every 30 minutes until ice is firm, 2 to 4 hours.

3. Break up frozen mixture with a wooden spoon. Place in a food processor and process, using pulses, until ice is smooth. Scoop into chilled parfait glasses or wine goblets. Serve at once.

Per Serving: Calories: 162   Total fat: 0 g   Saturated fat: 0 g
Cholesterol: 0 mg   Percentage calories from fat: 0%

Index

Acknowledgments

To my sons Peter and Jaime, who always told me I should write a cookbook.

Thanks to Anne Salisbury of R. C. Auletta & Co., who returned phone calls, answered my questions, and sent Perdue products for use in testing. To all my friends, neighbors, and family who served as tasters and critics, often asking, "Which chapter are we eating now?" And to Susan Wyler for giving me the opportunity to do this book and for her constant encouragement.

Notes

———————

———————